Using Folk Literature in the Classroom

Encouraging Children to Read and Write

by
Frances S. Goforth
and
Carolyn V. Spillman

ORYX PRESS
1994

The rare Arabian Oryx is believed to have inspired the myth of the unicorn. This desert antelope became virtually extinct in the early 1960s. At that time several groups of international conservationists arranged to have 9 animals sent to the Phoenix Zoo to be the nucleus of a captive breeding herd. Today the Oryx population is over 800, and nearly 400 have been returned to reserves in the Middle East.

© 1994 by The Oryx Press
4041 North Central at Indian School Road
Phoenix, Arizona 85012-3397

Published simultaneously in Canada

Printed and Bound in the United States of America

∞ The paper used in this publication meets the minimum requirements of American National Standard for Information Science—Permanence of Paper for Printed Library Materials, ANSI Z39.48, 1984.

Library of Congress Cataloging-in-Publication Data

Goforth, Frances S., 1932-
  Using folk literature in the classroom : encouraging children to
read and write / by Frances S. Goforth and Carolyn V. Spillman.
  Includes bibliographical references and index.
  ISBN 0-89774-747-X
  1. Folk literature—Study and teaching (Elementary) 2. Reading (Elementary) 3. English language—Composition and exercises—Study and teaching (Elementary) I. Spillman, Carolyn V. II. Title.
LB1583.8.G64   1994
372.64—dc20   94-18808
                                                                     CIP

CONTENTS

❈ ❈ ❈ ❈ ❈ ❈ ❈ ❈ ❈

v

PREFACE

❀ ❀ ❀ ❀ ❀ ❀ ❀ ❀

"Although the explicit teaching of skills destroys the aesthetic (personal, affective) stance, aesthetic reading may yield much incidental learning or reinforcement of skills ..."[1]

Louise Rosenblatt
"What Facts Does This Poem Teach You?"

Over the years, teachers have worked hard to "teach" children to read; for many teachers, passing on the enjoyment of books has been a major goal, with "reading" and "stories" at the crux of the curriculum. It has become increasingly clear to us, however, through our own experiences as teachers and researchers over the past decade, that although "reading" and "stories" are core components of literacy development, many children, although functionally literate, fail to catch the fervor of reading.

We believe that when readers connect their own background to ideas found in a story, they have a base for beginning a relationship with that text. Once that relationship is begun, there is a natural need for further dialogue—construction of meaning—between the reader's knowledge and the images and ideas called forth from the text. Such construction or transaction encourages the reader to make meaning of the selection and to respond to the story in further ways.

The literary transaction process just described—*connect* with literature, *construct* meaning, and *create* responses—is the basis for this book. It is a process that children may learn through guidance from a teacher; it is also a mental structure that may become natural to a reader and is probably a framework used by avid readers as they transact with a text. Knowing how to transact with a text may be a key to a lifelong love of reading.

It is our goal to help teachers plan ways to guide children toward the literary transaction process and to implement the process with folk literature. Children who are guided through a relationship with folk literature will find meaning for their personal lives, insights into cultures of long ago and today, clues to language origins, and connections from the past to contemporary vocabulary; they will personalize the structure of "story" and may unlock the door to fantasy for a lifetime of enjoyment. Whatever the specific benefits may be, children who learn to transact with literature will never be without a story.

This book is directed toward classroom teachers and those preparing for the teaching field. It will also be an important resource tool for the librarians and media specialists in public and school libraries.

The prevailing philosophy in this book is that children and the adults who guide them into literature are the decision makers on the selection of stories and the response options to them. The recommended folk literature and possible activities should be viewed as a scaffold. Adults and children together should plan and negotiate stories and the responses to them. Ultimately, however, the teacher or librarian needs to be a few steps ahead of the students. This book will provide those few steps.

We philosophically embrace the ideas of meaningful, authentic learning experiences, integration of curriculum, thematic studies, and independence in thinking and decision making. The literary transaction process and its implementation through folk literature may be developed in concert with the philosophy of the teacher or librarian who uses this book.

The first two chapters provide a background for the world of folk literature and the structure of the literary transaction process. The first chapter explains why folk literature should be used in the classroom or library setting. In the second chapter, educators and media specialists will find out how the literary transaction process matches current reading and language theories.

Chapters 3–7 present summaries of 54 stories and verses from 20 countries representing 15 subgenres of folk literature. These chapters provide suggestions for connecting children to the texts and guiding them toward responses. Each chapter is a thematic unit for primary or intermediate grades. Each unit contains three themes with three folk literature selections per theme. The country of origin of each selection is listed along with the subgenre. Within these teaching themes and units are suggested connections, constructions, and creations. These responses take the forms of ideas for setting background, networking ideas to connect to children's prior knowledge, probing questions to promote higher-level thinking and meaningful responses, and opportunities for children to respond personally to the selections.

The unit web at the beginning of each chapter provides a quick overview of the unit. Following the unit web, literary goals are discussed, followed by suggestions for integrating these narratives with the total curriculum. As teachers review these units, they will decide which tales and instructional strategies to use. To fully develop the literary concepts, the themes should be followed, although other tales or strategies may be selected, substituted, or modified for individual classes.

To help the teacher or librarian locate the stories, several sources are listed at the beginning of each story summary. Frequently, related stories or additional references are also listed. The first title listed is the version we used in preparing the literary suggestions. The version used is, in most cases, inconsequential since the framework of the tale is usually similar in all variations. Whether the tale is found in an old anthology or a new picture book, the suggestions for sharing the story are relevant. It is the teacher's or librarian's decision to make regarding the mode of delivery: using a picture book, reading the story from an anthology, telling the story in storytelling form, or other techniques. We recommend a variation of these modes as it is as valuable for children to hear a tale without seeing the pictures as it is for them to view the beauty of the illustrations.

The instructional strategies we suggest for each story are not set in stone. Teachers may wish to pick and choose among the many different activities to find the ones most suited for their students. For easy access and comparison, Appendix A lists some of the more complicated activities. It categorizes the suggested response modes into four types: visual manipulative (VM); visual artistic (VA); verbal oral (VO); and verbal written (VW). The entries are also numbered to help locate them. Within the units, these responses are set in boldface type followed by a reference to type and number of the activity, e.g., **probes** (VO 72).

Appendix B provides more information on specific subgenres of folk literature. The charts of subgenres succinctly characterize the language, story elements, and environmental context of each subgenre. Examples of each type are cited. They will be useful reference tools for adults and may be used by older children to compare subgenres.

This book is unique, not only in its organization, but in its intent. It is a guide for a thinking practitioner who ultimately makes instructional decisions. The strategies and suggestions may be used as described or modified as needed. This book is not intended to basalize literature, but to present a framework through which teachers may help students experience folk literature to the fullest extent.

It is our hope that readers will become excited about the use of folk literature in the classroom, and as a result of the experiences conceived or inspired by this book, thousands of children will discover the value and joy of reading, hearing, and viewing all literature.

ENDNOTE

1. "What Facts Does This Poem Teach You?" Rosenblatt, L. 1980. *Language Arts.* pp. 392-93.

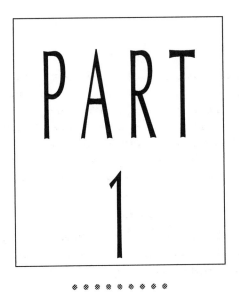

Introduction to Folk Literature

CHAPTER
one

Folk Literature

The words "*Once upon a time . . .*" invite listeners and readers to enter the world of folk literature. To children, folk literature means fairy tales, nursery rhymes, chants, riddles, and other assorted tales that may seem familiar. The familiarity arises from remembrances of early cradle songs, playful childhood rhymes, and those best-loved tales that seem to begin in a faraway place and end "happily ever after." Many of these tales and verses were first told orally hundreds of years ago and were repeated through the years and across cultures before being recorded in written format for modern children to read.

The term *folklore* was coined in the mid 1800s as a reflection of the people: their manners, customs, observances, superstitions, ballads, tales, and proverbs. Folklore is a broad term encompassing not only traditional materials presented in words, but also traditional tools, physical objects, symbols, beliefs, and rituals. Folk literature, as a branch of folklore, is a window through which children in today's world may view cultures of long ago. Within this genre of literature, there are several forms, or subgenres, in both prose and poetry. A selection of these subgenres is described in charts in Appendix B.

ORIGINS OF FOLK LITERATURE

It is unrealistic to view folk literature apart from its cultural context, for it is only through awareness of the origins of the stories and verses that they can be fully appreciated.

The path of folk literature through history reflects various strata of human development. To learn more of the "folk" from whom the materials evolved, scholars have studied vestiges of stories and verses from prehistoric people to contemporary societies[1] and know that folk literature spans the range of human history. They have examined folk literature, passed down from generation to generation, and have found that all levels of society, from peasants to literate classes, preserved their rituals, values, and heritage through their folklore.[2]

The emotions of people are also evident through their stories. Motivated by fear, many of the ancient stories were concerned with the unseen power of nature. Stories that explain natural phenomena such as thunder, lightening, clouds, and rain are examples of the impact of nature on literature during the early stages of human history. At one stage of human development, all objects, animate and inanimate, were believed to have feelings, emotions, wishes, and fears. Remnants of this era are found in the folk literature that personifies animals and objects with human characteristics.

Many stories reflect seemingly irrational behaviors, which may have been perfectly rational in the cultures from which the tales originated thousands of years ago. Strong actions required for survival that today may be viewed as particularly violent were more accepted in cultures where living required a tougher stance. The Jack and the Beanstalk and Molly Whuppie stories are examples of differences in accepted behaviors of today and many years ago. In a society that claims to value fairplay and equal opportunity, Jack and Molly are sometimes viewed as taking advantage of the giant. Because communities in previous ages were constantly indebted to or in fear of powerful "giants"— rulers and landlords—people (the folk) were more likely to identify with Jack and Molly. Various religious beliefs and social customs of the cultures also influenced the stories as they were originally told or adapted for different cultures.[3]

Although many of these stories were born thousands of years ago and were changed many times to fit the culture, they are current because today's children can relate to and identify with the emotions, fears, hopes, and dreams of the characters and their situations. Current contexts—children who suffer oppression under adults, people whose dreams are difficult to obtain, joys of challenges met, and tedious fears when risks are taken—make ancient folk stories bear truth. Through these timeless connections, folk literature may be said to be "contemporary as well as historical."[4]

The storyteller, who relates to the human needs and feelings, brings credibility to the stories. The reader or listener transacts with a story, bringing as much to the story as there was from the beginning; thus these stories, first told years ago, are as current as the storyteller or reader invites them to be.

ORAL AND WRITTEN TRADITIONS IN FOLK LITERATURE

Scholars continue to debate the question of whether folk literature consists of only materials passed down in the oral tradition (by word of mouth) by the "folk" and by professional singers and storytellers from one generation to another; or if stories written and passed through the literary tradition should also be classified as folk literature.

Distinguished professionals from many fields of study have spent a lifetime compiling, classifying, and interpreting the vast body of traditional literature found in literate and nonliterate societies from all corners of the world. Most agree that when the printed word became readily accessible, many of the oral variations were collected, often embellished to interest and entertain their audiences, and recorded in print; they were then frequently returned to an oral form to continue the cycle. This process is seen today as stories and songs from previous days and cultures are adapted and changed to fit contemporary artists and their societies.

Although we recognize that current folklorists are rigorous in their distinctions of whether stories and verses were transmitted orally or in the literary form, for the purposes of this book we consider folk literature to be either oral or written.

BENEFITS GAINED FROM EXPERIENCES WITH FOLK LITERATURE

As children discover the fantasy world of folk literature, they feel safe exploring in their minds unknown and faraway places. They delight in the antics of the imaginary creatures and their ability to move in and around fanciful worlds. Students also relate to the illusory heroes who, seemingly without difficulty, accomplish the impossible. They better understand their own behavior and that of peers and adults after encountering similar actions portrayed in the folk literature of diverse societies.

Experiencing Pleasure in the Language of Folk Literature

Children seem to naturally enjoy manipulating and experimenting with their language. The variety of predictable language patterns and expressions, ranging from the rhythmic chants of nursery rhymes to the storyteller's "Snip, snap, snout, this tale's told out," gives students an invitation to join in and make the language a part of their own daily oral and written conversations. Students are intentionally and unintentionally influenced by the diverse vocabulary, unusual and appealing rhythm, and interesting combinations of language they encounter in folk literature. The memorable dialogue of strange characters is repeated and remembered long after the story is finished. Aesthetic appreciation of the sounds and nuances of the language is a pleasant product of working with folk literature.

Increasing Students' Literary Options

As experience with the language of folk literature increases children's awareness of possible language choices, so it also broadens their literary options. Those who experience fantasy, fiction, and nonfiction literature will, when given the opportunity, choose selections from these various genres. Usually their selections are based on what pleases them at the moment, their present emotional and intellectual development, and their prior literary experiences. Students who experience a variety of literary genres and have an opportunity to self-select a variety of literary types, become discriminating in the selection of literature. In addition, after experiencing multiple forms of literature, they recognize and understand the various structures of fiction, nonfiction, prose, poetry, and drama.

Negotiating Fantasy and Reality

Students who experience folk literature find new worlds grounded in fantasy but still reflecting realistic human conditions. Some adults feel children "must" understand the real world and not be allowed to escape into a "make-believe" world of folk literature. On the contrary, students usually move easily in and out of the two worlds because they recognize the differences between them and know which one they want to live in at that moment. When children move from one world to another, they use their imaginations and problem-solving skills to anticipate and predict the behavior of characters, and in their "mind's eye," they help the characters solve their conflicts and problems. This experience helps them solve real life experiences.

Transacting with Literature on a Personal Basis

Students who read, hear, and view literature that was told or written hundreds of years ago learn that all people, throughout history, have felt joy, fear, love, jealousy, loneliness, pride, and hope, just as they may feel these emotions periodically. They begin to recognize that folk heroes often need two or three trials before accomplishing their goals. They discover that in folk literature disappointments do not signal the end of a struggle, but that through these frustrations the characters find the strength to continue until they are successful. These fictional role models may give children alternative approaches to solve personal conflicts within their own world. From the actions of the stereotypical characters found in folk literature, readers may recognize the consequences of "acceptable" and "unacceptable" behavior. In this way they begin to understand why their society considers certain behaviors to be right and others wrong, and they can then determine the most appropriate social behavior to emulate. These stories from so long ago bring personal meanings to students as they combine their own experiences and background with the ideas and concepts found in the stories.

Widening the View of the World

An interest in other cultures is also developed through the use of folk literature. As children understand the themes of tales from various cultures, they may compare the similarities and differences among people and their cultural traits. Students who are exposed to the literature of other regions see how people in different societies react in their different environments. They learn not only something of the values and lifestyles of others, but also of historical places and people who played an important role in the development of a country. There is a close connection between history and literature, causing some to consider folklore as living history.[5] Whether or not the characters in folk literature are based on true-life heroes, they portray the cultural standards valued by an early society. Even though these universal standards may have changed slightly in contemporary society, they are compatible with the desired values of most modern cultures and will be remembered as students are involved in the past and present study of our world. [6]

CONCERNS ABOUT USING FOLK LITERATURE

Because of the adult themes, content, violence, magical objects, and activities, folk literature may be considered by some adults as unacceptable literature for children. C. S. Lewis, the creator of *The Narnia Chronicles* and a well-known theologian, suggested three reasons why adults object to introducing young people to folk literature.[7] First, adults are concerned that children who experience tales will not be able to understand the differences between real and fantasy worlds. Second, some well-meaning adults believe that, by reading tales, children are escaping the real world. Third, adults are concerned that the tales will cause children to have haunting, disabling, pathological fears. Lewis respects children's ability to distinguish between worlds. He insists children often find the fantasy world more orderly than the real one. They feel safe encountering uncomfortable (frightening) situations or characters in a fantasy world, because they know these situations or characters are not in their real world. Indeed, Lewis asserts, children receive more detrimental, negative impressions from realistic genres and media than from fantasy.

Today, diverse groups ranging from fundamental religious groups to witches and warlocks question the use of folk literature selections. Religious groups object to the supernatural elements found in the selections, while others question their authentic portrayal in tales and poetry. It is likely these groups will continue to object to the use of folk literature in the classroom. Wise teachers will attempt to circumvent such censorship by knowing the literature used with students and determining whether the selection will comply with the beliefs of the families in their classrooms and schools.

A GLANCE TOWARD THE FUTURE

Parents in the past shared their personal cultural and family stories with their children to preserve the heritage of their culture and family history. Unfortunately, many children today are growing up in homes where family and cultural stories, poems, games, and songs are not valued and are, therefore, not passed on to them. We now see generations of children growing up without experiencing their "roots" through folk literature. At the same time they are being excluded from the world of imagination, and they lack the chance to try their "wings" in the world of fantasy. Thus, we have a challenge to give children "roots and wings" by sharing folk literature in the classroom.

ENDNOTES

1. Yearsley, M. 1924. *The Folklore of Fairy Tale*. London: Watts & Co; Fine, G. A. 1987. "Joseph Jacobs: A Sociological Folklorist." *Folklore* 98: ii.

2. Bluestein, G. 1972. *The Voice of the Folk*. Amherst, MA: University of Massachusetts Press.

3. Yearsley, 1924. p. 16.

4. Fine, G. A. 1987. Joseph Jacobs: A Sociological Folklorist. *Folklore*, 98:ii. p. 187.

5. Boswell, G., and J. R. Reaver. 1962. *Fundamentals of Folk Literature*. Oosterhout, The Netherlands: Anthropological Publications. p. 207.

6. Boswell and Reaver, 1962. p. 206.

7. "On Three Ways of Writing for Children." Lewis, C. S. 1952. In *Only Connect* edited by S. Egoff, G. T. Stubbs, and L. F. Ashley. 1969. New York: Oxford Press. pp 207-20.

CHAPTER
two
* * * * * * * *

Folk Literature in the Classroom

Folk literature attracts our interest because of its many connections to the human condition and its parallels to everyday contemporary life. When we identify with the plight of a character, with the emotions and lessons learned, time spans are eliminated and fantasies are plausible. These universal happenings in folk literature **connect** us to the stories of long ago.

The stories have endured for countless generations because listeners and tellers have found meaning in them. The **construction** of meaning occurs as we shape and personalize tales and verses across cultures, through storytellers and audiences who reflect on their own experiences and juxtapose them on the narratives.

Once experienced, these tales and verses implore us to react — to respond. Some responses may be as quiet as a gentle reflection on our own life or as raucous as a spontaneous cheer. Whenever a response occurs, regardless of its origin or its form, a **creation** has emerged.

A LITERARY TRANSACTION PROCESS

Knowing that individuals respond to the old tales and verses by **connecting** emotions and previous experiences to the texts, by **constructing** meaning while personalizing the stories, and by **creating** various types of responses to stories, our goal is to describe these processes—connect, construct, create— and to present ideas that will facilitate students' transactions with folk literature selections. To reach that goal, we explain how we perceive what

9

happens when a reader and a story come together; when they transact to form an individual, personalized meaning for the reader. We call that transaction a **literary transaction process.**

The three phases of a literary transaction process, i.e., **connect, construct,** and **create**, are recursive and may merge into one another. Each is used to assist a reader's transaction with a text. Any one may be experienced independently by an individual, or facilitated by the teacher or a peer.

The first of the three phases occurs as the reader *connects* prior background knowledge or experiences with the concepts suggested by the text. Later, the individual uses such concepts to *construct* meanings evoked by the text. Another phase occurs when the reader *creates* a response to a literary selection. The entire process is nonlinear, except for the beginning phase when a person first *connects* personal knowledge with the text.[1] By moving through these three phases, a reader **transacts** with a text to complete a total process. A literary transaction process is individual-oriented; different people will express different reactions to the same piece of literature. Such a process cannot be dictated, but must remain fluid and dynamic to promote personal choice and meaningfulness.

Figure 1 visualizes the literary transaction process as we perceive it. The relationship among the three phases, i.e., **connect, construct,** and **create**, is represented in overlapping circles. The shaded section of the figure represents the actual transaction between the person and the text and reflects the dynamic nature of the nonlinear, recursive process.

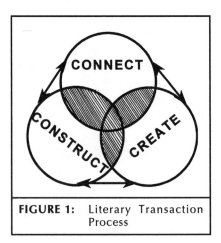

FIGURE 1: Literary Transaction Process

Connect

The literary transaction process begins when we encounter a literature selection. Initially, we react to a story or verse depending on our prior experiences with literature, personal cultural influences and values, background knowledge, social experiences, and what is important to us at the time we come in contact with a particular text. This background of experiences and knowledge represents our personal "schemata." These interrelated concepts of the world represent the ideas, feelings, and knowledge regarding a concept or subject and are hierarchically stored in our brain.[2] We retrieve our "schemata" by selecting appropriate background information and experiences to guide our understanding of the structure, content, and relationships suggested by the emerging literary work. We then relate these "schemata" to a network of ideas stimulated by our perceptions of the author's attitude, emotions, and ideas to infer or anticipate what is to follow.[3] We begin to **connect** with the text.

Accepting individual differences in literary and personal experiences and knowledge, we can use various materials such as visuals, information books, and poetry to clarify related content for students. Oral techniques such as book talks, storytelling, dramatic techniques, book discussions, or various brainstorming strategies can be used to help students connect to the concepts or ideas suggested in a particular literary selection.

Construct

We **construct** meaning or personal interpretations of the literature we hear, read, or see by tapping into our "schemata," and applying that knowledge and our experiences to the ideas, information, and concepts evoked by the images and language patterns of the text.[4] Because of the reciprocal nature of the reading event between the reader and the text and the belief that meaning is not inherent in the text alone, students should not be expected to analyze the author's intentions according to adult expectations. Initially, they need time to reflect and express personal reactions to a selection, and to construct intellectual insights and understandings of the author's work.[5]

The meanings of words are acquired from the context in which they appear. These meanings may change as the language appears in different contexts.[6] Because of the social and cultural aspects of acquiring and using language, students need many opportunities to share their original reactions to a literary work. These personal interpretations must be respected by others. As individuals interact with others and acquire a thorough understanding of the concepts evoked by the text, they will continue to support their original responses or choose to modify them.

Throughout the literary transaction process the teacher assumes the role of facilitator or moderator. The teacher models suitable probes and prompts to stimulate students' critical thinking and guide students to thoughtfully consider the responses and interpretations of others and construct meanings elicited by the literature.

Create

At the same time or before we connect to a selection and construct meanings, we may **create** oral or written responses or interpretations to it. The creating phase gives us an opportunity to share with others our personal reflections or "transaction" to a selection.

Creations should reflect students' spontaneous responses to a selection. Depending on their transaction with a literary selection, children will choose different visual or verbal literary response modes (L.R.M.'s) to express their natural creations.

The create phase of a literary response process replaces the typical book report. The primary focus of such reports is to determine whether the student actually read the selection and if so, whether the individual can literally retell and interpret (according to the adult's interpretation) the author's intention. Inherent in the philosophy of traditional book reports is the belief that meaning is found only "in" the text and the reader is responsible for finding and expressing accurately (as is understood by the teacher) the author's "meaning" in the text. This philosophy does not consider the transactional belief that meaning is constructed through the reciprocal nature of the event between the reader and the text. Therefore, the traditional book report is not compatible with a literary transaction process and is replaced by the construction and creation phases of the process.

INSTRUCTIONAL TECHNIQUES AND STRATEGIES

Inherent in all instructional approaches is a theoretical framework that appropriately supports the suggested techniques and strategies.[7] Our perception of a literary transaction process is based on Rosenblatt's Transactional Theory of the Literary Work. (See theory below.) Also included in our approach are elements of literature-based instruction representing instructional purposes integral to the use of folk literature in the elementary classroom.

Transactional Theory of the Literary Work

In 1938 Louise Rosenblatt conceptualized the interrelationship between the reader and a text in her book, *Literature as Exploration*.[8] At this time literary critics were espousing the theory that meaning resided solely in the text and the reader was responsible for finding the meaning, i.e., the author's interpretation. Rosenblatt insisted that meaning is not "in" the text alone, but of equal importance is the reader—what the person brings to the piece of literature, and what portion of the book he or she chooses to explore. This reciprocal contribution made by both the author's text ("a set of signs capable of being interpreted as verbal symbols") and what the reader brings to the text became the focus for many research studies and writings.[9] Forty years later, Rosenblatt proposed The Transactional Theory of the Literary Work in her book, *The Reader, the Text, the Poem*.[10] In this book, she further refined the social, dynamic transactional process of the reading event as an ongoing interchange between the reader and the text. When a person encounters a text, he or she focuses attention to the text and taps into personal experiences, knowledge, interests, development, and cultural and social influences to transact with that particular text.

Another aspect of the reading event identified by Rosenblatt is the "stance" or focus of attention a person adopts toward the ideas and feelings flowing from the transaction with the text. Two predominate "stances," **aesthetic** and **efferent**, were identified. A reader assumes a predominant **aesthetic** stance when attention is focused on the images, emotions, and thoughts "lived through" during the reading event. A reader assumes a predominant **efferent** stance when attention is focused on the information to be "carried away," extracted, and retained after the reading event.[11] Typically, a person moves freely between stances depending on his or her purpose for reading, the content suggested in the text, the style of writing, the person's interest at the time, or the teacher's instructional focus. In summary,

> *Transactional Theory states that meaning is not "in" the text or "in" the reader, rather, meaning happens during the reciprocal transaction between the reader and the text.*

Literature-Based Instruction

Throughout the nation, teachers are realizing the potential power of literature and are incorporating literature-based instruction.[12] As indicated by the name, entire pieces of literature, representing all literary genres, are used as the primary instructional material in a literature-based program.

Transactional Theory is recognized as a major theoretical foundation to "reader response," an influential approach to the use of literature in the classroom.[13]

Instructional Stances Adopted by a Teacher

Transactional Theory is now recognized as a major theoretical foundation for literary study. Literature-based instruction, using transactional terminology, classifies the instructional stance adopted by a teacher, as aesthetic teaching and efferent teaching.[14]

Aesthetic teaching encourages students to assume a predominately aesthetic transaction with literature. The questions, probes, and prompts used by teachers and students elicit individual reactions to images and emotions evoked in the selection. Adequate time is provided for students to read self-selected literature and select literary response modes to express their personal, aesthetic interpretations of literature.

Efferent teaching encourages students to focus attention on information taken from the reading experience, that is, to assume a predominately efferent stance toward the literature. A teacher adopts this instructional stance if students need additional instruction in literature, language, or specific content. Mini-lessons are often used that encourage students to explain, analyze, and summarize their interpretations of literary selections.

Initially, an aesthetic instructional stance is adopted by a teacher who implements a transactional viewpoint. This influences students to assume a predominantly aesthetic stance when reading, hearing, or seeing folk literature. An efferent instructional stance is then adopted depending on the needs of students, the content included in the selection, and the teacher's instructional purpose. As in all literature-based instruction, teachers are free to shift back and forth from one instructional stance to another.

Aesthetic and efferent teaching are compatible with literature-based instruction. Typically, literature-based instruction includes components as cited in the box on page 15.

SUMMARY

A Literary Transaction Process incorporating the **connect, construct,** and **create** modes was described in this chapter. Reflecting the transactional approach to instruction, the process highlights the personal "transaction" readers have with literature. It is compatible with literature-based instruction and designed to help students develop literacy (reading and writing) and oracy (listening and speaking) proficiencies. In addition, students' knowledge about other curricular areas is enhanced through literary experiences.

INSTRUCTIONAL COMPONENTS: LITERATURE-BASED INSTRUCTION

- Entire pieces of literature, representing a variety of literature and a variety of meaning-bearing selections, are used for instruction.
- Individual and cultural differences are recognized and represented in the literature used.
- The teacher establishes a student-centered environment, considering the students' needs and interests when selecting literature, instructional goals, and activities. Students assist in the selection of literature.
- Independent and collaborative reading, writing, discussion, and conferences with teachers are incorporated in the teaching approach.
- Students learn how to adopt to the reading stance appropriate to the situation.
- Students are encouraged to respond personally to various communication situations.
- Students are introduced to literature through daily teacher read alouds and other oral techniques, i.e., storytelling, book talks, book discussions, dramatic presentations, supplemented with visual aids and audio-visual aids.
- Students are encouraged to use all language modalities in natural ways when reading, viewing, writing, discussing, and reacting to literature and related materials.
- Teachers are empowered to select the most appropriate organizational and instructional techniques, i.e., independent speaking, reading, writing, and viewing activities; a variety of implementation procedures, i.e., total class instruction and paired and literacy discussion groups; and cognition strategies, i.e., "thinking-aloud"; mini-lessons.

In the following chapters, 54 folk literature selections, representing all 15 subgenres, were selected and arranged according to motifs. The **connect, construct,** and **create** phases are suggested to help teachers implement a Literary Transaction Process. Descriptions of 104 literary response modes, representing each phase, are included in appendix A.

.... **ENDNOTES** ....

1. Rosenblatt, L. M. 1988. Writing and Reading: The Transactional Theory. ERIC Document. Technical Report #416. p. 6.
2. "Role of Reader's Schema in Comprehension, Learning, and Memory." Anderson, R. C. 1985. *Theoretical Models and Processes of Reaching.* Edited by H. Singer and R. Ruddell. Newark DL: Internaitonal Reading Association.

3. Lehr, S. 1991. *The Child's Developing Sense of Theme*. New York: Teachers College Press. pp. 4-10.

4. Hiebert, E. H. (ed.). 1991. *Literacy for a Diverse Society: Perspectives, Practices, and Policies*. New York: Teachers College Press. p. 295.

5. Rosenblatt, L. M. 1978. *The Reader, the Text, the Poem*. Carbondale, IL: Southern Illinois Press. p. 14-21.

6. Vygotsky, L. 1986. *Thought and Language*. Cambridge, MA: M.I.T. Press. p. xxxvii.

7. "Focus on Research: Exploring the Literature-Based Reading Revolution." McGee, L. M. 1992. *Language Arts* 69 (7):529-37.

8. Rosenblatt, L. M. 1938. *Literature as Exploration*. New York: Appleton-Century Crofts.

9. Rosenblatt, L. 1978. p. 12.

10. Rosenblatt, L. 1978.

11. Rosenblatt, L. M. 1977. "The Transactional Theory of the Literary Work: Implications for Research." Paper presented at the Buffalo Conference on Researching Response to Literature and the Teaching of Literature, Buffalo, NY, October. ED 209 667. pp. 8-10.

12. "Literature-Based Language Arts Programs: Present and Future." 1992. *Language Arts* 69 (7). Urbana, IL: National Council Teachers of English. (Entire November Issue.)

13. Purves, A., T. Rogers, and A. Soter. 1990. *How Porcupines Make Love II. Teaching a Response-Centered Literature Curriculum*. New York: Longman; Feeley, J. T., D. S. Strickland, and S. B. Wepner (ed.). 1991. *Process Readhing and Writing: A Literature-Based Approach*. New York: Teachers College Press: "Worlds of Possibilities in Response to Literature, Firm, and Life. Cox, C. and J. E. Many. 1989. *Language Arts* 65 (3):287-94; "Guiding Young Students' Response to Literature." Kelly, P. 1990. *The Reading Teacher* 43 (7):464-70; "Seven Readings of a Folk Tale: Literary Theory in the Classroom." Temple, C. 1991. *The New Advocate* 4 (1):25-35.

14. "Theory Becomes Practice: Aesthetic Teaching with Literature." Zarrillo, J. 1991. *The New Advocate* 4 (4):221-34; "Efferent and Aesthetic Teaching." Zarrillo, J. J., and C. Cox. 1992. *Stance and Literary Understanding: Exploring the Theories, Research, and Practice*. Edited by J. Many and C. Cox. Norwood, NJ: Ablex. pp. 239-45.

PART

2

Instructional Units

LETTER TO TEACHERS

Dear Teacher,

As former elementary teachers, we decided that a short summary prior to the units would be helpful to you.

We believe the materials suggested are relevant for diverse groups of children since the literature in the units crosses 20 different cultures or countries and represents 15 different subgenres of folk literature.

Knowing that your time is limited, a graphic overview in the form of a web is provided for each chapter. The countries from which the stories have come and their subgenres are given with each tale.

The chapters are designated for either primary or intermediate age elementary school students; you can determine the appropriateness for your students by reading the summary and noting our age recommendations.

The introduction to each chapter includes concepts related to literature through which students may connect one story to another. These literary outcomes are designated as recognition of: 1) literary elements of story structure, such as characterization, setting, plot, theme, style, and point of view; 2) characteristics of the subgenres of folk literature; and 3) strategies, such as response modes, through which students may increase their literacy.

For each unit, there are nine stories with suggested accompanying experiences. Each story is listed in an anthology or in a single edition book that will be found easily in public or school libraries. A summary of each story is included to give you an idea of the content as you plan for your students.

Based on the premise of this book that there are recursive and overlapping stages within a transactional process with literature, we have included suggested experiences for students at each of the stages. The experiences are noted as **Connect, Construct,** and **Create.**

Connect

These experiences are designated for building background and linking with previous knowledge. Careful consideration must be given to including some of these experiences prior to and during the reading of the story. Giving a book talk or using a visual will help students connect their background knowledge to the tale.

Construct

The construction of meaning occurs all during the story experience—during the connection, during the reading or listening of the tale, and following it— as the student makes personal meaning of the text. These experiences include probes from the teacher, but frequently students find their own meanings without outside assistance.

Create

The process described as creation may come in many forms: spontaneous verbal responses; artistic or graphic reflections; written or oral pieces of work; or in many cases, the creations are covert thoughts that are kept within the minds and hearts of the ones who have experienced the literature.

Appendix A contains directions for 104 of the literary response modes suggested for the 54 tales and verses. These response modes are divided into four types: visual manipulative (VM); visual artistic (VA); verbal oral (VO); and verbal written (VW). In the text these strategies are designated by boldface type followed by an identifying number, e.g. **probes** (VO 72).

The philosophy that underlies this book is that of promoting literature-based instruction. We hope that these stories might provide a foundation around which reading experiences and other curriculum will be integrated.

It is our hope that you will help students through this process, so they may learn to transact with literature on their own.

We would like you to take our framework and plan for the needs of your students.

We hope that you will take our ideas for experiences and breathe life into them, adapting them as appropriate for the children in your classroom.

Through these literary response modes your children will realize that even though folk literature may have been told thousands of years ago, it is real and alive today!

The Elves and the Shoemaker

The Golden Goose

The Gift of St. Nicholas

Mysterious Changes

CHANGES AND CHALLENGES (kindergarten-grade 3)

Little Burnt Face

Toads and Diamonds

Cinderella Clues

Riddles and Rhymes

Tattercoats

Clever Challenges

The Old Woman and Her Pig

The Bear Says "North"

CHAPTER
three

·•·•·•·•·•

Changes and Challenges Unit
Kindergarten-Grade 3

LITERARY OUTCOMES

The stories in this unit include fairy tales from the Grimm Brothers' *Märchen* ("The Elves and the Shoemaker") and English, French, and Native American variants of the Cinderella tale. An American adaptation of a saint's legend ("The Gift of St. Nicholas") provides an introduction to legends with a character known and loved by young children. Other stories in this unit include a fable from the Jataka Tales of India ("The Golden Goose"), a delightful story of an old woman and her pig in the cumulative pattern, and an introduction to tricksters with a bear and fox story. This unit also includes an all-time favorite subgenre: riddles.

The first theme includes stories with elements of mystery for young children. In addition to the mystery theme, there are contrasts in the structure of fairy tales, legends, and fables that even young children can recognize.

In the second theme, the major literary goal is to compare variants of the same folktale—Cinderella. Most children will have heard or have seen at least one version of Cinderella, so the basic story structure will be familiar, even to very young children.

Riddles found in the third theme, Clever Challenges, will provide a climate for recognition and perhaps creation of more examples of this subgenre.

This third theme of this unit also demonstrates the cumulative pattern with "The Old Woman and Her Pig." The challenge in this story is twofold: the old woman needs to get her pig home, and the storyteller needs help from the listeners in unraveling the cumulative effects of the pig's stubbornness. The children will expand their schemata as they note the connections among the items in this cumulative tale and will add the cumulative tale type to their story schema. Other cumulative stories may also be read to children to reinforce the accumulation technique.

The trickster story, "The Bear Says 'North,'" will be most pleasing to the second and third graders who have recently honed their sense of humor. Watch them find ways to say "East" to each other after this tale!

Some underlying ideas that may be developed through this unit of changes and challenges include:

- awareness that these stories teach "lessons" about life
- recognition that most folk literature was told before being written and most of these stories are very old
- recognition that these stories represent people's hopes and dreams
- awareness that people told and retold stories to fit their lives and that although the stories are basically the same, they are still different and reflect the culture from which the stories came
- recognition that we know little of the characters in folk literature and often do not know their names
- recognition of elements of story: who, when, where, and what
- awareness that folk stories are found in anthologies as well as single versions of a story in picture book format
- noting differences among fairy tales, legends, and fables
- noting that legends are told as "true," even when they have elements of fantasy in them

INTEGRATED CURRICULUM STRATEGIES

Curriculum integration opportunities lie within the areas of:

- contrasts of British, French, and Native American cultures and lifestyles
- unit on reptiles or cold-blooded vs. warm-blooded animals
- fire safety
- rainbows and prisms and other weather related phenomena
- use of question marks
- figurative language
- animals and their natural enemies
- pets and how to treat them

Mysterious Changes Theme

THE ELVES AND THE SHOEMAKER—GERMAN FAIRY TALE

"The Elves and the Shoemaker." Sutherland, Z., and Livingston, M. C. 1984. *The Scott-Foresman Anthology of Children's Literature*. Glenview, IL: Scott-Foresman. pp. 187-88.

"The Elves and the Shoemaker."Arbuthnot, M. H. 1961. *The Arbuthnot Anthology of Children's Literature*. Chicago: Scott-Foresman. p. 199.

"The Elves and the Shoemaker." Arbuthnot, M. H. 1961. *Time for Fairy Tales*. Glenview, IL: Scott-Foresman. pp. 35-36.

"The Elves and the Shoemaker." Grimm, J., and W. Grimm. 1959. *Favorite Fairy Tales Told in Germany*. Retold by V. Haviland and illustrated by S. Suba. Boston: Little, Brown. pp. 118-21.

"The Elves and the Shoemaker." Hutchison, V. 1992. *Chimney Corner Stories, Tales for Little Children*. Illustrated by L. Lenski. Hamden, CT: Shoestring Press. pp. 99-106.

Grimm, J., and W. Grimm. 1967. *The Elves and the Shoemaker*. Illustrated by K. Brandt. Chicago: Follett.

Grimm, J., and W. Grimm. 1961. *The Elves and the Shoemaker*. Retold by F. Pavel and illustrated by J. Hewitt. New York: Holt, Rinehart, & Winston.

Littledale, F. 1991. *The Elves and the Shoemaker*. New York: Scholastic.

Plume, I. 1991. *Shoemaker and Elves*. San Diego, CA: Harbrace.

Rowland, J. 1989. *The Elves and the Shoemaker*. Chicago, IL: Calico.

Recommended for students in kindergarten through third grade.

Summary

This tale was recorded by the Brothers Grimm who traveled around the German countryside in the early 1800s recording the tales of ordinary people. A familiar tale, it is about an old couple whose business is in trouble, but because they are very good, their kindness is repaid by unusual helpers.

Connect

Prior to reading the story, select some of the following strategies to help connect children's prior background knowledge and experiences to the story.

- Announce an upcoming slumber party for stuffed animals. Encourage children to each bring in one animal for the party. Provide a comforter and pillows. Leave books around for reading during the animals' slumber party. After the children leave for the day, arrange the room to appear as if a slumber party has occurred: move each animal to a different position, move books as if they have been read, and leave a couple of empty pizza boxes and empty soft drink cans in the area.

    The next morning, allow time for talking about the "mystery." Encourage theories from the children about the evidence of the slumber party and what the animals might have done during the night.

- Leave notes in the classroom for children to find that appear to have been written by others outside the class—maybe elves!

- Tell the children about a stack of paper that you left on the shelf last night and show them the **show-me cards** (VM 28) that were there this morning. How can this be? A stack of colored paper has turned into a set of show-me cards! Show-me cards may be used for students to display their individual answers to questions.

    Read "The Elves and the Shoemaker" to the children.

Construct

Following the reading of the story, if needed ask **probes** (VO 72) such as the following:

Is there a mystery in this story that is similar to our "mystery" of the show-me cards? How are the mysteries similar? How are they different?
How can we find out who made our show-me cards from our stack of paper?
What did the elves do when they were rewarded for their good deeds? Why did they do that?

- Find out if anyone knows what it means to do a "good office in return."
- Allow **predictions**.
- Paraphrase these terms in language that we hear today: "one good deed deserves another"; "treat each other kindly"; "treat others as you wish them to treat you." Direct children in **role playing** (VO 74), soliciting some examples of how they might treat each other as they wish to be treated.
- Talk about other stories or events in which something mysteriously changes form. (An example is *Blackboard Bear* by Martha Alexander.)

- Make a display of single version picture books of "The Elves and the Shoemaker." Encourage children to read them and look at the pictures independently.
- This activity is **K.W.L.: (Know, Want to Know, Have Learned)** (VM 14). Make a chart of what the students know about this story; make another chart of any questions for which they would like to find answers. Read the story again to the children with the questions displayed, so they can listen for answers in the story. Following the second reading, allow time for discussion of the questions that were generated. If some of their questions require inferences, encourage children to state their theories. Following the second reading, children may review the story by completing the "L" or "Learned" column.
- Lead the children in making character **comparison charts** (VW 85) as they dictate or write what they know about the characters. Guide them toward recognizing the fact that in fairy tales, we usually know very little about the characters. Often, we don't even know their names. Ask them to think of other fairy tale characters and what is known about them. Some other examples of stories with characters who are nameless and about whom we know little of their personalities are "The Three Pigs," "Red Riding Hood," and "Billy Goats Gruff."

Following is a suggested format for the chart:

STORY:	NAME OF CHARACTER:	PERSONALITY:

Create

- During periods of time for self-selected writing, called writing blocks, add an option to children's choices for topics and suggest they write mystery stories to place on a mystery bulletin board. Also suggest that they find books of mysteries to place on a table or shelf near the bulletin board.
- Let children experiment with sounds to accompany the storytelling and add background sound effects to the story using a tape recorder. Place cassette recorders at a center. A tape of the story may be on one recorder while the other recorder has blank tapes. Have the children plan sound effects and record onto the blank tape both the telling of the story and the sound effects. All of the tapes then may be left at the center for children to listen to

individually. Texts of the story may also be available for children to follow as they listen to the tapes.

■ Have children paint with watercolors a house for the elves or a new shoe shop for the shoemaker.

■ Imagine what it might have been like when this story was first told around a campfire with families sitting and listening in much the same way they sit and watch television today. **Role play** (VO 74) the storytelling while sitting around an **imaginary campfire** (VO 68).

■ Problem-solving tasks for the children in groups or individually include:

1) make a plan for keeping the elves there with the shoemaker. How could the shoemaker have done something differently so the elves would have stayed and lived with the shoemaker and his wife?

2) determine what the class should do about trying to find out how the stack of colored paper turned into show-me cards in the classroom.

THE GIFT OF ST. NICHOLAS—AMERICAN LEGEND

"The Gift of St. Nicholas." Arbuthnot, M. H. 1961. *Time for Fairy Tales.* Glenview, IL: Scott-Foresman. pp. 191-96.

Other Santa Claus, Christmas, or Holiday stories

Baum, F. 1985. *The Life and Adventures of Santa Claus.* New York: Dutton.

Giblin, J. 1985. *The Truth about Santa Claus.* New York: Crowell.

"The Gift of the Magi." 1987. *One-Minute Christmas Stories.* Adapted by S. Lewis and illustrated by J. Palmer. New York: Doubleday.

Lane, J. 1983. *The Life and Legends of Santa Claus.* Illustrated by Hokie. Harleysville, PA: Tonnis.

Porter, A. P. 1991. *Kwanzaa.* Illustrated by J. Porter. Minneapolis: Carolrhoda Books.

The following story, although not the same story as the "Gift of St. Nicholas," has some similarities and could easily be substituted:

"St. Nicholas and the Children." Martin, E., and L. Gál. 1984. *Tales of the Far North.* New York: Dial. pp. 81-88.

Recommended for children from kindergarten to third grade.

Summary

A young Dutch couple and their children, living in New Amsterdam, have difficulties because the cruel and rich burgomaster deliberately causes them financial hardships and trouble. After expending all their resources to pay the fees levied by the burgomaster, Claus is ready to sell his wonderful pipe. As he sits pondering the decision, he rubs his pipe and is amazed to see a little man with a round structure materialize. Upon being instructed to make the place warm and to provide food for a weary traveler, Claus and his wife are embarrassed by not having any wood or food in the house. To their surprise, though, the little man breaks his cane and places it in the fire; when he does, the cane turns into huge logs. When they say they have no food, the little man chastises them, smelling the wonderful aromas of just-cooked foods. They are overjoyed and have a wonderful time with the little man eating a delicious meal.

The next morning the burgomaster comes to have them arrested for wizardry, but before he can, their humble cottage turns into a palace and invisible hands grab the burgomaster and his troops, chasing them away, leaving Claus and his family to wonder about the little old man whom some call St. Nick.

Connect

(Teachers, be aware that some parents object to the study of any of the symbols of Christmas. This story may need special consideration before using it.)

■ Prior to reading this story display a picture of Santa Claus and ask children who this character is and what some of his other names are. Some children will have heard the names of Saint Nicholas, Saint Nick, or Father Christmas. Read the excerpt from Moore's *The Night before Christmas* that describes Saint Nick. Tell the children that stories about very good people who lived long ago are sometimes called "saint's legends" and that some people believe St. Nick was a good man who helped people in need.

■ Model a **think aloud** (VO 81) as you show children how you make connections between what you do and do not know about a character and how you make predictions and form questions to allow you to learn from your reading. You might ask yourself these questions out loud:

Could this story be about the St. Nicholas whom I call Santa Claus? Does that mean that this is going to be a Christmas story? I can imagine what St. Nick looks like and what he will be like in the story. The title of this story is "The Gift of St. Nicholas," so he must give someone a gift. Will he leave the gift under a tree? Will the gift be a surprise? Who will receive the gift?

■ Read or tell the story to the children. When you come to the character of the burgomaster, ask for predictions about what a burgomaster does. Many of the children may have seen the burgomaster in some of the Christmas specials on television and will recognize his character as the "villain."

Construct

- Immediately after reading or telling the story, give children an opportunity for spontaneous responses. One form of such responses is to group children into buddy teams and encourage **buddy buzzing** (VO 54). Following their questions or comments, hand out cards on which either the names of the characters or their pictures have been sketched prior to the classroom session. Characters include Claus; his wife, Anitje; their fat children; the burgomaster; soldiers; St. Nick.
- Lead a story retelling as children who are holding cards tell what they know about the characters. As soon as a child has had a turn to tell something about the story, he or she should pass the card to another child who can tell another part of the story including that character.
- Guide discussion through appropriate **probes** (VO 72) such as the following: *Why are people sometimes "jealous" of others? What right did the burgomaster have to build roads through Claus's pond and garden? Imagine how Claus and his family felt when they had no money or food on Christmas Eve. Show by the expression on your face how Claus must have looked when he rubbed the pipe and the blast of cold air brought in St. Nick. Who left the note under the door that said, "Don't ever sell the pipe"?*
- Paste felt tabs on the backs of the cards and leave them at the **flannel board** (VM 11) so children may retell the story independently. Add cards for the pond, the garden, the roads, the large brick house, the little cottage, the pipe, and the great house with its fine silver and large ice pond. Children who tell the story again may enjoy these prompts.

Create

- Have younger children draw the faces of Claus, his wife, the burgomaster, or St. Nick and write or dictate a sentence or story about the facial expression.
- Fraction activities may be integrated with this story as children draw roads "through ponds and gardens" to show halves, thirds, or fractional parts in the curriculum.
- Suggest that older children investigate the history of New Amsterdam (New York) and determine what the area was like 300 years ago as compared to today. At some grade levels, the social studies curriculum will include a study of the beginnings of the New England states.
- This story may be followed with the reading of some other legends, such as Johnny Appleseed. To help children realize that legends are usually told

about people who actually lived, have them group-write a legend about someone whom they all know (another teacher, custodian, principal). Post this legend on a chart for all to read. Children may follow the group legend with individual ones, and they also may be posted near the chart.

THE GOLDEN GOOSE—INDIAN JATAKA FABLE

"The Golden Goose." Saltman, J. 1985. *The Riverside Anthology of Children's Literature.* Boston: Houghton Mifflin, p. 235.

Gaer, J. 1955. *The Fables of India.* Illustrated by R. Monk. Boston: Little, Brown. pp. 164-66.

"The Golden Goose." Babbitt, E. C. 1950. *More Jataka Tales.* Illustrated by E. Young. New York: Appleton Century Crofts.

"The Golden Goose." Rugoff, M. 1949. *A Harvest of World Folk Tales.* New York: The Viking Press. pp. 435-36.

Hilbert, M. 1978. *The Golden Goose.* Illustrated by M. Santa. Chicago: Follett.

Similar fable

"The Goose That Laid Golden Eggs." Mitsumasa, A. 1989. *Anno's Aesop: A Book of Fables.* New York: Orchard, p. 36.

(There are different stories by the same name. For example: Bell, A. 1988. *The Golden Goose by Jacob and Wilhelm Grimm.* Illustrated by D. Duntz. New York: North-South.)

This story is recommended for children from kindergarten through third grade.

Summary

This fable from the Jataka Tales tells the story of a goose whose feathers are gold. The goose gives away feathers to help a family until the family becomes greedy and plucks the remaining feathers. The feathers that grow back after being plucked are white—not gold.

Connect

■ Prepare the children for the reading of this fable by introducing them to fables. Young children can understand that fables are stories that were told to teach lessons. The lessons in each fable are clear, even to young children.

Quickly tell Aesop's fable of the Greedy Dog (sees reflection in water holding a bone and thinks he may get two bones if he can take away the bone from the dog in the water; loses his bone) to help children quickly realize that fables:

> are short
> usually have animal characters
> usually show a weakness in a character
> teach a lesson

- To help children focus on the lesson found in "The Golden Goose," review the way the shoemaker and his wife (from "The Elves and the Shoemaker") wanted to do something good for the elves who had helped them.
- If needed, ask **probes** (VO 72):
   Do you suppose everyone "does one good turn for another"? What are some reasons that people would not be kind and good to someone who was helpful to them?

Right before reading the story ask the children to listen to the story to find out if the family will be as good and kind as the shoemaker and his wife were.

- Read or tell "The Golden Goose" to the children.

Construct

- For comparison of this story's characters with those in "The Shoemaker and the Elves," draw a large **Venn diagram** (VM 33) on which one circle is labeled "The Shoemaker's Family" and the other circle is entitled "The Goose's Family." Using information supplied by the children, discuss each incident, event, or motivation suggested by the children and determine whether it will be placed in the circle for either of the families or on the overlap portion, which would indicate it was true for both families. Accept all reasoning for the placement of an idea and if controversy exists, call for a vote to decide on the placement. Through such discussions, meaning for these stories is cultivated.

Create

- Encourage children to make their own **Venn diagrams** (VM 33) of comparisons of characters and stories.
- For a bulletin board of "feelings" supply materials for children to make varying degrees of happy and sad faces. Attach pieces of velcro to the backs of the faces. Write some questions on sentence strips and attach them to the background of the bulletin board. Velcro may also be applied to the space

beside each question and children may manipulate the faces to show the feelings of each character at different times in the story. Some typical questions are:

How did the goose feel when she was able to do something good for her family? How did the family feel about the goose when they first discovered her gold feathers? How did the goose feel when the family began plucking her feathers? How did the family feel when they discovered that the feathers growing back were white instead of gold? How did the goose feel when her feathers were white instead of gold?

- Dramatize or write a follow-up to the story in which the family apologizes to the goose for plucking the feathers.
- Dramatize or write a goodbye letter from the goose to the family citing "goose abuse."
- For an integrated math lesson, arbitrarily determine that a goose feather weighs one ounce. Find the current value of one ounce of gold and have children write in their math journals story problems and the answers to the value of various numbers of gold feathers. For example, a child might write: The goose lost two feathers by the pond and they were found by a frog. He took them to the Frog Bank. How much money did the Frog Bank give him for two feathers?
- In second or third grade classes, consider conducting a court of law in which the family is tried for "goose abuse." Children may choose to defend or prosecute the family and write their own legal briefs for the case.

Cinderella Clues Theme

TATTERCOATS—ENGLISH FAIRY TALE

Jacobs, J. 1989. *Tattercoats*. Illustrated by M. Tomes. New York: Putnam.

Greaves, M. 1990. *Tattercoats*. Illustrated by M. Chamberlain. New York: Crown.

"Tattercoats." Arbuthnot, M. H. 1961. *The Arbuthnot Anthology of Children's Literature*. Glenview, IL: Scott-Foresman. pp. 158-59.

"Tattercoats." Arbuthnot, M. H. 1961. *Time for Fairy Tales*. Glenview, IL: Scott-Foresman. pp.19-21.

"Tattercoats." Jacobs, J. 1894. *More English Fairy Tales*. London: David McNutt. pp. 67-72.

"Tattercoats." Sutherland, Z., and M. C. Livingston. 1984. *The Scott-Foresman Anthology of Children's Literature*. Glenview, IL: Scott-Foresman. pp. 155-57.

Recommended for children from kindergarten through grade three.

Summary

In this British version of Cinderella, a gentle goosegirl's clothes are changed from rags into shining robes as she wins the prince's heart and becomes his bride.

TOADS AND DIAMONDS—FRENCH FAIRY TALE

"Toads and Diamonds." Sutherland, Z., and M. C. Livingston.1984. *The Scott-Foresman Anthology of Children's Literature*. Glenview, IL: Scott-Foresman. pp. 199-200.

"Diamonds and Toads," Opie, I., and P. Opie. 1992. (reissue). *The Classic Fairy Tales*. New York: Oxford. pp. 98-99.

"Toads and Diamonds." Hutchison, V. 1927. *Candlelight Stories*. Illustrated by L. Lenski. New York: Minton, Bolch., pp. 93-100.

"Toads and Diamonds." Lang, A. 1889.*The Blue Fairy Book*. London: Longmans, Green, & Co. pp. 295-98. (Republished in 1969 by Airmont; republished in 1965 by Dover.)

Summary

This French variant of Cinderella contrasts the kind maiden who is rewarded with pearls and diamonds falling from her lips while her haughty sister only finds toads and snakes.

LITTLE BURNT FACE—NATIVE AMERICAN FAIRY TALE

"Little Burnt Face." Sutherland, Z., and M. C. Livingston. 1984. *The Scott-Foresman Anthology of Children's Literature*. Glenview, IL: Scott-Foresman. pp.388-89.

"Little Burnt-Face." Arbuthnot, M. H. 1961. *The Arbuthnot Anthology of Children's Literature*. Glenview, IL: Scott-Foresman. pp. 392-93.

"Little Burnt-Face." Arbuthnot, M. H. 1961. *Time for Fairy Tales*. Glenview, IL: Scott-Foresman. pp. 199-201.

"Little Burnt Face." Butler, F. 1989 (reissue). *Sharing Literature with Children, A Thematic Anthology.* Prospect Heights, IL: Waveland. p. 180.
Martin, R. 1992. *The Rough-Face Girl.* New York: Putnam.

Summary

The Native American maiden in this story is scarred from hot coal burns by her eldest sister who has always claimed her youngest sister had fallen into an open fire. The maiden is good and has a gift that will enable her to "see" the Great Chief when no one else can. Through her view of the Great Chief, her skin is bathed in dew and becomes perfect as she becomes his bride. The wicked and vain sisters are disgraced.

Other Cinderella Tales

Brown, M. 1988. *Cinderella.* New York: Macmillan.
"Cinderella." Hutchison, V. 1992. *Chimney Corner Stories, Tales for Little Children.* Illustrated by L. Lenski. Hamden, CT: Shoestring Press. pp. 117-29.
"Cinderella.: Opie, I., and P. Opie. 1992 (reissue). *The Classic Fairly Tales.* New York: Oxford. pp. 117-22.
Climo, S. 1989. *The Egyptian Cinderella.* Illustrated by R. Heller. New York: Harper Trophy.
Huck, C. 1989. *Princess Furball.* New York: Greenwillow.
Louie, Ai-Ling. 1982. *Yeh-Shen: A Cinderella Story from China.* Illustrated by E. Young. New York: Philomel.
Mills, L. 1993. (Translated from P. Asbjornsen and J. Moe). *Tatterhood and the Hobglobins: A Norwegian Folktale.* Boston: Little, Brown.
Perrault, C. 1990. *Cinderella.* New York: Puffin.
Shorto, R. 1990. *Cinderella, The Untold Story.* Illustrated by T. Lewis. Secaucus, NJ: Birch Lane Press/Carol Publishing.
Wagman, W. 1993. *Cinderella.* New York: Hyperion.

Note: For a collection of 25 Cinderella tales from around the world, see Sierra, J. 1992. *The Oryx Multicultural Folktale Series: Cinderella.* Phoenix, AZ: The Oryx Press.

Recommended for children from kindergarten through grade three.

Connect

■ Prior to reading these stories, prepare a display of **realia** (VA 46), including fancy dancing shoes (silver or gold), pumpkin, replica of horse drawn coach, box of ashes from a fireplace, mop or scrub brush, rawhide strap, bow and arrow, and mirror. Give children an opportunity to handle objects and speculate on how they relate to each other.

- Bring in a collection of "Cinderella" tales from many countries and add to the table with the realia.
- Make a poster announcing an upcoming "Cinderella" afternoon. Encourage children to look for other "Cinderella" tales.
- Ask parents to tell children "Cinderella" tales, and collect additional "Cinderella" realia.
- On "Cinderella afternoon" have a collective storytelling session of the basic "Cinderella" story. Ask for a volunteer to begin the storytelling. Hand the volunteer a "magic wand," which will be held while storytelling. After a child has made a contribution to the story, he or she passes the wand to another volunteer who continues the story. The process continues until the story has a satisfactory ending.
- Encourage picture drawing or discussion of these areas:

    What is a fairy godmother? Why do Cinderella stories have such a helper? How must it feel to be in dirty, ragged clothes? How does it feel to be dirty and not to be able to take a bath? How does it feel to be in fine, dressy clothes? How does it feel for others to make fun of you? In folk literature what happens to "good" people? What happens to "bad" people?

After completing these connecting activities, read the three stories over the period of one day, if possible. Since the goal of this theme is comparison, the stories need to be read as close in time to each other as possible.

Construct

- Immediately following the reading or telling of each story, allow spontaneous reactions. If a question is required to initiate the reactions, the following **probe** (VO 72) may be used:

    Do you think this story is a Cinderella story? Why or why not?

Following the reading of all tales, make a **motif comparison chart** (VM 18) such as the following:

	Tattercoat	Toads & Diamonds	Little Burnt Face
What was her name? What did she look like? How was she treated? Who helped? How did the story end?			

■ Have children sit around an **imaginary campfire** (VO 68) and talk about the following:

Why were all three tales told by people of long ago? How are all three stories alike? How are all three stories different?

■ Use the following **probes** (VO 72) with older, more mature groups:

Why do you think the original storytellers allowed "bad" things to happen to such a "good" person? Why did the storytellers make family members so mean to each other? Can you tell what is important to the people of all three countries by the stories they told?

Create

Children may be given choices of activities for responding to these stories or the teacher may select experiences for guided responses. Some suggestions are as follows:

■ Add to the **realia** (VA 46) collection started before the reading of the stories.
■ Build a carriage or make a bow and arrow from cardboard, string, and construction paper.
■ Plan and make a "Cinderella" **board game** (VM 3).
■ Bring in dolls and dress as "Cinderella" characters.
■ Divide class into cooperative groups and have each group paint watercolor scenes from one of the tales and then compare the pictures and illustrations.
■ In cooperative groups, draw a **wordless text** (VM 35) for one of the tales.
■ Make a Native American headdress that Little Burnt Face might have worn on her wedding day.
■ In small groups, combine the three tales into one. Using simple costumes to represent one of the "Cinderella" characters, dramatize the combined version to another class.

- Act out "Toads and Diamonds," showing emotions by having paper "diamonds" fall from children's mouths.
- Write a letter from one of the stepsisters to "Cinderella" after she marries.
- Write a response journal entry [**literature response logs, also called lit log,** (VW 92)] from the wicked stepmother's point of view, explaining her behavior to Cinderella.
- Write a song or chant for Little Burnt Face before and after meeting the chief.
- Create a motif comparison chart (VM 18), comparing these three Cinderella variants. Add other Cinderella stories to the comparison as an extension.

Clever Challenges Theme

RIDDLES AND RHYMES—CHILDHOOD AND NURSERY RHYMES

Opie, I., and P. Opie. 1955. *Oxford Nursery Rhyme Book.* New York: Oxford University Press.

"Folk Rhymes." Butler, F. 1989 (reissue). *Sharing Literature with Children: A Thematic Anthology.* Prospect Heights, IL: Waveland. pp. 5-14.

Hastings, S. 1990. *Miss Mary Mac All Dressed in Black: Tongue Twisters, Jump-Rope Rhymes, and Other Children's Lore from New England.* Little Rock, AR: August House.

Opie, I., and p. Opie. 1991. *Tail Feathers from Mother Goose: The Opie Rhyme Book.* Avenal, NJ: Outlet Book Company.

Yolen, J. 1992. *Street Rhymes around the World.* New York: Wordsong.

These rhymes and riddles are recommended for children in kindergarten-grade 3.

Summary

The riddles and rhymes recommended for this theme are found in nursery rhyme books and books of Mother Goose rhymes. Typically these riddles give clues and reveal clever inferences to well-known objects about which the riddles or rhymes are written. Many of these childhood rhymes have been passed from child to child and preserved through generations. This emphasis on traditional riddles will transfer into modern literature as children's interests grow in this form of writing. Encourage children to examine the vast assortment of contemporary riddle books available.

Connect

- Before reading any of the riddles to the children, display a "challenge" bulletin board. On the board, have a riddle (without the answer) that is typically passed from child to child and one that your students might recognize. An example is the riddle about teeth:

  Thirty white horses upon a red hill
  Now they stamp
  Now they chomp
  Now they stand still.
  What are they?

- Just prior to the reading of some riddles in class, ask children to meet the challenge and solve the puzzle in the riddle. Read one or two more and ask for solutions. Children may know a few riddles to share. Encourage them to bring in riddle books for a display table.
- Background for riddles may include sharing a challenge: find out who was "Mother Goose."
- Plan a Mother Goose display table for children to bring their rhyme and riddle books from home.
- Record many of the old rhymes for children's independent listening and reading at the **listening post** (VO 70).

Construct

- Allow free responses after reading riddles, so that children have time to think of the answers to the riddles or of other challenges that are brought to mind. Encourage responses by having structured "think time" in which children have from three to five minutes for thinking, drawing, writing, or making up new riddles.
- After the sharing of riddles is complete, distribute pads of paper that have been stapled together to make small booklets. Suggest a writing block time in which everyone will practice writing some riddles and will produce a riddle booklet. Some children may want to copy riddles rather than create them. This activity is valuable for children to learn the form of the riddle as well as the appropriate punctuation to follow a question.

Create

- Make collages to represent selected riddles.

- Design jacket covers for the riddle booklets created earlier.
- Read poems about insects from *Joyful Noises* by Paul Fleischman and try to make insect riddles.
- Pantomime or act out the riddles.
- Write "school" riddles about the playground, the library, the principal, the teacher, or a class pet.
- Some discussion questions or ideas for **literature response journals**, also called **lit logs**, (VW 92) follow:

    Why I liked or disliked characters in a riddle.

    I really want to know about …?

    My favorite animal character. Predict what the animal did after the riddle was over? Where did he/she go?

- Write an original riddle.

THE OLD WOMAN AND HER PIG—ENGLISH CUMULATIVE FOLKTALE

Kimmel, E. A. 1992. *The Old Woman and Her Pig*. New York: Holiday.

Galdone, P. *The Old Woman and Her Pig*. 1960. New York: Whittlesly.

"The Old Woman and Her Pig." Arbuthnot, M. H. 1961. *Time for Fairy Tales*. Glenview, IL: Scott-Foresman. pp. 7-8.

"The Old Woman and Her Pig." Hutchison, V. 1992. *Chimney Corner Stories, Tales for Little Children*. Illustrated by L. Lenski. Hamden, CT: Shoestring Press. pp. 11-18.

"The Old Woman and the Pig." Morel, E. 1970. *Fairy Tales and Fables*. New York: Grosset & Dunlap.

"The Old Woman and Her Pig." Richardson, F. 1972. *Great Children's Stories*. Northbrook, IL: Hubbard.

This story is recommended for children in kindergarten-grade 3.

Summary

In this cumulative tale from Joseph Jacobs' *English Fairy Tales*, the old woman is sweeping her house when she finds a crooked sixpence. She is so pleased that she goes to the market and buys a pig. Her troubles begin when she tries to coax the pig over the stile. Because the pig will not cross the stile, the little old woman asks for help from a stick, dog, fire, water, ox, butcher, rope, rat, cat, and cow. Through the cumulative action of each object, the pig jumps over the stile and the little old woman goes home that night.

Connect

Prior to reading the story try some of the following activities:

- To illustrate the cumulative concept, arrange a set of dominoes side by side so that when the first one is pushed over, the rest will follow suit and fall. Explain that this happening is sometimes called a chain reaction or a domino effect. In literature, it is called a "cumulative story."
- Line children around the room so the beginning and ending of the line will be evident. Show them the cumulative effect with this procedure: On a given signal, child one will lightly tap child two on the shoulder and say "one." As soon as child two feels the tap, he or she will tap child three and say, "two." The same action will carry through until all children have been tapped. Then the last child will turn around and tap the child who just tapped him or her and the process will reverse with tapping and calling the numbers out in reverse order.

After these activities get ready to read the story as follows:

- In preparation for the story, make a fence from brown construction paper and attach felt to the back for use with the **flannel board** (VM 11). Ask the children to decide how they would get a pet animal over the fence if they were leading it and could not pick it up. Allow suggestions and short discussion.
- Place a small block covered with brown paper in front of the fence on the flannel board and ask the children if this step or stile could be used to climb over the fence.
- Tell them that in this story, the stile plays an important role. Place a construction paper or fabric "old woman" on the flannel board and begin telling or reading the story. Other objects needed for the story are a pig, dog, stick, fire, water, cow, butcher, rope, rat, ox, and cat. As you read about each character or object and its response to the old woman's request, involve the children in chanting the response by saying, "But the pig said, 'NO!' or "But the dog said, 'NO!' continuing through to the cat who asked for a saucer of milk as a condition for her cooperation. At that point, the story reverses and each character becomes conditionally cooperative. The children will see the relationships as the objects are moved on the board in reverse direction toward the preceding object.

Construct

- Discuss the meaning of the word "stile" after the reading and allow time to clarify the word and its use. Some children may want to talk about the term "sixpence" (silver coin from England worth a few pennies).
- Divide children in small groups of four to six. Have them close their eyes and see pictures in their minds as you reread the story. After the rereading, have each child draw a picture of some part of the story. The paper will be prepared with a rectangle drawn in the center of a quarter sheet of newsprint. Ask children to draw their pictures inside the rectangle. After pictures are drawn, have children share in groups by holding up pictures and allowing others to comment on what they see (**say what I saw** [VO 76]).
- To reinforce meaning from the story, ask these **probes** (VO 72):
  Why do you suppose the pig was being stubborn about going over the stile? Why were the other animals not being cooperative? What do you like best about the way this story is written? What do you not like about the way the story is written?

Create

- Demonstrate how to wrap each picture the children drew earlier around a wooden or cardboard block. (If possible, have the same size blocks.) Many children will be able to fold sides and ends of paper and close with tape. For younger ones, adults in the classroom may be needed for assistance. The picture in the rectangle should be centered on the front of the block. Place the blocks in order of the story in domino fashion (there will be duplicates) and give children opportunities to tip the first block to begin the cumulative effect. These blocks may be placed in the block center or the story center for later experiences of sequencing and manipulating.
- Leave newsprint in the art center prepared with rectangles in the center of each quarter section so children can draw additional pictures of cumulative stories and make their own set of dominoes for a story.
- Leave books *One Fine Day* by Nonny Hogrogrian and the traditional tale of *This Is the House that Jack Built* prominently displayed for children to read and look at the pictures. These may become models for additional cumulative stories to be written by the children.

THE BEAR SAYS "NORTH"—FINNISH ANIMAL TRICKSTER TALE

"The Bear Says 'North.'" Saltman, J. 1985. *The Riverside Anthology of Children's Literature*. Boston: Houghton Mifflin Co.

Fillmore, P. 1922. *Mighty Mikko: A Book of Finnish Fairy Tales and Folk Tales.*
Illustrated by J. V. Everen. New York: Harcourt.
Note: Trickster tales that could be used in this unit include:
Hastings, R. 1991. *Reynard the Fox.* New York: Tambourine.
McDermott, G. 1992. *Zomo the Rabbit: A Trickster Tale from West Africa.* New
York: Harcourt.

**This story is recommended for children from kindergarten through third
grade.**

Summary

In this simple animal trickster tale, children will recognize the cleverness
of Mikko, the fox, as he tricks Osmo, the bear, into setting free a grouse
being held in his mouth. These animals are not well known to children
in America but can easily become favorites. Follow-up stories may
include some of Reynard, the fox, which are probably related to this story.

Connect

■ Before beginning this story, place a large chart on the wall with these
headings:

HELPERS	HURTERS	TEASERS

■ Review the roles played by characters throughout this unit as helpers,
hurters, or teasers. They will remember the Cinderella stories well with the
strong character traits of either good or bad. Develop the meaning of the
word "teasing" by allowing children to remember teasers in their families or
among their friends. The words "playing tricks" will be familiar to the
children, so share with them the word "trickster," and tell them that a
trickster is one who plays tricks or teases others.

Help them see the difference between one who hurts others as opposed to
one who plays tricks.

■ Write the names "MIKKO" and "OSMO" on posters which become character tags to be worn by children who assume the role of that character. Place
the "Mikko" tag around a child's neck and tell the class that this is Mikko,

the fox, who is a trickster. He loves to play tricks on his friend, Osmo, the bear. Place the tag for Osmo on another child and have both children stand with the tags while you read or tell the story.

Construct

■ To construct meaning with the children, retell the story, allowing other children to wear the character tags and to make facial expressions to indicate how they feel at different times during the story. Then give each child a happy and sad face drawn earlier on a tongue depressor. Half the class will represent the feelings of Osmo and half will represent Mikko's feelings. During the third retelling, stop at points in the story and ask for an **EPR** (**every pupil response**) (VO 66) . When you ask for EPRs from Mikko's group, those children representing him will display a face to show how he feels at that point in the story. The same will be done for Osmo's group when you stop and call for EPRs on how Osmo feels.

■ Discussion will follow as children disagree on how either animal feels at a given point. Some questions to use if **probes** (VO 72) are necessary:

What other words could you use to describe Osmo's feelings at the beginning of the story? What made those feelings change? Have you ever felt frustrated? What causes frustration? What made Mikko happy? Have you ever known anyone like Mikko?

■ Have the children say these words together while reading them from a chart: "North," "South," "East," "West." Elaborately form your mouth in the proper position for saying each of the words and give the children time to do likewise. It is only through understanding the position of one's mouth and teeth in pronouncing those words, that the humor of the story can be experienced.

Create

Tell children that African storytellers from the past often used a **storytelling bone** (VM 30) to remind them of the stories of their families and villages. These bones from large animals were carved with pictures and hieroglyphic symbols to prompt storytelling.

■ Children may collaboratively create a classroom storytelling bone from papier-mâché. Once it is completed, they can paint symbols to represent various episodes from their class history or from stories recently read. The bone subsequently may be passed from one student to another for telling the whole or parts of the stories.

■ Writing in **literature response logs (lit logs)** (VW 92) is another suggested activity. Some topics, if needed, are:

> *How I Outsmarted a Trickster*
> *When I Tricked My...*
> *The Funniest Story I Know...*

■ During **writers' workshop** (VW 104), children may be encouraged, although not assigned, to write other stories of Osmo and Mikko or to write other "animal trickster" stories.

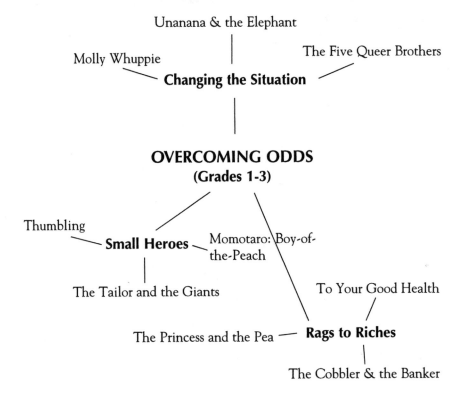

Unanana & the Elephant

Molly Whuppie   The Five Queer Brothers

Changing the Situation

OVERCOMING ODDS
(Grades 1-3)

Thumbling

Small Heroes — Momotaro: Boy-of-
the-Peach

The Tailor and the Giants   To Your Good Health

The Princess and the Pea — **Rags to Riches**

The Cobbler & the Banker

CHAPTER
four
∗ ✷ ∗ ✷ ∗ ✷ ∗ ✷

Overcoming Odds Unit
Grades 1-3

LITERARY OUTCOMES

Throughout this unit, the protagonists, through their cleverness or "gifts," overcome almost impossible situations. From powerless to powerful, from poor to rich, the motif of contrast is strong through these stories. Children will enjoy these tales that reflect a balance of less- and well-known stories.

Literary outcomes for unit theme include:

- recognizing the importance of the number "three" in folk literature, i.e., three tasks, three major characters. One tale, "*The Five Queer Brothers*," is an exception with the five brothers and five tasks.
- an awareness of the protagonists' determination to reach their goals by outwitting "stronger" or "larger" antagonists
- noting unusual language and repetitive dialogue
- comparing the fantasy elements of the tales with the realistic elements
- realizing that there are many variations of folk literature selections
- an awareness of the characteristics of fairy tales, legends, folktales, and fables
- recognizing the theme of each selection

INTEGRATED CURRICULUM STRATEGIES

Integration of curricular areas may be accomplished through these suggested instructional strategies:

- understand the similarities of personal needs throughout various cultural groups, i.e., European, African, Oriental
- awareness of the justice system that rewards "good" over "evil"
- awareness of the traditions that surround royalty
- recognizing the similarities and differences of human needs in cultural or regional groups

Changing the Situation Theme

MOLLY WHUPPIE—ENGLISH FAIRY TALE

"Molly Whuppie." Sutherland, Z., and M. C. Livingston. 1984. *Scott-Foresman Anthology of Children's Literature*. Glenview, IL: Scott-Foresman. pp. 159-62.

"Mollie Whuppie." Briggs, K. M. A.1970-1971. *Dictionary of British Fairy Tales*, London: Routledge & Kegan Paul. pp. 154-55, 400-03.

"Mollie Whuppie." De la Mare, W. 1980 (reissue). *Tales Told Again*. Illustrated by A. Howard. London: Faber Fanfares. pp. 193-200.

"Molly Whuppie." Haviland, V. 1972. *The Fairy Tale Treasury*. Illustrated by R. Briggs. New York: Dell.

"Mutsmag." Chase, R. 1948. *Grandfather Tales*. Boston: Houghton Mifflin. pp. 40-51.

Recommended for students in second and third grades.

Summary

A young girl outwits a giant to get a sword, a purse with gold, and a ring to give to the king. She and her two sisters marry the king's three sons for her reward. This fairy tale contains many motifs associated with the subgenre, i.e., magic, the small outwitting the large, a smart human heroine, a stupid giant, the familiar repetitive phrase "Fee, fie, fo fum, I smell the blood of some earthly one," and three sisters, three sons, three tasks.

Possible objections: destitute parents abandoning three daughters; the giant killing his own daughters; the giant beating his wife.

Connect

Prior to reading the story, the teacher should select strategies to help children expand their previous knowledge and experiences.

- Tell an old but more familiar tale with the same theme, i.e., "the small and weak outwitting the strong." A likely example that children may recognize is "Jack and the Beanstalk."
- **Cluster** (VM 9) the physical descriptions and actions of giants in other stories around the word "giants."
- Group-write a description of giants in folk literature on a chart. Display the chart for children to see as you begin to read the story of Molly Whuppie.
- Give a book talk such as:

    Molly Whuppie was a little girl with two sisters, and Molly felt responsible for taking care of them. (Do any of you take care of little brothers or sisters?) When they met a mean giant, Molly had to outsmart him. (Is it possible for a little girl to outsmart a big, mean giant?) Then when Molly told the king how she saved her two sisters and herself from the giant, the king asked her to help him! The king wanted Molly to get three things from the giant—his sword; his purse; and his ring. As a reward she and her sisters would be married to the king's sons. (Would Molly need help? Who do you think would help her?) Display a long strand or hair: Molly had help from a "bridge of one hair," from the giant's wife, and a sack. (How do you think it happened?)

- Display a **word wall** (VM 34) containing unique language, such as "bread and treacle," "sup," "chinkling," "billet," "chickabiddies," "niche." These words may be highlighted before, during, or after presenting the selection.
- Before, during, or after presenting the selection, encourage students to use their **literature response logs (lit logs)** (VW 92) to record their thoughts in writing or picture form.

Construct

- Let children discuss this story after hearing it read aloud. Encourage them to ask questions about the story.
- If needed, use **probes** (VO 72) such as:

    How did you feel at the beginning of the story? Which character would you choose as your BEST friend? Why? Did you wonder why the giant didn't follow Molly over the "BRIDGE OF ONE HAIR"? (In Norse mythology and other folktales, such as in Scottish folktales, only witches can ride on a bridge made from a single hair.) *What would you have done in Molly's place? Have we read about this giant in another story? Which one?*

- **Role play** (VO 74) an imaginary scene: the giant talking to his own little girls and calling them "chickabiddies." Was he a good father? Role play other incidents not discussed in tale, i.e., actions of sisters.
- Talk about special names your students are called by their parents and others. Record the names on a chart. If duplicates names are recorded, prepare a bar graph of the names.

Create

- Have a group of students prepare a **readers' theater script** (VO 73) and read it to another class.
- Prepare a fairy tale **literary ladder** (VM 16).
- Construct a castle where the king lived, and label the rooms where Molly and her sisters stayed. Build a house where the giant lived. Make his kitchen, bedroom, and basement.
- Write a dramatic script from the giant's point of view. Speculate on the fate of his wife and children and write an original version of what happened to them. First, outline the story as a whole group, then have small groups paraphrase a section of the outline on an overhead transparency. Have the whole group edit and revise the outline, and finally, small groups may rewrite their story segments on charts to be displayed around the classroom. Script can be presented to other groups of students.
- Make an **accordion book** (VM 1) retelling the tale. Place in school media center or class literature center.

UNANANA AND THE ELEPHANT—AFRICAN LEGEND

"Unanana and the Elephant." Sutherland, Z., and M. C. Livingston. 1984. *The Scott-Foresman Anthology of Children's Literature*. Glenview, IL: Scott-Foresman. pp. 314-17.

"Unanana and the Elephant." Arnott, K. 1962. *African Myths and Legends*. New York: Walck. pp. 68-73.

Recommended for students in first (older) through third grade.

Summary

Unanana is a brave, intelligent mother who must save her two beautiful children from the elephant with one tusk. She is helped in her plight by a baboon, a gazelle, and a leopard. This African folktale has humans and beasts who can talk to each other and a clearly stated theme: "don't be satisfied with your fate." The tale contains three helpful animals, three major incidents, a small hero outwitting a large antagonist, good winning over evil, and the cultural lifestyle of Unanana is portrayed.

Connect

- Display pictures of animals typically associated with Africa: elephants, lions, monkeys, and others that may be found in picture files or magazines. Link children's knowledge of wild animals in Africa to this story.
- Locate Africa, and students' personal nation, state, and city on a map. Measure distance between Africa and personal location. Discuss differences in geography, religion, and lifestyle of people.
- Introduce African folktales, Unanana and her problems to the children using **probes** (VO 72) such as these:

    Unanana is an unusual name. Can you guess where she might live? Read the title and ask where children think the home of elephants might be? (Elicit a few guesses from the children.)

- Present a book talk, such as:

    This is a very old African folktale. Unanana lived in North Africa. She was a mother of two beautiful children who had a problem and knew that she must solve it. In this tale, some of the characters are real and some are make-believe. Four animals appear at different times to help her. They are: a baboon, a gazelle, and a leopard. Wonder how they will help her?

- Display a **word wall** (VM 34) in the shape of an elephant, containing unique language. Highlight the words before, during, or after presenting the selection, i.e., "The walls of the elephant's stomach were like a range of hills . . ." and "ravenously."
- Before, during, or after presenting the selection, encourage students to write in their **literature response logs (lit logs)** (VW 92).

Construct

After completing some of the activities above, read the story to the children. This is a complex story and may need to be discussed during the reading. Use your judgment. If discussed during reading, consider the children's attention span and the potential loss of momentum or interference with the flow of the story. You may want to consider giving a more detailed book talk to help the children understand the story without interruptions.

■ Suggested **probes** (VO 72) are given for particular incidents. If the teacher does not choose to stop, probes may be used at the conclusion of the tale:

First, stop after Unanana returns home after working and use probes such as: *Why do you think Unanana wanted to know how the elephant swallowed the children? Wonder what she will do now? Wonder why the elephant has one tusk?*

Next, stop just before she meets the elephant with one tusk: *Why did the baboon, gazelle, and leopard give her directions? Are they tricking her? Are the animals friends of the elephant? How do you know ?*

Next, stop just after the elephant swallowed Unanana, her pot, and her knife. *Why did Unanana want the elephant to swallow her, her pot, and her knife? Who is the smartest character, Unanana or the elephant? How do you know? What will Unanana do now?*

Finally, stop after the elephant complained about feeling uncomfortable: *What will happen to the elephant now? How did Unanana feel about the other humans and animals who had been swallowed by the elephant?* (Scornful.) Discuss the theme. *Did Unanana surprise you? Why?*

After reading the conclusion of the story: *Who was the smartest character? Why did Unanana do what she did?* (Again talk about the theme.) *Why wasn't the little family still poor?* (Discuss "gratitude.") *Would you want the feast they had? Why?*

■ Prepare a **real and make-believe chart** (VM 25). Record students' answers to the following questions:

Identify the make-believe characters. Identify the real characters. What events were real and which were make-believe? How do you know? Was this story true?

Create

■ Make masks of the various animals.
■ Use masks, and have students **role play** (VO 74) favorite incidents.
■ Prepare a **mobile** (VA 44) representing the characters or events in the tale. Place a sentence describing the events or characters on the back of each visual.
■ **Thought-Splash** (VO 82) the following questions:

Was Unanana right to do what she did? Did she reach her goal? (Theme: don't accept meekly what happens to you.) *What would you have done if you were Unanana?*

■ Have groups of students select a response and write a plan of action.
■ Students select an idea suggested above, write a plan of action, and list in appropriate sequence a plan of action for Unanana. Each group should give their plan to the teacher and improvise it for the class. (The teacher may

follow the plan to help the groups stay on task while presenting their improvisations.)

■ Children and teacher will prepare a **literary ladder** (VM 16) in the shape of Africa and place it on the bulletin board. NOTE: This story is an excellent example of a folktale, i.e., make-believe and reality; "threeness" of characters, incidents; stereotypical "good" and "bad" characters; "good" winning over evil; early African lifestyle.

THE FIVE QUEER BROTHERS—CHINESE FOLKTALE

"Five Queer Brothers." Nelson, M. A. 1971. *A Comparative Anthology of Children's Literature*. New York: Holt, Rinehart, & Winston. pp. 294-95.

Bishop, Claire H. 1938. *Five Chinese Brothers*. Illustrated by K. Wiese. New York: Coward-McCann.

"The Five Queer Brothers." Sian-Tek, L. 1948. *More Folk Tales from China*. New York: J. Day.

Mahy, M. 1991. *The Seven Chinese Brothers*. New York: Scholastic Hardback.

"Six Servants." Grimm, J., and W. Grimm. 1972. *The Complete Grimms Fairy Tales*. New York: Random House. pp. 600-07. (Six men use their supernatural abilities to solve a problem.)

Recommended for students in kindergarten through third grade.

Summary

This amazing tale is about a Chinese woman and her five sons who look exactly alike. Each son has a different talent. One can gulp the sea, one has a body as hard as steel, one has legs that can stretch to any length, one cannot be burned, and the fifth can live without breathing for many days. The five abilities come in handy when the first is arrested and placed on trial.

This Chinese fairy tale contains many characteristics expected of the subgenre; however, the number "five," instead of the expected "three," plays an important role in this tale. The theme "teamwork helps change a bad situation" is implied. The superhuman abilities are vital to the tale, and these abilities are intriguing to primary age children.

Connect

■ Give a book talk such as the following:

This Chinese fairy tale is a wonder story, a story with imaginary actions that make you stop and wonder. There are some elements (parts) that are realistic, but not the Five Queer Brothers' abilities! The five brothers look alike, but each has a special ability. Therefore, the neighbors called them "queer" (different). When something happened to one brother, the other four came to his rescue—just as brothers and sisters will do!

- Display a **word wall** (VM 34) containing unique language, such as: "executioner," "consented," "condemned," "exasperated."
- Before, during, or after presenting the selection, encourage students to write in their **literature response logs (lit logs)** (VW 92).

Read the story aloud to the students.

Construct

- **Probes** (VO 72) may be asked, such as:
    Were you surprised that the judge let the boy go home to see his old mother? Why? Will the brother's life be saved? How? (Discuss the reason the brother was brought before the judge.) *Was there a better sentence the judge could have given the brother? Did the brothers do the right thing in tricking the judge? How would you describe the brothers? the judge?* (Discuss the theme.)
- Some further questions that could be asked are as follows:
    What do you think happened a year after the tale ended? Did the judge find out about the "Queer Brothers' abilities? How might this story be different if it had come from another country? Does it make any difference that it is a Chinese fairy tale?

Create

- Read C. Bishop's book, *The Five Chinese Brothers*. Compare this book version to other versions of the tale. (Talk about the stereotyped illustrations found in the book and the differences in the plots.) Compare this book with Mahy's *The Seven Chinese Brothers* and "Six Servants" by the Grimms. Discuss the importance of the numbers five, six, and seven in folk literature and life.
- Read other collections of Chinese folk literature. Compare and contrast these tales with tales from other cultures, i.e., note story structure.
- Present a **round table discussion** (VO 75) discussing differences and similarities between Chinese folk literature and the folk literature of other cultures.
- Prepare a **character attribute chart** (VM 6) such as the one on the following page.

CHARACTER	ABILITY	PROBLEM	SOLUTION
MOTHER	good, caring mother		
OLDEST SON	could gulp a mouthful of the sea, gulped the sea so that children could play on bottom.	they would not come back; he had to let go; the children were drowned; he was arrested; put in prison; sentenced to have head cut off	allowed to go home to say goodbye to old mother
SECOND SON	body was as hard as steel	took the first brother's place in prison; could not be executed; ordered to be drowned	allowed to go home to say goodbye to old mother
THIRD SON	legs could stretch to any length	took the second brother's place in prison; could not be drowned; stretched legs to touch bottom of the sea; ordered to be burned	allowed to go home to say goodbye to old mother
FOURTH SON	could not be burned	took the third brother's place in prison; tied at stake and set on fire; he was ordered buried alive	allowed to go home to say goodbye to old mother
FIFTH SON	could live without breathing for many days	took the fourth brother's place in prison; buried (brothers dug him up)	the judge ruled that he must be innocent since could not be killed; he was innocent and released; the brothers were reunited and lived happily with their mother

- Divide the class into five groups, and give each group a brother. Have groups prepare a defense of the character's actions to present before a judge who later found out about his ability. A child will play the judge.
- Have each group prepare a **wanted poster** (VA 51) for their selected brother. Share posters with others and place them on the bulletin board. Students can suggest a bulletin board title.
- Conduct a trial. Assume the brothers and their mother were arrested by the judge. Let each child select a role, plan their actions, and invite several classes to view the trial. *Will the brothers and the mother be released by the jury?*

- Write a **news report** (VW 95). Divide the class into six groups. Give each group one of the brothers or the mother and write about the incidents from the particular character's point of view. These reports can be placed in a newspaper format or in a bound book.

Rags to Riches Theme

THE PRINCESS AND THE PEA—DANISH FAIRY TALE

"The Princess and the Pea." Andersen, H. C. 1987. *Andersen's Fairy Tales*. New York: Grosset & Dunlap. pp. 80-81.
Ardizzone, E. 1974. *Ardizzone's Hans C. Andersen*. Translated by S. Corrin. New York: Atheneum. pp. 64-66.
"Princess and the Pea." Haugaard, E. 1974. *Hans Andersen: His Classic Fairy Tales*. Illusrated by M. Foreman. New York: Doubleday.
"The Princess and the Pea." Rackham, A. 1930. *The Arthur Rackham Fairy Book*. Philadelphia: Lippincott.
Stevenson, S. 1992. *The Princess and the Pea*. New York: Doubleday.

Recommended for students in kindergarten through third grade.

Summary

When a prince decides he wants a "real" princess for his wife, a rainstorm and his mother come to his rescue. A short, familiar literary fairy tale whose theme characterizes, with satire, the attributes of a "real princess." Encourage the students to find other fairy tales recorded or written by Andersen, along with biographies about his life.

Connect

Prior to reading the story use a strategy such as the following:

- Display a pea in a clear plastic bottle. Ask students why they think the pea will be important to the character in the tale.
- Display a banner on the literature bulletin board, titled:
  WANTED: A REAL PRINCESS!
- Discuss what it takes to become a princess. Make a list of all the princesses they can remember—both real and in fantasy. Use a **K.W.L., know, want**

to know, have learned (VM 14) to find out what the children know about princesses who are alive. Request that children bring pictures of royal festivals or fair princesses. Place pictures on the bulletin board.

- Make a collage using visuals representative of royalty.
- Discuss the meaning of "monarchy"; discuss the way real royalty are selected in other countries and compare to our form of government. Many children will relate to the selection of kings, queens, princesses, princes for fairs or local festivals. Point out that in this tale, we are talking about real royalty who are born into families of kings and queens.
- Prepare a chart titled, A REAL PRINCESS IS ... Elicit and record, the childrens' descriptions of a real princess. [After reading the tale elicit characteristics of a real princess as described in the tale. This strategy can be used before or after the tale is shared to discuss the personality of the prince also.]
- Talk about the author, Hans Christian Andersen, who lived almost 200 years ago in Denmark. (Point out Denmark on a world map.) When Andersen first began to write, he recorded Danish folktales that he had heard early in his life. Later, he wrote original stories, similar to the folktales. These tales are called literary fairy tales, because we know who wrote them. Remind children that the old folktales were told by unknown storytellers. An entire Folk Literature Unit could be designed using Andersen's tales. Older children can compare and analyze his tales.
- Display a **word wall** (VM 34) containing unique language from the story, such as: "reproachful," "torrent," "forlorn," "plight," "draught."
- Before, during, or after presenting the selection, encourage students to write in their **literature response logs (lit logs)** (VW 92).

Read the story aloud to the children.

Construct

- If needed, begin discussion with **probes** (VO 72), e.g.:

  *Do you think the prince was hard to please? Do you think that the girl was really a PRINCESS? How would you have felt if you had been on the road all alone? Wonder why the prince wanted to find a REAL PRINCESS? What action would the prince take, if, after marrying the girl, he found out she was not a **real** princess? Were you surprised the queen helped the prince find a wife? If you were a prince what would you do to find a real princess? Why do you think Andersen wrote this tale?* (Help the students discover the theme of the tale and why Andersen might have written a satire about royalty.)
- Discuss the requirements for a princess cited in the tale.

Create

After reading and discussing the story the children could select from some of the following strategies.

- Prepare a bumper sticker the prince might use to advertise for a real princess.
- Write a magazine advertisment for a real princess. Include the prince's requirements for a princess and what he has to offer her.
- Paint a picture of the real princess; the prince; his castles.
- Prepare a **diorama** (VA 38) of the prince's kingdom.
- Locate other literary fairy tales written by James Thurber, George MacDonald, Carl Sandburg. Compare the characteristics of traditional fairy tales and literary fairy tales.
- Write a fairy tale told from the "real princess'" point of view describing how the prince found her.
- Write a **magazine story** (VW 93) describing the prince's search for a real princess. Write a new ending telling how he "found" his bride. (Be sure to include his requirements and something about the prince, his lifestyles, likes, and dislikes.)
- Write a description predicting what happened at the castle 10 years after the marriage.
- Illustrate the scenes from previous activity and place tale and illustrations in a bound book.
- Write a script for a creative drama extending the tale, changing the setting to the twenty-first century, and modifying the plot and characters. Present the play to another class. (Display and discuss the components of a script.)
- Design a "pea proof" mattress. Describe the size, the shape, and what is inside it. Make a sketch. Write an advertisement for the product. (Shannon Thorpe's idea, 1989)

TO YOUR GOOD HEALTH—RUSSIAN FOLKTALE

"To Your Good Health." Lang, A. 1962. *The Crimson Fairy Book*. New York: McKay. pp. 18-25.

"To Your Good Health." Sutherland, Z., and M. C. Livingston. 1984. *Scott-Foresman Anthology of Children's Literature*. Glenview, IL: Scott-Foresman. pp. 287-89.

Recommended for students in first through third grades.

Summary

A clever shepherd refuses to wish the king good health *every time* he sneezes, until he receives the hand of the princess, even though he is placed in the pit of a white bear, in the den with wild boars, into a vault of scythes, and offered silver woods, a golden castle, and a diamond pond.

The theme of this Russian folktale is "despite the odds, work for your goals." The tale is unusual because it contains eight attempts to change the hero's mind (four negative incidents and four offerings). The introduction and conclusion are typical of folktales, as are the three stereotyped characters, and other literary elements.

Connect

- Prior to reading the story, prepare the children for a quiet think time when you might ask **probes** (VO 72)such as the following:

  Have you ever wanted something so much that you said you would do ANYTHING to get it? What was it? What did you have to do to get it? Did you get it? (Elicit several answers.)
- Give a book talk (see summary). Note this is a Russian tale.
- Encourage students to write in their **lit logs** (VW 92).

Read the story aloud to the children.

Construct

- Elicit typical phrases used following a sneeze, e.g., "Bless you." Discuss other customs such as covering your mouth.
- Use **probes** (VO 72) if it is necessary to lead a discussion of the story, for example:

  How did this story make you feel? What did you think would happen when the shepherd was thrown in the pit of the white bear? (other incidents). *Why did the shepherd REALLY refuse to bless the king?* (Reread the introduction and the conclusion.) *Do you think he had a plan before he went to the castle? Should he have taken the king's gifts? Why or why not? Describe the lord chamberlain, the shepherd, the princess, and the king.*

Create

- Have students prepare a **character attribute chart** (VM 6).
- Prepare a **literary circle** (VM 15) of the 8 incidents in this tale.
- Have students write **what if? incidents** (VW 102). To help them get started, discuss with class:

What if the shepherd had said, "Bless you," the first time the king sneezed? How would that have changed the story? What if the shepherd had been thrown into a cave with different animals? How would he have survived? What if the king had not offered him the silver woods? How could the tale be changed?

- Divide class into groups, and have each group prepare a **readers' theater script** (VO 73). Then have groups read and act scripts to one another.
- Compare incidents in the tale to the new what if? incidents. Write a new conclusion based on the what if? incidents.
- Prepare a bound book including readers' theater script, what if? incidents, and new conclusions. Let children illustrate text. After reading and enjoying the book, place it in the school media center.

THE COBBLER AND THE BANKER—FRENCH FABLE

"The Cobbler and the Banker." La Fontaine, J. *A Book of Fables*. New York: Warner. pp. 50-51.

"The Financier." Spector. 1988. *The Complete Fables of Jean de la Fontaine*. Evanston, IL: Northwestern University. pp. 355-56. (Verse in English and French.)

Related Stories and Fables

Aesop. 1989. *Aesop's Fables*. Illustrated by L. Zwerger. New York: Picture Book Studio.

Brown, M. 1961. *Once a Mouse*. New York: Scribner.

Fables La Fontaine. 1954. New York: Viking.

La Fontaine. 1982. *The Hare and the Tortoise*. Illustrated by B. Wildsmith. London: Oxford.

Lobel, A. 1980. *Fables*. New York: Harper.

Recommended for students in second grade and above.

Summary

A cobbler exchanges his happy life for a bagful of gold and decides that "money is everything." This fable, written 300 years ago, uses the typical format attributed to Aesop , i.e., a humorous, short story followed by a lesson or moral. It is different from most fables because real people are portrayed, not animals. Also, it does not emphasize the moral as much as many traditional fables.

Connect

- Display a literature center with an assortment of books of fables for children to read and discuss.
- Prior to reading the story try some **probes** (VO 72) such as the following:

    *Has anyone ever offered to pay you to **stop** doing something? If I offered you a bag of gold to stop singing while you were in class, what would you do? Why? How would your life change if you took the money?* (Encourage the children to think about the positive and negative aspects of the change.)

- Discuss fables and the author; for example, you could say:

    Our tale today is a fable. This fable was written about 300 years ago by a Frenchman named La Fontaine. He used the fable format developed by Aesop, but made some changes to his fables.

    Describe a fable.

- Discuss bankers and cobblers and what they do. Divide students in triads. Give each triad a prediction paper. Ask the students to think about a cobbler, a banker, and a bagful of gold and to write on their papers a prediction about each. Instruct them to fold the papers and place them in a **prediction pitcher** (VM 23). Compare predictions after reading the fable.
- Display a **word wall** (VM 34) containing unique language from the story: "fitful doze," "providence," "saleable commodity," "simplicity."
- Let students write in their **literature logs** (VW 92).

    Read the story aloud to the class or group.

Construct

- If needed for discussion after reading the story, use **probes** (VO 92) such as:

    Do you think it was right for the banker to give the cobbler the bagful of gold? Why? Was the cobbler wise to give the bagful of gold back to the banker? Do you think the cobbler's family was happy he gave the money back? Why? Is money the most important thing in the world? What is the moral (theme) of this fable? Whom would you have liked to have known—the cobbler or the banker? Why? Why do you think this story was told for the first time a long time ago? Is it the kind of story that would be told today? Why?

Create

- Have an assortment of books of fables available for children to read.
- Prepare a fable chart. Label the columns AESOP, LA FONTAINE, LOBEL. Elicit from the children the facts they discovered by looking at the collections of fables, i.e., *What do you notice about the way all fables are written?*

Record appropriate information in each column. Read and discuss other fable collections to the class. Have the students identify similar characteristics. If additional facts are found, add them to the chart.

- Group-write a fable after selecting a moral and reviewing the fact chart. Encourage students to use people instead of animals as characters.
- Let children illustrate the original fables using a variety of media.
- Place fables and illustrations in a bound book. Display the finished product in the literature center.
- Compare and discuss illustrations found in different fable collections. Vote for favorite illustrations and keep track of votes. Have children explain their choices. Talk about the importance of illustrations, i.e., clarifying fable, supplementing sparse narrative, setting, costumes of early days reflected in the illustrations, etc.
- Pantomime favorite fables for other class members.
- Prepare and present a **subgenre commercial** (VW 99).

Small Heroes Theme

THE TAILOR AND THE GIANTS—AMERICAN FOLKTALE VARIANT

"Jack the Giant Killer." Cole, J. 1982. *Best-Loved Folktales of the World.* Illustrated by J. K. Schwarz. Garden City, NY: Doubleday. pp. 198-206.

Compton, K., and J. Compton. 1993. *Jack and the Giant Chaser: An Appalachian Tale.* Illustrated by K. Compton. New York: Holiday.

"Jack the Giant Killer." Rackham, A. 1930. *The Arthur Rackham Fairy Book, A Book of Old Favourites with New Illustrations.* Philadelphia: Lippincott. pp. 111-27.

"The Tailor and the Giants." Roberts, J. W. 1955. *South from Hell-fer-Sartin.* Lexington: University of Kentucky Press. pp. 126, 137-40.

Thomson, P. 1992. *The Brave Little Tailor.* New York: Simon.

"The Valiant Little Tailor." Ehrlich, A. 1985. *The Random House Book of Fairy Tales.* Illustrated by D. Goode. New York: Random House. pp. 102-17.

"The Valiant Little Tailor." Grimm, J., and W. Grimm. 1972. *The Complete Grimm's Fairy Tales.* New York: Pantheon. pp. 112-20.

"A Widow's Son." Glassie, A. 1985. *Irish Folktales*. New York: Pantheon. pp. 267-69.

Recommended for students in first through fourth grades.

Summary

A little tailor kills seven flies with one blow and embroiders "killed seven with one blow" on a belt and proudly sets forth to tell the world. A giant sees the statement and interprets it to mean the tailor has killed seven men with one stroke. The little tailor travels with the giant and on his adventure squeezes water from a rock (cheese), throws a rock so far it never comes back (thanks to a bird), carries a big tree out of the forest (with the help of the giant), frightens three giants with his bragging stories, kills the four giants, and marries the king's daughter.

The theme *"a clever small person outwits giants"* is one that children find fascinating, since they must deal with "giants" daily.

This American variant of the European tale is written in limited Southern dialect with situations that are typical of a Southern, nineteenth-century setting. This very popular folktale is found throughout the world in longer versions and adventures.

Connect

- **Cluster** (VM 9) a tailor's responsibility.
- Predict how the paths of a tailor and a giant will cross.
- Just as you are ready to read the story to the children, have a puppet appear who is boasting of incredible deeds. The children will quickly recognize the boasting. Ask the puppet to listen to the story with the children.

Construct

- If needed, ask the following **probes** (VO 72), such as:
  Why did the little tailor go down the road to brag about killing seven at one stroke? Wonder what would have happened had he met someone other than a giant? Describe the little tailor, the giants, the king, and the princess. Which character would you like to be? Why? Help children discover the theme ("the small outwitting the large"). *How was the little tailor able to outwit the giants? Could this really happen?*
- After the reading, allow and exchange between the puppet and the children by first initiating a question to the puppet: *Do you know anyone like the tailor?* The puppet's answer will be evasive, then the children can compare the puppet's boasting with that of the tailor.

- Have children help fill in a **character attribute chart** (VM 6) such as the following:

CHARACTER	SIZE	WIT	WISDOM	ACCOMPLISHMENTS
LITTLE TAILOR				
GIANTS				
KING				
PRINCESS				

Create

- Have several variants of the tale. Divide children into groups, and give each group a different variation. Have each group list events in each tale and tell how the little tailor solved his problem. Each group should share information about their variants. Let the class compare the tales.
- Prepare a **Venn diagram** (VM 33) listing differences and similarities among the variants.
- Present a **chain-the-tale** (VO 55).
- Design a **tale-a-timeline**(VM 32). Title the timeline, "Tale-a-Timeline-with-the-Tailor."
- Write a future event about the little tailor and his wife. Remember "... *and they married and lived happily ever after.*" Find a version in which they did not marry and live happily ever after. Choose your own ending.
- Prepare the tale for use in a **storytelling festival** (VO 78).

MOMOTARO: BOY-OF-THE-PEACH—JAPANESE FAIRY TALE

"Momotaro." Butler, F. 1987. *The Wide World Around.* White Plains, NY: Longman. pp. 15-21.

Hooks, W. 1992. *Peach Boy.* Bank Street Ready to Read Series. New York: Little Rooster.

"Momotaro." Uchida, Y. 1977. *The Dancing Kettle and Other Japanese Folk Tales.* New York: Harcourt-Brace-Jovanovich.

"Momotaro: Boy-of-the-Peach." Sutherland, Z., and M. C. Livingston. 1984. *Scott-Foresman Anthology of Children's Literature*. Glenview IL: Scott-Foresman. pp. 330-32.

"Momotaro or the Peach Boy." Cole, J. 1982. *Best-Loved Folktales of the World*. Illustrated by J. K. Schwarz. Garden City, NY: Doubleday. pp. 503-05.

"One-Inch Fellow." Briggs, R. 1972. *The Fairy Tale Treasury*. Selected by V. Haviland. New York: Dell. pp. 162-169.

Related References

Dahl, R. 1961. *James and the Giant Peach*. New York: Alfred A. Knopf.

Joyce, W. 1985. *George Shrinks*. New York: HarperCollins.

MacDonald, M. R. 1993. *The Oryx Multicultural Folktale Series: Tom Thumb*. Phoenix, AZ: The Oryx Press.

Mosel, A. 1972. *The Funny Little Woman*. New York: Dutton.

Recommended for students in second through third grade.

Summary

Momotaro, the "Son of a Peach" or "Strong Boy," appears from inside a large peach to cheer an old Japanese couple. At age 15 Momotaro leaves his foster-father to perform a task that fate has given him—to rid the countryside of a band of ogres (devils). On his way to Devil Island, Momotaro meets a dog, a monkey, and a pheasant. The creatures are natural enemies, but each must reform to go with Momotaro on his adventure. After traveling a long way over land and sea, the strange companions reach the island and the devils.

What happens on the island is exciting and represents the typical Japanese folktale: adventure, suspense, and theme: *a "good" small hero succeeding over "evil," and receiving his just reward.*

Connect

- Several days before reading the tale display a large papier-mâché peach in the literature center. Invite the students to contemplate why it is there.
- Share the picture book *The Funny Little Woman* by A. Mosel. Talk about the little woman and the terrifying oriental creature called "Oni." Read aloud R. Dahl's *James and the Giant Peach* to the class before or after sharing this tale.
- Give a book talk. (See summary.)
- Bring rice cakes for the children to eat while writing predictions to probes, such as the following:

What kind of creatures did Momotaro meet? Did they look like the Oni? In this tale Momotaro met a dog, a monkey, and a pheasant. They do not like each other, but they all want to go with Momotaro. Will they travel peacefully? Will they help or hinder Momotaro?

- Place signed predictions in the **prediction pitcher** (VM 23).
- Display a **word wall** (VM 34) containing unique language. Some terms to be considered are "scythe," "lamented," "plunder," "subdue," "precipitous," "enterprise," "Daimios," "precipice."

Read the story and have the children respond to it in their **lit logs** (VW 92).

Construct

- Divide children in pairs and have them spontaneously respond to the story, using **buddy buzzing** (VO 54).
- **Probes** (VO 72) may be used to guide the discussion of this story, e.g.:
  Could a boy really appear to old folks in a giant peach? Why did he appear? How does Momotaro know where to go? How do the characters differ in the stories? How do you feel about each story? Why do you think each story was written? Do you think any of the authors had ever heard any of the stories before writing or telling their own?

Create

- Put students in small groups and have them retell the tale and list the major incidents.
- Let partners select an incident and sketch it on a piece of pellon or felt with permanent colored markers. Place the completed visuals, in proper plot sequence, on a **hook 'n loop board** (VM 13).
- Have partners paint a visual description of the tale on a mural.
- Group children into triads and have them write a conversation between the rulers of the country trying to decide what they should give Momotaro as a reward for ridding the countryside of the demons.
- Plan a celebration to honor Momotaro. List what will happen at the celebration. Share plans with others to make the final preparations.
- Prepare a scroll from the Daimois whose daughter was saved from the demons by Momotaro, thanking him for her return. Draw treasures the Daimois would give him and place them in a treasure box.
- Prepare a **flannel board** (VM 11) with the **objects** representing the incidents in the tale. Have children use the flannel board objects to tell the tale to another class.
- Prepare and present a creative drama of the tale.

If possible, locate Japanese costumes for the drama and present it to another class. Also, if possible, videotape the drama and play on a schoolwide television station.

THUMBLING—GERMAN FAIRY TALE (MÄRCHEN)

"Thumbling." Grimm, J., and W. Grimm. *1972. The Complete Grimms Fairy Tales*. New York: Pantheon. pp. 187-93.

"Hop o' My Thumb." Griffith, J. W., and C. H. Frey. 1981. *Classics of Children's Literature*. New York: Macmillan. pp. 24-29.

"Hop o My Thumb." Rackham, A. 1930. *The Arthur Rackham Fairy Book, a Book of Old Favourites with New Illustrations*. Philadelphia: Lippincott. pp. 15-29.

Hughes, M. 1992. *Little Fingerling*. Illustrated by B. Clark. New York: Ideals.

MacDonald, M. R. 1993. *The Oryx Multicultural Folktale Series: Tom Thumb*. Phoenix, AZ: The Oryx Press. (A collection of Tom Thumb stories from cultures throughout the world.)

"Thumbelina." Ehrlich, A. 1985. *The Random House Book of Fairy Tales*. Illustrated by D. Goode. New York: Random House. pp. 194-205.

Related References

Schories, P. 1991. *Mouse House*. New York: Farrar, Straus, Giroux.

White, E. B. 1945. *Stuart Little*. Illustrated by G. Williams. New York: Harper.

Recommended for students in upper first grade through upper elementary.

Summary

A boy no bigger than your thumb was born to a poor peasant couple. As the boy grew older, he grew no larger, but because he was clever, intelligent, and adventurous he went into the world to bring riches to his family. During his adventures he found himself in the hole of a mouse, in a cow's belly, and in a wolf's paunch. The central theme is again "the small outwitting the larger."

This story is a perfect example of a "Märchen" (fairy tale), i.e., brief introduction, three major events, imaginary and real stereotyped characters, except for the protagonist who is a sensible, clever, wise, and nimble creature. The setting is the countryside, anywhere, and the hero is rewarded for his deeds. This story is the seminal "little person" tale and one that many children will recognize through other stories, movies, or videos.

Connect

- Introduce the title of the tale and say: *This tale is about a boy, born to a peasant couple, who was no bigger than your thumb.* Discuss what it must be like to be a little person using **probes** (VO 72) such as:

    If you are no bigger than a thumb how could you eat with a fork or spoon? or would you? How could you get anyone to hear you when you spoke? How could you write?

    Encourage probes from the students.

- Prepare a **semantic map** (VM 26) with the words "big as your thumb" written in the center. Cluster descriptions around the title of things in the real world that are about the size of a thumb. Display the map in the literature center.
- Share other variants or related stories: *"Thumbelina"* by H. C. Andersen; Monica Hughes, *Little Fingerling;* or the English tale *"Hop-o'My-Thumb."* (This study could become a unit entitled "Tiny Heroes." Information about the Grimm Brothers or Andersen could be included in the unit with other tales about tiny heroes. Your media specialist will be of assistance.)
- Display a **word wall** (VM 34) containing unique language, such as: "gee up, gee up!" (when driving a wagon, "gee up" means "gitta up, go"; "gee" means go right; "haw" means go left); "vexation"; "subterranean passage"; "ran as if Wild Huntsmen were behind them"; "Thumbling, unperceived, betook himself to the granary"; "Truly, there is much worry and affliction in this world!"; "In this little room the windows are forgotten ... and no sun shines in, neither will a candle be brought." (describing the cow's stomach); "fodder"; "dunghill"; "the wolf's paunch."
- Read the story and have students respond to the story in their **lit logs** (VW 92).

Construct

- Concurrent with this story or unit on "Tiny Heroes," read aloud E. B. White's *Stuart Little.* Elicit from the students the differences and similarities of the two selections.
- Use a **Venn diagram** (VM 33) to visually portray the differences between the tale and the book.
- If *Stuart Little* is read, **probes** (VO 72) such as the following might be helpful before reading "Thumbling":

I wonder if E. B.White read "Thumbling" before he wrote "Stuart Little"? Which story is older? "Thumbling" was told by old German storytellers to the Brothers Grimm (the tales are very old stories passed from one generation to another), who published them in 1812. When was "Stuart Little" written?

- After reading the tale, discuss ideas about the tale, such as :

  Did this story make you think of another fairy tale? ("Little Red Riding Hood"). Could this adventure happen in our world? How do you know? Remember in the beginning I told you that this was a German Märchen or fairy tale. In Märchens the hero is rewarded. How was Thumbling and his family rewarded? Märchens contain fantasy or imaginary events and characters. What was real and what was make-believe in this tale?

Give more information about the Brothers Grimm and their German Märchen (fairy tales). See your media specialist for additional information.

- If needed, include **probes** (VO 72), such as:

  Do you think the people and animals could hear Thumbling from the cow's and wolf's stomach? How did you feel when the parents cut the wolf's stomach open? What was your favorite part of the story? What would you do in that same adventure? Would your parents like to have a son like Thumbling? How do you know? Would you like to have a son like him?

Create

- Have students retell the tale aloud to each other and the class.
- Discuss the tale. Talk about the characterization, i.e., growth of the characters who are either static (staying the same) or dynamic (growing); and the description of the characters, i.e., flat (stereotyped) or round (well developed). Elicit one word statements about each character. Map the characters' problems and solutions on a **character and plot chart** (VM 7), such as the following:

CHARACTERS	CHARACTERIZATION	PROBLEM	SOLUTION
THUMBLING	helpful; clever; wise; round & static; GOOD	FOLLOWS?	AS FOLLOWS?
MOTHER & FATHER	happy; peasant farmers; flat & static; GOOD	needed help with chores	Thumbling drove cart sitting in horse's ear
TWO STRANGERS	greedy; flat & static; EVIL	bought Thumbling to display him for money	Thumbling escaped down mouse hole
THIEVES	greedy; flat & static; EVIL	wanted to rob rich pastor	Thumbling cried loudly at pastor's home; thieves ran away
PASTOR'S MAID	flat & static; STUPID	heard Thumbling; couldn't find him	Thumbling went to sleep in the barn
COW	flat & static; MINDS OWN BUSINESS	swallowed Thumbling in hay	Thumbling cried out in cow's stomach; cow then considered evil and was killed; stomach thrown in dung heap
WOLF	flat & static; GREEDY	swallowed cow's stomach and Thumbling	Thumbling took wolf to his father's house; Thumbling cried from wolf's stomach; mother & father heard him and killed wolf; opened stomach; rescued Thumbling

- Give groups of children **character tags** (VO 58). Have them retell a part of the story involving their character. Various children within a group may share the retelling.
- Write diary entries for Thumbling. Describe his adventures.
- Make drawings from thumb prints. Display drawings on the bulletin board with the title "Our Thumbling Prints."
- If needed, discuss **probes** (VO 72), such as the following:

    Suppose Thumbling came to our class, what would you do? Is there a job a thumb-sized boy could do in our class? Would you like him to be in your cooperative group or be on your soccer team? What could you do that he could not do, i.e., get a drink at the water fountain or sit at a desk?

- Record students' responses to the probes on a **brainstorming board** (VO 53).
- Draw comic book sketches showing Thumbling's adventures with you at school (or home). Include dialogue in the comic bubbles.

- Write procedures for teaching Thumbling to participate in a contemporary activity, e.g., playing baseball or a video game.
- Pantomime directions written for the procedure for others. See if they can guess the procedure.
- Write a **news report** (VW 95) describing a selected incident. Read the report to others. Select reports that cover all of the incidents in the tale.
- If possible, videotape reporters reading their reports. Show tape on the school video system or in the school media center as a "You were there ... historical news."
- Read the wordless text *Mouse House*. Make a **wordless text** (VM 35) of the tale.

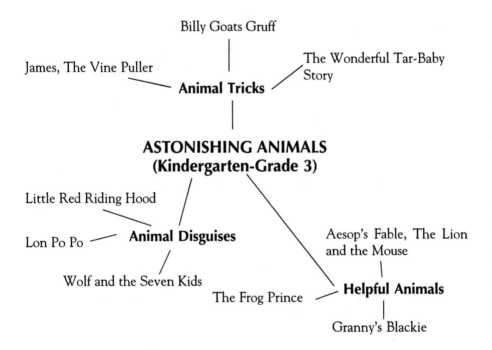

CHAPTER
five
⊛ ⊛ ⊛ ⊛ ⊛ ⊛ ⊛ ⊛

Astonishing Animals Unit
Kindergarten-Grade 3

LITERARY OUTCOMES

Three stories in this unit demonstrate "trickery" among animal characters in folk literature. After reading or hearing many stories of trickery, children will become aware of various motives and outcomes of trickery in literature. They will learn to compare the tricksters' motivations, noticing the survival strategies of the Goat family and of Brer Rabbit, when he was being held by Brer Fox, as opposed to the turtle's cleverness in tricking larger animals for the fun of it in "James, the Vine Puller."

Children will gradually learn to accept and appreciate language differences in literature as they recognize that the language reflects the culture from which the story originated. A version of the Tar-Baby, in dialect, is referenced.

Children may begin developing a schema for Grimm Brothers tales through the "Wolf and the Seven Kids" and "The Frog Prince." Teachers may want to have several collections of Grimm Brothers tales available for children's perusal. A major premise children should learn from these stories is that characters are either very good or very bad. Usually, the bad characters are punished.

Two variants of "Red Riding Hood" provide a foundation for comparing like stories, which will lead to prediction of sequence and literary comparisons.

The literary element of characterization will be expanded through the stories from the theme on helpful animals. The characters of these animals may be compared to those of the tricksters.

The format of Greek and Indian fables may be compared through the two styles of fables in this unit.

INTEGRATED CURRICULUM STRATEGIES

Throughout this literature unit, there will be opportunities to include additional integrated experiences in these areas:

- repetitive language
- dramatization
- comparatives (small, smaller, smallest or small, middle-sized, and large) and descriptive language
- oral language in the form of speaking, chanting, retelling
- mathematical concepts of measuring, counting, estimating
- physical development in balancing, stretching, pulling
- use of critical thinking and problem solving
- brainstorming, questioning, personal writing, and group cooperation.
- braiding (as in rope making)
- uses of animals for labor
- size relationships (lion and mouse; Grannie and elephant; turtle, elephant, and whale)

Animal Tricks Theme

BILLY GOATS GRUFF—NORWEGIAN FOLKTALE

"The Three Billy Goats Gruff." V. Haviland. 1985. *Favorite Fairy Tales Told around the World*. Illustrated by S. Schindler. Boston: Little, Brown. pp. 229-34.

Greenway, J. 1991. *The Three Billy Goats Gruff*. Illustrated by L. Lustig. New York: Andrews & McMeel.

Roberts, T. *The Three Billy Goats Gruff*. Illustrated by D. Jorgensen. Westport, CT: Rabbit Ears Press. (Billy goats go "clip-clop" instead of "trip-trap.")

Rounds, G. 1993. *The Three Billy Goats Gruff*. New York: Holiday.

"The Three Billy Goats Gruff." Arbuthnot, M. H. 1961. *The Arbuthnot Anthology of Children's Literature*. Glenview, IL: Scott-Foresman. p. 227.

"The Three Billy Goats Gruff." Arbuthnot, M. H. 1961. *Time for Fairy Tales.* Glenview, IL: Scott-Foresman. pp. 72-73.

"The Three Billy Goats Gruff." Sutherland, Z., and M. C. Livingston. 1984. *The Scott-Foresman Anthology of Children's Literature.* Glenview, IL: Scott-Foresman.

Recommended for students in kindergarten through third grade.

Summary

This Scandinavian folktale, originally collected and published by P. C. Asbojornsen and J. Moe, appeals to young children and their fascination with trolls and with justice brought to those who are bad. In this classic tale, the largest and oldest billy goat brother, middle-sized and middle-aged brother, along with the youngest and tiniest of the Gruff brothers encounter the ugly troll as they cross over the bridge to find green grass. The repetitive language used by each goat brother as he converses with and attempts to outwit the troll to get to the green grass is fun for children as they quickly learn the phrases and the appropriate intonation.

Connect

- Preparation for the story may include making a background display by mounting a cardboard box with flaps still attached on a wall, resting on the floor. If side flaps are extended and taped to the surface of the wall, the bottom of the box will serve as the face of the troll. Add paper saucers for eyes and cover a four-inch section of rubber hose with masking tape for a nose. The box must be mounted near the floor (below eye level), so children will not be endangered by the nose. Construction paper or yarn may cover the taped flaps and serve as the troll's ears and hair.
- Ask questions that will allow children time to speculate on what kind of monster head is taped to the wall. Some sample **probes** (VO 72) include the following:

  What stories do you know that have monsters in them? What roles do the monsters usually play in stories? What are some names of monsters that you have heard from stories?

Write down the names the children know for monsters and make a list of all the names. The list may be made on chart paper and attached near the monster's head. Included on the list will probably be words such as giant, beast, savage, brute, ogre. If the word "troll" is not included, it may be added by the teacher.

- Help children understand the words "tripping" and "tramping" prior to reading. Children will enjoy dramatizing the meaning of these words, even before they have heard the story.
- After children have been prepared for the story, it may be told or read with the help of a **flannel board** (VM 11) and felt characters: small, middle-sized, and large goats, a bridge, and a troll. Children may later make their own flannel board characters to add to the collection.

Construct

- During or after the reading or telling of the tale, provide an opportunity for each child to respond to the story. A structured way to do this is to signal children to their response time by holding up a cardboard sign that reads **buddy buzz** (VO 54). Prior to this session, children will have been paired in buddies and will have been taught the procedure for buddy buzz.
- After initial responses during buddy buzz, ask for volunteers to share their responses with the class.
- As a class, retell the story by allowing one child to begin, moving from child to child as others volunteer the continued sequence. At the end of each added segment, ask for "thumbs up" or "thumbs down" from the class on the agreement of placement of the segment. Allow for discussion and for children to justify their contributions to the retelling if other children question the sequence.
- The following **probes** (VO 72) may be used for higher-level comprehension of the story:
  What are some reasons that the grass on the Gruffs' side of the bridge was not as green as on the other side? Why do you suppose the troll was under the bridge? Do you think the Gruffs had made a plan ahead of time for telling the troll to wait for the largest goat? Why or why not? Read something from the story that makes you believe what you do. When the goats were safely on the other side, how did they feel? How did they trick the troll? What might have happened if they had not tricked the troll?
- Groups of four children may play a **file folder game** (VM 10), "Tricking the Troll," made by the teacher. Goals should include: recalling the sequence of the story; reinforcing concepts of comparatives, such as small, middle-size, and large and young, younger, youngest.

Create

- Place a balance beam on the floor near the troll's head. Let children walk the balance beam in a line while chanting "tripping, tripping, tripping" or "tramping, tramping, tramping" with corresponding body movements.

- The balance beam "bridge" may serve as the focus for frequent creative dramatizations of the story by children during center time. They select their own parts and make up their own lines to the story as they re-enact it.
- Have children freely manipulate the felt characters used with the **flannel board** (VM 11) in the original telling of the story. Encourage them to tell the story to a partner, using the flannel board over the next few days.
- Make file folders, markers, rulers, and stacks of index cards available for children to create their own **file folder games** (VM 10) related to the story. Once created, the game will be approved by the teacher and then placed on a table for other children to use.
- Let children design the cover for a **lit log** (VW 92) to use as they experience the stories in this unit. When the cover is finished they may staple it onto prepackaged unlined or lined pages of paper.
- Give opportunities, in oral, written, dramatization, or artistic form for a personal response to the story from each child. If prompts are needed for oral or written responses, here are some suggested **probes** (VO 72):

    I know how the (goats) (troll) felt in this story, because...
    I had a bully in my neighborhood.
    I tricked... once. This is how it happened.

For dramatizations, try these ideas:

- Children may practice walking over the bridge as quietly as possible to avoid disturbing the troll.
- In pairs, children can pretend to be Mama goat and Big Billy, talking about how to practice safety on the roads and bridges.
- The total story may be dramatized, changing parts frequently to give all a chance to participate. Additional roles may be added as other characters (animals or people) are inserted into the story and also have to cross the bridge.

For artistic response, consider these suggestions:

- Students paint with tempera paints landscape scenes that the goats may have seen.
- Students draw bridges and compare the bridges they pictured in their minds while hearing the goat story.

JAMES, THE VINE PULLER—A BRAZILIAN ANIMAL TRICKSTER TALE

Stiles, M. B. 1992. *James, the Vine Puller: A Brazilian Folktale.* Minneapolis, MN: Carolrhoda. (In this story, the small animal is a turtle.)

Porter, Wesley. 1979. *The Hare, the Elephant, and the Hippo.* Illustrated by J. Behr. New York: Westport Group Book. (Note the change in this story from a whale to a hippo and from a turtle to a rabbit.)

"The Rabbit, The Elephant and The Whale." Foster, J. R. 1955. *Great Folktales of Wit and Humor.* New York: Harper & Brothers. pp. 303-05.

Related Tales

"Tortoise Triumph." Elliot, G. 1987. *Where the Leopard Passes: A Book of African Folk Tales.* Illustrated by S. Hawkins. New York: Schocken. pp. 120-126.

These stories are recommended for students in grades one through three.

Summary

James, the turtle, out of jest, challenges a whale to bet that he (the turtle) is stronger than the whale. Of course, the whale takes on the bet. The turtle then finds the elephant and entices him to participate in a tug-of-war with him. The turtle, trickster that he is, ties one end of the rope to the elephant and the other to the whale. The contest is really between the whale and the elephant, but neither knows that. They tug and tug until the rope breaks, giving the turtle an opportunity to chastise both the larger animals and to gloat as he believes that he has proven himself as strong as either of them.

Connect

■ Before reading or telling the story, ask children, "What is the strongest animal in the world?" From their responses, make a **character attribute chart** (VW 6) to post on the wall with the title, "Strongest Animal Guesses." Elicit responses of elephant and whale if they are not forthcoming. Then ask, "How many of you believe the turtle is the strongest animal in the world?" Few will want to put turtle's name on the chart!

■ Ask children for suggestions for determining which animal is strongest. They may suggest measuring to see which one is largest, weighs the most, or has the longest legs, or legs at all. (Prior to the reading of the story, arrange for the physical education teacher to teach the children the game tug-of-war.) Someone will probably mention tug-of-war as a way of determining the strongest animal. Accept all responses and list them on a chart.

■ Read or tell the story to the children.

Construct

■ **Chalk, talk, and walk** (VM 5) this story to assure the development of meaning.

■ For chalking and talking, have the children retell the story in this way: Break the story into parts and write the following parts on sentence strips: 1) turtle is amazed at size of whale; 2) turtle challenges whale to test of strength; 3) turtle challenges elephant to test of strength; 4) tug-of-war; 5) turtle talks to elephant; 6) turtle talks to whale. Divide children into six groups, give each group a sentence strip and give them time to talk and think about their sections of the story. For younger children, a group leader may report on the collective ideas while the teacher writes the dictation on charts. Each section's dictation will be written on separate sheets of chart paper. (With older children, the teacher may decide that groups should write their own chart retelling the story for their sections.) Hang the chart stories around the room in sequence. Read the story in unison.

■ For walking, each group will plan a short dramatization of its part of the story. After planning and practice time, children will present the story to each other.

■ Display the word "TRICKSTER" on posterboard and ask children for a definition. Take their words and collaboratively compose a definition that they understand. The following **probes** (VO 72) may help clarify their thinking:

Suggest other characters you have read about that you believe are tricksters. What does a trickster have to do to receive such a label? Would you want to be labeled a trickster? Why or why not? Why did authors from long ago write stories about tricksters?

■ Let children continue writing in their **lit logs** (VW 92) on tricksters. It is advisable to allow free choice of topic in their response logs, but if prompts are needed, here are some possibilities:

Being small is not so bad. How it feels to be tricked.

Create

Children should have some choices in their responses to the story, especially for homework or free time activities. After the teacher has directed several responses, children may determine ways they would like to respond. Following are some teacher-directed response activities:

- Attach a rope across a bulletin board for a background display onto which a construction paper background has been stapled. Let each of the six groups make pictures and place objects on the bulletin board to display the story. This activity will require some planning time as well as working time to draw pictures, write conversations, make objects and place them on the board. When finished, the charts that tell the story may be placed around the bulletin board.

- Discuss the phrase "big head, little tail," as a description of the elephant. Show a picture of an elephant and talk with the children about why the turtle might call the elephant by this phrase. Older children may wish to think of similar descriptions for other animals, such as "big mouth, flapping fins" (whale); "long neck, hard shell" (turtle). These descriptions may be illustrated also.

THE WONDERFUL TAR-BABY STORY—AFRICAN-AMERICAN ANIMAL TRICKSTER TALE

"The Wonderful Tar-Baby Story." 1961. Arbuthnot, M. H. *Time for Fairy Tales.* Glenview, IL: Scott-Foresman. pp 216-18.

Arkhurst, J. C. 1964. *The Adventures of Spider.* New York: Scholastic.

Hamilton, V. 1985. *The People Could Fly.* New York: Alfred A. Knopf.

Lester, J. 1990. *Further Tales of Uncle Remus: The Misadventures of Brer Rabbit, Brer Fox, Brer Wolf, the Doodang, and Other Creatures.* New York: Dial.

Lester, J. 1987. *The Tales of Uncle Remus, The Adventures of Brer Rabbit.* Illustrated by J. Pinkney. New York: Dial.

Related Tales

"How Br'er Rabbit Outsmarted the Frogs." Young, R., and J. Young. 1993. *African American Folktales for Young Readers.* Little Rock: August House. pp. 66-75.

"The Wonderful Tar-Baby Story." Sutherland, Z., and M. C. Livingston. (1984) *The Scott-Foresman Anthology of Children's Literature.* Glenview, IL: Scott-Foresman. pp. 377-78 (In dialect).

Recommended for children in kindergarten through grade three.

Summary

This story is one of the best known of the African-American folktales, told by Joel Chandler Harris as he heard them from African-American storytellers more than a hundred years ago. In the Uncle Remus stories, Brer Rabbit (Brother Rabbit) is a resourceful, lovable trickster, who uses trickery to save himself from Brer Fox. The version of the story referenced is a retelling by May Hill Arbuthnot as she attempted to de-emphasize the dialect and still maintain the rich language from the Harris version of the story. For those who can do justice to the original dialect, such a version is also found in the Scott-Foresman Anthology. Other modern versions of these tales of trickery among the animals are available in illustrated books.

Connect

- Before reading or telling this tale, revisit the concept of "trickster" with the children and note the list of examples children have found in which one animal tricks another. Remind them of the previous story in which the turtle was a trickster. Introduce another trickster to them: Brer Rabbit.
- Prediction **probes** (VO 72) might include:
    Who might be the trickster in this tale? What reasons can you think of that the rabbit might have for tricking another character?
- Note that brer means brother. Find out if any children have heard of other animals called "Brer," such as Brer Fox or Brer Bear. Tell the children that these stories were told long ago by African American men who frequently called each other "Brother." They also used the English language in a special dialect that is hard for some of us to understand. Alert the children that the language will sound different, but that the differences show us how people talked in some parts of the world long ago. Help them realize that the rich language is part of what makes the Uncle Remus stories unique.
- Put on a hat of any kind that may be called a **storytelling hat** (VM 31). Tell the children that when you are wearing this hat, they can expect you to use language that is different—just like saying "brer" for brother.
- Read the first two sentences of the story and stop and ask **buzz buddies** (VO 54) to explain to each other what a Tar-Baby might be. Ask again: "Who will the trickster be? Brer Fox or Brer Rabbit?"
- Read the rest of the story to the children.

Construct

■ Have a comparison chart or overlay for the overhead projector prepared with
the following heading for comparing tricksters in this story:

BRER RABBIT	BRER FOX

Using the chart for recording, ask children to share their thoughts on the
"tricks" of each animal in this story. List them on the chart as children mention
them. Talk about why each animal tried to trick the other (fox for food; rabbit
for survival).

■ Group the children into six groups. Ask each group to write (or with younger
children, to talk about) one question about the story that they would like to
have asked the original teller of this story. After appropriate working time
(two to five minutes) ask one group to ask its question. Allow time for
speculation on what the answers might be. Move through the other groups
with questions and answers. The questions may be collected, mounted, and
displayed with the chart showing the tricks of each animal.
■ Here are some questions they may ask or which may be used as **probes** (VO
72):
   *Why would the author make a rabbit and a fox enemies? If this story were about
   people, who would the characters be? Why? In what cases do you think trickery is
   justified? Why did Brer Rabbit tell the fox not to do exactly what he wanted him to
   do?*

Create

■ Following the reading of the story, children may draw pictures of some of the
following parts of the story:
   what the Tar-Baby looked like;
   what Brer Rabbit looked like when he was stuck on the Tar-Baby; and
   what the brier patch might have looked like.

These drawings may be placed with the chart of tricks played by each animal
and the questions the groups asked about the story.

- Provide modeling clay for children to make individual Tar-Babies. Some children may prefer to make Brer Fox or Brer Rabbit. These models may be glazed and arranged in displays in the classroom or around the school.

Animal Disguises Theme

WOLF AND THE SEVEN KIDS—GERMAN FOLKTALE

"The Wolf and the Seven Little Kids." Kherdian, D. 1992. *Feathers and Tails*. Illustrated by N. Hogrogian. New York: Philomel. pp. 53-59.

Jennings, L. 1986. *The Wolf and the Seven Little Kids*. Illustrated by M. Ursell. Kent, TN: Hodder & Stoughton.

Ross, T. 1990. *Mrs. Goat and Her Seven Little Kids*. New York: Atheneum.

Shannon, G. 1992. *The Oryx Multicultural Folktale Series: A Knock at the Door*. Phoenix, AZ: The Oryx Press. (A diverse collection of folktales with the theme of a stranger knocking at the door.)

"The Wolf and the Seven Little Kids." Arbuthnot, M. H. 1961. *Time for Fairy Tales*. Glenview, IL: Scott-Foresman. p. 34.

Recommended for children in kindergarten through grade three.

Summary

This story holds children spellbound as the wicked wolf, in disguise as mother goat, tricks the seven little kids into opening the door and proceeds to swallow six of them whole. The seventh one tells his mother when she returns and she tracks down the wolf, who is sleeping by the river. She cuts his stomach open with scissors and out pop all six kids, alive and well. They fill the gaping hole with rocks, which later causes the wolf to fall into the water while trying to drink. The kids shout, "The wolf is dead!" A gory story from the Grimm Brothers, this tale is a favorite of many children.

Connect

- Before reading or telling the story, introduce the children to the terms "goat" and "kids." Make a list of other animals and the names for their young:

horse	colt
dog	puppy
cat	kitten
lion	cub

- Select a favorite puppet from the classroom; one that the children have used and know well. Dress the puppet differently or put a mask on its face to disguise it. Change the voice that is usually associated with the puppet and then let the puppet take off the disguise, while you revert to the usual voice, thus showing the children how a disguise works. Allow children to talk about other disguises.
- Tell children the name of the story and ask **probes** (VO 72) such as these:
  Imagine how the mother goat and the kids looked. How did the wolf look? What are some ways the goat children—kids—might have recognized the wolf? What would happen if he were disguised and the kids did not know he was a wolf?
- Read or tell the story to the class.

Construct

- Children may experience strong emotions with this story and will need several opportunities to express their thoughts.
- Encourage open discussion of the story by asking some **probes** (VO 72) such as the following:
  Why did the mother goat tell the kids they could recognize the wolf by his rough voice and black feet? Imagine how the kids felt when the wolf was at the door pretending to be their mother. Pretend to be the seventh kid who hid in the clock-case. How did he feel when the wolf was inside the house? Pretend to be mother goat when you found your kids missing. Pretend to be the wolf with rocks in your stomach.
- To help children begin thinking about the origins of folktales, ask:
  How do you think the early people who heard and told these stories felt? Do you think the stories frightened them too?
- Provide time for children to respond to this story in their personal **lit logs** (VW 92) after much group discussion. Encourage children to write anything they wish to express in their response logs.

Create

- Compare the use of the term "kids" to the common usage of the term in our society referring to children. Have children prepare a survey to gather information from other classes in the school regarding children's opinions about being called "kids." Some planning for the survey will include:
  learning how to write good questions;

deciding how many children to survey and what ages;
implementing the actual survey, i.e., face to face or by distribution of
questionnaires;
learning how to compile data;
learning how to disseminate information.

- Have children learn the song, "Who's Afraid of the Big, Bad Wolf?" They
  may also learn the wolf's song from "The Three Pigs' Musical" in which the
  wolf sings, "I want a big, fat pig to eat."
- Write the words to one of the above songs on a chart tablet and use it as a
  pattern as the children copy cat (VW 86) their own song about this story.
- A direct mini-lesson on the use of commas in sequence could spring from this
  story at an appropriate time.
- Many children enjoy comparing this story to "The Three Little Pigs." A
  comparison chart on which likenesses and differences may be noted will help
  organize the comparison.

Story	Characters	Villain	Outcomes

LITTLE RED RIDING HOOD—FRENCH FOLKTALE
LON PO PO—CHINESE FOLKTALE

Coady, C. 1992. *Little Red Riding Hood*. New York: Dutton.
Young, Ed. 1989. *Lon Po Po*. New York: Philomel.
Grimm, J., and W. Grimm. 1983. *Little Red Cap*.Translated by E. Crawford;
Illustrated by L. Zwergwer. New York: Morrow Jr. Books.
"Little Red Riding Hood." Morel, E. 1970. *Fairy Tales and Fables*. Illustrated by
G. Frijikawa. New York: Grosset & Dunlap. pp. 11-13.
Bornstein, H., and K. Saulnier. 1990. *Little Red Riding Hood: Told in Signed
English*. Illustrated by B. Pomeroy. Washington, DC: Kendall Green.
Eisen, A. 1988.*Little Red Riding Hood*. Illustrated by L. Ferris. New York: Alfred
A. Knopf.
Goodall, J. 1988. *Little Red Riding Hood*. New York: McElderry.
Marshall, J. 1987. *Red Riding Hood*. (Big Book). New York: Puffin.

Vozar, D. 1993. *Yo, Hungry Wolf, A Nursery Rap.* New York: Doubleday for Young Readers.

"The Chinese Red Riding Hoods." Sutherland, Z., and M. C. Livingston. 1984. *The Scott-Foreman Anthology of Children's Literature.* Glenview, IL: Scott-Foresman. pp. 322-23.

"Little Red Riding Hood." Saltman, J. 1985. *The Riverside Anthology of Children's Literature.* Boston: Houghton Mifflin Company. pp. 275-76.

"Little Red Riding Hood." Martignoni, M. E. 1955. *The Illustrated Treasury of Children's Literature.* New York: Grossett & Dunlap. pp. 175-77.

Recommended for students in kindergarten through grade three.

Summary

"The Red Riding Hood" and "Lon Po Po" stories are masterpiece disguise stories which children love. In both stories, the wicked wolf disguises himself as Grandmother and tricks the child(ren) into letting him in the house. In a twist of plot, found in "Lon Po Po," the children also become tricksters and are delighted when the wolf meets his rightful punishment.

Connect

The previous story of the "Wolf and the Seven Kids" is a good foundation for the following Red Riding Hood stories. Review the common threads of disguise and deception prior to beginning these stories, which are variants of the same story, and lend themselves to comparison.

- Stop after the introduction of the story and ask for help in telling the story. Many children will have heard the Little Red Riding Hood story, so they can help tell it. The part children enjoy the most is the dialogue when Red Riding Hood asks the wolf (disguised as Grandmother), "What big teeth you have, Grandmother." Children will enjoy asking the series of questions leading up to the wolf's attempt to eat Red Riding Hood.
- If children need **probes** (VO 72) to keep the dialogue moving, ask: *What did Red Riding Hood ask the wolf (disguised as Grandmother)? How did the wolf answer? What did she ask next?*
- Review the term "disguise" and talk about how the wolf put on Grandmother's clothes to fool Red Riding Hood. Compare this disguise to the one in "The Wolf and the Seven Kids."
- Show children the cover of Ed Young's *Lon Po Po* and indicate to them that this story is like Red Riding Hood. Ask for predictions on how the stories might be the same or different. Record some of the predictions on a chart before reading the story.

- Read or tell the story to younger children.
- For children with appropriate reading levels, divide the class with two to three children per group. Make a copy of the story and cut it into the number of groups in the classroom. Distribute the sections of the story to the children for reading. Each group will only read an isolated segment of the story. When groups are finished, ask which group might have the beginning of the story. Have someone from that group read aloud to the class. Then ask if someone has a section that seems to follow what was just read. Someone from the group will read aloud. Continue until the story has been completed. This reading technique is called a **cooperative reading activity (C.R.A.)** (VO 63).

Construct

- Following the reading of the story, allow time for personal responses either by children talking in small groups or writing in the **lit log** (VW 92). If prompts are needed try the following:
   One time I was frightened by a.... The story I liked better was (Red Riding Hood) (Lon Po Po), *because...*
- As a large group, compare the two stories. Prepare a comparison chart on which the children's comparisons may be written, either through dictation or by allowing children to write their own comments on the chart.

We Know:	Red Riding Hood	Lon Po Po
# of Children		
About Granny		
About Wolf		
Alike		
Different		

- Discuss various names for Grandmother: Granny, Nana, Grandmommy, Lon Po Po. After names have been listed on chart or board, make a bar graph showing the frequency of each Grandmother name used by the children in the class.
- Form literary discussion groups consisting of four to six children to compare the two stories and to consider these questions:
   Why are the stories so much alike? Why would people from long ago have liked the stories? Why do you like the stories? Why do you not like the stories? What is the message in these stories?

Create

- Dramatize Lon Po Po, changing characters frequently, allowing all children a role during the dramatization.
- Make **pop-up stories** (VM 20) from file folders in which some aspect of one of the stories is shown.
- Have older children rewrite the dialogue between the wolf and child(ren).
- Begin constructing a bulletin board titled "Folktale Animals Road" by taking brown paper and stretching it across a wall, chalkboard, or bulletin board. Children will begin drawing folktale animal characters on the road. Before a character may be drawn on the road, the class must decide if the character is really a "folktale animal" character who belongs there. Criteria for "folktale animal" characters will be developed by the class as the teacher guides the selection of criteria.

```
Folktale Animals:
    are found in a folktale
    must be an animal
    may be in disguise
    will be very good or very bad
```

Helpful Animals Theme

THE FROG PRINCE—GERMAN FOLKTALE

Black, F. 1991. *The Frog Prince*. Illustrated by W. Parmenter. New York: Andrews & McMeel.

Darrell, M. (ed.) 1972. *Once Upon a Time: The Fairy Tale World of Arthur Rackham*. New York: Viking. pp. 43-46.

"The Frog Prince." Gag, W. 1936. *Tales from Grimm*. New York: Coward-McCann. pp. 179-88.

"The Frog King, or Iron Henry." Rugoff, M. 1949. *A Harvest of World Folk Tales*. New York: Viking Press.

Grimm, J., and W.Grimm. 1989. *The Frog King and Other Tales of the Grimm Brothers*. New York: Dutton.

Isadora, R. 1989. *The Princess and the Frog*. New York: Greenwillow.

Lewis, N. 1989. *The Frog Prince*. Illustrated by B. Schroeder. New York: North-South.

Ormerod, J. 1990. *The Frog Prince*. New York: Lathrop, Lee, and Shepard.

"The Well of the World's End." Williams-Ellis, A. 1987. *Tales from the Enchanted World.* Illustrated by M. Kemp. Great Britain: Hodder & Stoughton. pp. 53-61.

Recommended for students in kindergarten through third grade.

Summary

This story is a classic fairy tale from the Märchen of the Grimm Brothers. It is a romantic tale of a princess who drops a golden ball into a well. She promises many things to a frog who offers to retrieve the ball. After the helpful frog delivers the ball, the princess forgets her promise until her father, the king, expects her to keep her word. She does and eventually the frog turns back into a prince, breaking a spell placed on him long ago by a witch. The story has a happy ending with a strong moral of "keep your promises" and "play fair."

Connect

■ Begin the connecting activities with a **probe** (VO 72):
   What does it mean to keep a promise?
■ Elicit suggestions from children and allow some of their own examples of keeping or not keeping promises.
■ Tell them the title of the story, "The Frog Prince," and ask for predictions:
   What kinds of promises could a frog prince make? If there is a prince in the story, will there be a princess? What kinds of promises could the princess make?
■ Read or tell the story to the children.

Construct

■ Before class make a paper plate puppet for each of the characters: frog, prince, princess, and king. After reading the story, hand a puppet to a child who will tell about that character. Retell the story by continuing to pass around the puppets until everything has been remembered and talked about in the group. For example, hand the princess puppet to a child first. The child will probably tell that the princess was playing with a golden ball. Then hand the frog puppet to another child. Rules, such as telling only one thing, or waiting for a turn, may have to be discussed before beginning.
■ Revisit the earlier discussion on "keeping promises." Ask children to discuss at their tables or in groups these questions:

Why did the princess make a promise she did not intend to keep? Why do you suppose this story was first told?

■ Place several copies of the story and a tape recording of the reading in a center for children to enjoy independently.

■ Make a set of cards using the following vocabulary for children to use while they read or listen to the story in the center. Indicate that children should order cards according to the word's use in the story, first, second, third, etc.

frog	playfellow	prince
marveling	bulge	bewitched
princess	well	king
deftly	content	horrid
ball	greed	foot-end
goggle-eyed	croak	scorn

Create

Centers will give children a choice of activities for responding creatively to the story. Allow choice as children may want to experience several of the centers.

■ Center 1:   Children make their own set of paper plate puppets to take home and tell the story to family members.

■ Center 2:   Children draw pictures of frog prince "before" and "after." Using a folded paper, the frog will be on one side and the prince on the other. Children draw picture of choice regarding story using crayons and watercolors.

■ Center 3:   Read and listen to tape of a parody of the story called, "The Frog Prince Continued." Find the book and read it onto a tape.

■ Center 4:   Play a "Frog Prince" **file folder game** (VO 10) in which the object is to avoid turning into a frog. Children must read and count blocks for moving tokens.

■ Center 5:   Make a bed **checkbook box diorama** (VA 39) for the frog (so he won't have to sleep with the princess). Materials: checkbook boxes, scraps of fabric, paste, ribbon, glitter. When finished, write a letter to frog telling him about it.

■ Center 6:   Select one of the following: Write another ending to the story; write an entry in personal **lit logs** (VW 92) about this story; write a story about a character in disguise; write a story about when you were in disguise; write about keeping or breaking promises; write a fairy tale.

THE LION AND THE MOUSE

Barnett, C. 1990. *Lion and the Mouse*. New York: NTC Publishing Group.

"The Lion and the Mouse." Aesop, 1947. *Aesop's Fables*. Illustrated by F. Kredel. New York: Grosset & Dunlap. pp. 137-38.

"The Lion and the Mouse." Alley, R. W. 1986. *Seven Fables of Aesop*. New York: Dodd-Mead. pp. 16-19.

"The Lion and the Mouse." Arbuthnot, M. H. 1961. *Time for Fairy Tales*. Glenview, IL: Scott-Foresman. p. 225.

"The Lion and the Mouse." MacDonald, S., and B. Oakes. 1990. *Once Upon Another*. New York: Dial for Young Readers. (Read the book one direction for "The Lion and the Mouse." Another story is there if the book is turned upside down.)

"The Lion and the Mouse." Morel, E. 1970. *Fairy Tales and Fables*. Illustrated by G. Frijikawa. New York: Grosset & Dunlap. pp. 70-71.

"The Lion and the Mouse." Santore, C. 1988. *Aesop's Fables*. New York: Jellybean Press. p. 12.

Paxton, T. 1991. *Androcles and the Lion: And Other Aesop's Fables*. Illustrated by R. Rayevsky. New York: Morrow Jr. Books.

Stevens, J. 1989. *Androcles and the Lion: An Aesop Fable*. New York: Haliday.

Recommended for students in kindergarten through grade three.

Summary

When a lion is awakened by a mouse running over its face, the lion considers killing the mouse. The mouse talks him into sparing his life, saying he will someday repay the kindness of the lion. The lion sets the mouse free and is then caught in a hunter's trap a short time later. The mouse comes upon the entrapped lion and gnaws the ropes, setting the lion free.

Connect

■ Prior to reading the story, show the children pictures of a mouse and a lion. Compare and talk about the differences in size, appearance, and characteristics between the two animals. Attach the pictures side by side on the top of a chart page and draw a line down the center separating the two pictures. Ask the children to suggest ways a lion could help a mouse, or a mouse could help a lion. Record the suggestions under the appropriate animal's picture. Some possible suggestions are a lion could protect a mouse from other animals, save the mouse from drowning, rescue the mouse from a treetop, or shelter the mouse from a rainstorm; a mouse could help a lion by warning him of danger or gnawing a hole for him in something. List all of the ideas given by the children. Then read the story to them or, if appropriate, have the text typed and duplicated for each child to have a personal copy of the fable to read.

Construct

■ After children have read or have heard the reading of this fable, provide an opportunity for children to talk about the story in groups of two or three. These literary discussion groups may respond to one of the following questions:

Why did each animal decide to help the other? What do these old saying mean: "Turn about is fair play" or "One good turn deserves another" or "Treat others as you would like to be treated"?

■ Share with the children some information about fables (see chart in appendix B) and particularly about Aesop for older children. Lead the children in a shared writing experience.

Some topics for the group composition might be:

Why did the original author of this fable tell this story? If the author were living today, how might the story be the same or different?

■ Pictures of the lion and the mouse, along with the shared writing piece, may be added to the "folktale animals" bulletin board.

Create

Give children choices among these response activities:

■ Dramatize the fable several times, giving many children an opportunity to create their own dialogue. Videotape the dramatizations for children to view later or to show to another audience.
■ Encourage individual creations of modern day fables. Share Arnold Lobel's *Fables* as a model for older children's creations.
■ Art project: Crisscross (crosshatch) yellow crayon markings on white paper to resemble a rope net. Paint over it with thick black tempera paint. After the paint dries, scratch the black paint with a flat surface tool to design the shape of the net that caught the lion. Then attach cutouts of the lion and mouse.

GRANNY'S BLACKIE

"Granny and Her Blackie." Arbuthnot, M. H. 1961. *Time for Fairy Tales.*
Glenview, IL: Scott-Foresman. pp. 163-64.
"Granny's Blackie." Babbitt, E. C. 1912. *Jataka Tales.* New York: Appleton-
Century Crofts, Inc. pp. 78-83.

Other Jataka Tales

De Roin, N. 1975. *Jataka Tales.* Boston: Houghton Miffin.

Recommended for children in grades one through three.

Summary

This story, from the Indian Jataka Tales, is similar to a fable but longer
and more complex. It is about a granny who receives a baby elephant from
a rich man and raises him among the children in the village. Blackie is
the elephant's name, and he takes the children for swing rides everyday
while Granny works and supports them. One day, Blackie realizes that
Granny is getting older, and he decides that he should go out and earn
money instead of Granny. He pulls wagons across the river when the
oxen are unable to do so. He is a smart business "person" in collecting all
the money due him. In the end, he is able to support Granny and himself,
allowing her to rest.

Connect

- Prepare the children for the reading or telling of this tale with a review of the
  names discussed earlier for grandmothers. Let them know that this story is
  another one with a grandmother as a character. This grandmother is called
  "Granny."
- Point to the bulletin board of "folktale animal characters" created earlier and
  note the helpful animals on the board. Tell them that Granny has an animal
  who helps her. Place the picture of an elephant on the board. Some
  prediction **probes** (VO 72) might include:
  *How might an elephant help a Granny? Why would an elephant help a Granny?
  How do you think the elephant and Granny are related? Would an elephant make
  a good pet? Why or why not?*

- With older children who have studied the form of fables, review the presence of morals in fables. Suggest that they compare this story to other fables they know and see if this tale, too, might be a fable.
- Read or tell the story to the children.

Construct

- After reading the story, group the children in triads, labeling each child as Granny, Blackie, or Observer. Granny will tell Blackie and the Observer what Granny did in the story; Blackie will tell Granny and the Observer what Blackie did; and the Observer will add any parts that are left out. Allow this type of discussion for five minutes following the reading of the story. These triad recaps give children opportunities to make their own meaning from stories as they retell a small segment of the tale. The observer plays an important role in clarifying disagreements and filling in details left out by the other two children. The child who is given the role of Observer needs to be mature with good listening skills.
- Total group discussion may include the following **probes** (VO 72):

    How did Granny raise such a kind and thoughtful elephant? Imagine what would have happened if Blackie had not decided to go to work instead of Granny continuing to work? What might have happened if Blackie had not insisted on getting paid what he was promised? Why or why not was he brave to refuse to move out of the road until he was paid what he had been promised? How must Granny have felt when she could not find Blackie? How must Granny have felt when he finally came home and told her about his job?

    (For those children who recognize this story as a fable: What is the lesson found in this story?)

Create

- Group children into the same triads as before and ask each group to plan a dramatization of the story. Have each group choose the medium for drama-tization, for example: paper plate puppets, finger puppets, readers' theater, pop-up character displays to show the story, or physical re-enactment of the story, with or without props. Give each group time to decide on the medium. Preparation may extend over a period of a day or two. After the triads make presentations to their own classroom, they may each select another class-room as an audience for a repeat performance.
- Writing in the **lit logs** (VW 92) may be independent writing or may be prompted with these questions and open-ended statements:

Who gave the greatest amount of help to the other, Granny or Blackie? Whom do you help and how? Describe how to make pop-ups, finger puppets, or paper plate puppets to someone who does not know how.

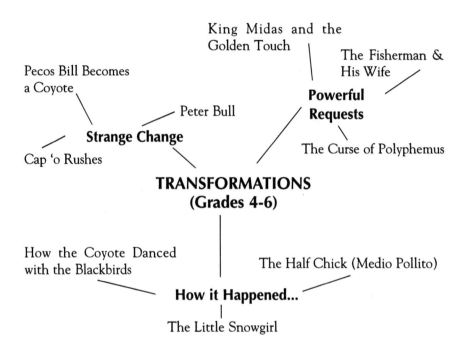

King Midas and the
Golden Touch

The Fisherman &
His Wife

Pecos Bill Becomes
a Coyote

Peter Bull

**Powerful
Requests**

Strange Change

Cap 'o Rushes

The Curse of Polyphemus

TRANSFORMATIONS
(Grades 4-6)

How the Coyote Danced
with the Blackbirds

The Half Chick (Medio Pollito)

How it Happened...

The Little Snowgirl

CHAPTER
six
* * * * * * * * *

Transformations Unit
Grades 4-6

LITERARY OUTCOMES

The literary selections in this unit include folktales from Denmark, Spain, Russia, and Germany; an American tall tale; and a Native American explanatory tale. Students are introduced to an English novella, a Greek myth, and an epic. The variety of subgenres will allow students many opportunities for comparison of different structures.

Through this unit, students will have an opportunity to recognize a "tragedy" in the plot of "The Little Snowgirl" and "irony" in "The Fisherman and His Wife." These two stories clearly represent the innocent tragedy as opposed to the ironic fate of one who brings on his or her own disaster.

These nine stories will help students understand the theme of "transformation" found in many folktales over the world. These tales and the study of transformations, as presented here, should fascinate most intermediate age students and add to their perspective on folk literature.

INTEGRATED CURRICULUM STRATEGIES

Here are some related topics for possible curriculum integration:

- Animal life, characteristics, habitats, classification
- Cultural and geographical study of the Old West, including history of Native American life, westward movement of the United States, discovery of gold
- Physical science: changes of matter—various states of matter

- History of Greece, Greek mythology
- Research and library skills
- Map skills and calculation of travel concepts
- Study of oceans, seas, and bodies of water
- Scandinavian countries, geography, history, culture, and literature

Strange Change Theme

PETER BULL—DANISH FOLKTALE

"Peter Bull." Lang, A. 1967. *The Pink Fairy Book*. New York: Dover.
"Peter Ox." Hatch, M. C. 1949. *More Danish Tales*. New York: Harcourt, Brace
& World. pp. 167-81.

Related stories of parents wanting children

Littledale, F. 1989. *Snow Child*. New York: Scholastic.
MacDonald, M. R. 1993. *The Oryx Multicultural Folktale Series: Tom Thumb*.
  Phoenix, AZ: The Oryx Press.
Shute, L. 1986. *Momotaro, The Peach Boy*. New York: Lothrop.

Recommended for students in grades four through six.

Summary

Peter Bull, a Danish tale, is about an old couple who want a child. When
they obtain a bull-calf, they treat him like a son. They employ someone
to teach him to talk. They are cheated by the clerk, who neither teaches
Peter Bull to talk nor takes care of him properly. The old couple is told
that he has run away. Later they read in a newspaper of a new merchant
who has settled in a nearby town, whose name is Peter Bull. After
contacting him and finding a man with the same broad forehead and red
hair, they conclude, and he concurrs, that they are his parents. They
move to the nearby town to be near their son.

Connect

Try the following activities prior to reading the story:

- Examine the origin of the word "transformation." It is formed from two words: *trans* meaning "over" and *forma* meaning "form."
- Ask students to predict what the two words mean when they are connected. Ask for ideas of what kinds of stories will be in a unit on "transformations." Use a **prediction pitcher** (VM 23).
- Ask the students if they ever wished their pets could talk and perform human activities.
- Show the cover of the picture book *The Velveteen Rabbit* by Marjorie Williams and allow discussion on how it would feel to have a toy become real or a pet become human.
- Discuss animal communication research (e.g., dolphin research; Koko, the gorilla) and suggest research projects in this area.
- **Thought-Splash** (VO 82) and chart some tales known by the students in which animals are changed into humans:

Story	Beast	Changed to
?	Frog	Prince

- Read "Peter Bull" to the students.

Construct

- For literary discussion groups prepare these generic **probes** (VO 72) on slates and place around the room:

    What does the author do to let you know where the story is happening? What do you know about the characters? How do you know? How did they change or stay the same during the story? How did the author start the story? How was the beginning event crucial for the rest of the story? What was the author's main message about the hero of the story? What other stories have given the same message? Compare the heroes of these stories. How are they alike or different? Are you reminded of things in your life when you read these stories? How does the author create suspense? How else could the author have created excitement and interest in the story? Were you surprised by the ending? Why or why not? Why did the author give the story such an ending?

    If you were reading this story to a younger child, what questions would you ask?

- Group topics for problem-searches:

If you were searching for someone, how would you go about finding the person? If you lost a child on a trip, how would you start a search? What rules should children be told to follow in the event of becoming lost?

- Search phone books for names that could be animal names, e.g., Peter Bull, James Wolf, Sally Salmon, Patsy Peacock, Dee Dove, Helen Hogg, Bob Buck.
- Teach the meaning of "motifs." Then prepare center activities for students to find and compare stories with the following motifs:

    lost objects or characters (Frog Prince, Cinderella);

    found objects or characters ("The Greedy Dog and the Bone," "The Gingerbread Man," "Aladdin," "The Magic Pot," "Thor and His Hammer").

Create

- Immediately following the reading of the story, ask each student to write a main idea from the story on an index card. Discussion of the story will follow as cards are shuffled, redistributed, and read aloud. Students may agree or disagree with the main ideas as they are read.

Students may work individually or in cooperative groups to complete some of the following responses:

- Create **mobiles** (VA 44) of the sequence of events in this story by stringing together abstract shapes of construction paper, each containing a drawing of an event in the story. The string of events may be attached to a clothes hanger for displaying.
- Write responses to the story in the **lit log** (VW 92).
- Make posters advertising the lost or found objects from stories that were compared to Peter Bull.
- Plan ways that Peter Bull's parents could have avoided losing their "child," and rewrite the story, including your plan.
- Make some "missing" posters to help search for Peter.
- Research some real-life missing children stories. Make a bulletin board of pictures from media flyers and newspaper stories of missing children. Make a list of safety rules for children to follow.
- Give a presentation to a kindergarten or first grade class on safety rules around strangers.

PECOS BILL BECOMES A COYOTE—AMERICAN TALL TALE

"Pecos Bill Becomes a Coyote." Saltman, J. 1985. *The Riverside Anthology of Children's Literature*. Boston: Houghton Mifflin. pp. 453-54.

"Pecos Bill and the Mountain Lion." 1961. *The LIFE Treasury of American Folklore*. New York: Time, Inc. pp. 274-75.

"Pecos Bill Turns into a Coyote." Bowman, J. C. 1937. *Pecos Bill, the Greatest Cowboy of All Time*. Chicago: Whitman. pp. 15-22.

Related Pecos Bill stories

Dewey, A. 1993. *Pecos Bill*. New York: Greenwillow.

Gleeson, B. 1988. *Pecos Bill*. Illustrated by T. Raglin. Saxonville, MA: Rabbit Ears Books. (Unpaged, but referenced story is on 2 pages. Also: videocassette from Sony Video Software; cassettes from Windham Hill Records.)

Kellogg, N. 1992. *Pecos Bill*. New York: Morrow.

Lyman, N. 1980. *Pecos Bill*. Mahwah, NJ: Trall.

"Pecos Bill." Osborne, M. 1991. *American Tall Tales*. Illustrated by M. McCurdy. New York: Alfred A. Knopf. pp. 75-85.

"Pecos Bill and His Bouncing Bride." Sutherland, Z., and M.C. Livingston. 1984. *The Scott-Foresman Anthology of Children's Literature*. Glenview, IL: Scott-Foresman. pp. 365-67.

Small, T. 1992. *The Legend of Pecos Bill*. New York: Little Rooster.

Recommended for students in grades four through six.

Summary

"Pecos Bill Becomes a Coyote," an American tall tale, explains how Bill becomes lost from his parents and 17 brothers and sisters and becomes the pet of the coyotes, led by the granddaddy of all coyotes, Grandy. In this story, all the animals, except two, pledge to help Cropear (Bill's coyote name because he had short ears) grow to adulthood safely.

Connect

- Prepare a background setting display to include a map of Texas and the Pecos River, which meanders through New Mexico into Texas where it joins with the Rio Grande in southwest Texas.
- In a short book talk tell the students that this story is about a family who crossed Texas in the early 1800s and lost a child, who was later known as

Pecos Bill, at the Pecos River. Ask if they have known of children becoming lost from their parents. Allow time for these stories to be shared.

■ Have duplicate copies of the story for paired reading and allow time for both reading and discussing the story in pairs.

■ Prepare a **word wall** (VM 34) to display unusual words related to tall tales and particularly to this story: e.g., "tall tales," "exaggeration," "cowboy," "Rio Grande."

Construct

■ The following **probes** (VO 72) may be used to direct the paired discussions:

Why did Pecos Bill believe his name was Cropear? Where could he have gotten this name? What do coyotes look like? Do they have crop ears or long ears? Would coyotes raise a child in the wild?

Why was Pecos Bill called the greatest cowboy of all times in this story?

How could Bill have been lost from the wagon and his mother not know it? How do you suppose she felt when she realized Bill was missing? How do you think she felt when she went back to the river and could not find him? Why did his family call him Pecos Bill after that?

How do you think Grandy looked? Why did the author of this story call Grandy the leader of the Loyal and Approved Packs of the Pecos and Rio Grande Valleys? What did the author do in this story to make it believable?

■ Direct students in a **descriptive name tag** (VW 87) activity in which students find words used to describe the way something looks, such as how Cropear in Pecos Bill refers to his short ears. Other characters in this story or other stories could be given descriptive names.

Create

■ Use this story to begin a focus during the unit on the literary element of "setting." Coordinate a study of the geography of the West or social studies history of the westward movement that will allow students to understand the setting for this story and that real places are described.

■ Students may make a background setting display to strengthen their knowledge of the setting for this story and to use if they share the information with another group or another class. This display would, of course, be different from the one prepared by the teacher prior to reading the story.

■ Examine and compare the setting of this story with that of "Peter Bull," and note what is known about the setting of each story.

■ Use a comparison chart to compare the subgenres of the two stories (folktale and tall tale) and list how they are alike and different. (Major differences are the setting and the exaggerated language of tall tales.) Student may create charts to place near the background setting board to show the comparisons. From this comparison, the students will be able to use the criteria for American tall tales and write one; some students may prefer to create an original transformation story. (For more details on comparison, see appendix B.)

- Revisit the theme of children being lost from their parents that is found in both Peter Bull and Pecos Bill stories. Encourage students to write in their **lit logs** (VW 92) about how these events might have been prevented.
- Dramatizations that students will enjoy creating and presenting to others are:

  recreate Pecos Bill's meeting with Grandy

  re-enact the scene of Bill's mother and brothers and sisters returning to the river to find him

  dramatize Bill's education with Grandy

  make puppets and retell Bill's associations with the rabbit, the bear, the rattlesnake, and the wouser.

CAP O' RUSHES—ENGLISH FOLKTALE

"Cap o' Rushes." Sierra, J. 1992. *The Oryx Multicultural Folktale Series: Cinderella*. Phoenix, AZ: The Oryx Press. pp. 40-43.

"Cap o' Rushes." Williams-Ellis, A. 1987. *Tales from the Enchanted World*. Illustrated by M. Kemp. Great Britain: Hoddler & Stoughten. pp. 8-16.

Jacobs, J. No date. *English Folk and Fairy Tales*. New York: Putnam. pp. 51-56.

Minard, R. 1975. *Womenfolk and Fairy Tales*. Boston: Houghton Mifflin. pp. 77-82.

Related Tales

"Cap o' Rushes." National Association for the Preservation and Perpetuation of Storytelling. 1991. *Best Loved Stories Told at the National Storytelling Festival*. Jonesborough, TN: NAPPS. pp. 91-95.

"Mossy Coat." Garner, A. 1984. *Alan Garner's Book of British Fairy Tales*. Illustrated by D. Collard. New York: Delacorte. pp. 47-57.

Recommended for students in grades four through six.

Summary

This novella is basically a Cinderella story without the magic. In this tale, a sensible young girl is turned away from her home by her father when she gives him a pragmatic answer to the question of how much she loves him. Her answer, much different from that of her two sisters, is "as much as fresh meat needs salt."

When turned out, she has to find food and shelter, so she hides her fine clothes and makes herself a cape from head to toe of rushes from the bog. In these clothes, she is able to offer her services of washing pots and pans to a household that also has some daughters.

Eventually, a dance is announced at which the son of the master of the land will attend. After everyone has gone, she changes into one of her fine dresses and attends the ball. For three consecutive nights she does this, each time winning the heart of the young man, but leaving to be at home before the others arrive. After the third night, when he gives her a ring, the man becomes very ill. Cap o' Rushes, as she is called, asks the cook to let her make a soup for his recovery. In this soup, she places the ring. He recognizes the ring, calls for her, and they announce their engagement. One of the guests at the wedding is her father, who does not know she is the bride. She asks the cook to leave all salt off the meat, and it is upon eating nonsalted meat that her father realizes how much she loves him.

Connect

- Begin an introduction to this story by reminding the students that in the two previous stories, characters were lost from their families. Ask them if they can think of any stories in which children were "turned out" by their families. They may think of "Hansel and Gretel," "Snow White," or "Cinderella." Ask them to think of similarities with these stories as they hear Cap o' Rushes.
- If there are marshes near your location, bring in some examples [realia (VA 46)] of rushes or long-stemmed weeds for students to develop an idea of how the cape in this story was made by braiding the leaves.
- Read the story to the students.

Construct

Following the reading of the story, engage the class in the construction of a mood path to retell the story. To begin a mood path, list a series of colors and obtain student agreement that certain colors represent certain moods. For example: Blue = sad; Red = mad; Green = contented; Yellow = happy.

Then as students retell a segment of the story, ask them to label that portion of the story with one of the colors. Discussions will occur as students negotiate their reasoning for a given color, i.e., emotion.

The story may be divided with students in pairs or small groups illustrating segments and coloring an inch strip at the top of the page the color of the mood.

When all illustrations are posted sequentially, the story may be retold and the mood of each scene will be evident to those looking at the pictures.

- The folk literature subgenre, novella (novelle is the plural), is represented by this story. More information on the novella is available in appendix B. Upper-elementary students will enjoy this Cinderella story without the magic.
- A **Venn diagram** (VM 33) is a good technique for comparing the Cinderella story to this story. Through this activity, students will be able to see how Cap o' Rushes is ill-treated by her father, rather than stepmother, and how Cap o' Rushes works to solve her own problems rather than passively accepting magical happenings to improve her life. Venn diagrams may be completed by small groups of students and then compared or completed as a large group activity using an overlay for all to see.
- Divide the class into literary discussion groups (four to six students) and use these probes if necessary:

   How would you have answered the question about how much you loved your father? Why do you think the author used the salt and fresh meat analogy in this story? Where do you suppose the story took place? Why do you think that? How does the author let you know that Cap o' Rushes is an independent young lady?
- Speculate on whether the original author of this story was a man or a woman. Why?

Create

- Let students select from these beginnings and write in imitation diaries, either from a fictional or personal perspective.

   Entry 1) It is easy to misunderstand what someone else is saying. It happened to me one time, so I can understand how her father misunderstood what she said. This is how I was misunderstood.

   Entry 2) I find working with my hands is rewarding. I love to weave rushes into baskets and hats. I was lucky that I knew how to do that when I had to change out of my good clothes to convince someone that I needed a job. I just wove a set of clothes from the rushes. I think the family thought I was weird because . . .

   Entry 3) I didn't believe that a pretty girl could also cook well until . . .

   Entry 4) Fresh meat needs salt as much as a fish needs water.

   A fish needs water as much as a cat loves mice.

   A cat loves mice as much as . . .

Powerful Requests Theme

KING MIDAS AND THE GOLDEN TOUCH—GREEK MYTH

"The Golden Touch." Arbuthnot, M. H. 1952. *Time for Fairy Tales, Old and New.* Glenview, IL: Scott-Foresman. pp. 229-35.

"The Golden Touch." Sutherland, Z., and M. Livingston. 1984. *The Scott-Foresman Anthology of Children's Literature.* Glenview, IL: Scott-Foresman. pp.430-36.

"The Golden Touch." Saltman, J. 1985. *The Riverside Anthology of Children's Literature.* Boston: Houghton Mifflin. pp. 494-502.

Hewitt, K. 1987. *Nathaniel Hawthorne, King Midas and the Golden Touch.* San Diego: Harcourt, Brace & Jovanovich.

Newby, R. 1990. *King Midas: With Selected Sentences in American Sign Language.* Washington, DC: Kendall Green.

Recommended for students in grades four through six.

Summary

"King Midas and the Golden Touch," a story from Greek mythology, is about a king who is more fond of gold than anything else in the world—except maybe his daughter, Marygold. He requests that everything he touches turn to gold and is granted his request. After turning Marygold into a golden statue, he realizes that his wish is actually a curse.

Connect

- Introduce the theme of powerful requests to students. Ask the students if they have ever wished for something that they later regretted. Allow examples from the students' lives to support their points.
- Make a wish basket. Cover a basket with gold paper and give each student a slip of gold paper for making a wish to deposit in the wish basket. Ensure privacy by providing a stapler for students to close their wish slips.
- Display a poster showing the old proverb: "Take time to stop and smell the roses." Give time for students to talk in pairs about what it means and how it can relate to the first story in this unit.
- Read the story to the students or allow silent independent reading if their reading levels are adequate.

Construct

- Divide this story into four sections:
  1) before King Midas was given the Golden Touch;
  2) while he was talking to the magic power, making his request;
  3) when he began turning everything into gold; and
  4) when he discovered the consequences of his request.

  Divide the students into four groups, giving each a section of the story, and ask them to prepare a character report card for King Midas for that section of the story. Criteria for grading should be developed by the whole class so the standards will be consistent. Following the grading of the character, group representatives should share their findings and their reasonings with the whole group.

- Further constructing of meaning may occur through these **probing** (VO 72) questions:

  How did the author communicate with us, the readers? What was the most significant part of the story? What part of the story was the most difficult to accept? What was the motivation behind Midas's actions? How did the ending fit the rest of the story? Were you satisfied? Why or why not?

Create

- Students may create a bulletin board of "powerful wishes." Each student will have a section on the board for adding objects, drawings, or writings regarding his or her own wishes. Students may retrieve their wishes from the wish basket to use on the board.

- These wishes may be tied to goal setting. In personal journals students may list their readers' and writers' workshop goals for the next grading period. Such an activity will allow students to see the difference between setting and accomplishing goals as opposed to waiting for requests to be filled.

- Students may create and illustrate a list of rules for King Midas to follow to stay out of trouble.

- Students may paint a scene from "The Golden Touch" using a **golden scratchboard** (VA 42) technique. They will enjoy the gilded edges of their design after scratching it onto the surface.

- Read *The Chocolate Touch* (Catling, P. Bantam, 1981) and write a comparison with "The Golden Touch."

- An option in **writers' workshop** (VW 104) may be for students to write "golden stories" of themselves accomplishing the wish in the golden wish basket.

THE FISHERMAN AND HIS WIFE—GERMAN FOLKTALE

Richardson, I. M., (ed). 1988. *The Fisherman and His Wife*. Illustrated by G. Troll. New York: Lippincott.

"About a Fisherman and His Wife." Shub, E. 1971. *About Wise Men and Simpletons, Twelve Tales from Grimm*. Illustrated by N. Hogrogrian. New York: Macmillan. pp. 5-16.

Craig, J. 1986. *The Three Wishes*. Illustrated by Y. Salzman. New York: Scholastic.

"The Fisherman and His Wife." Arbuthnot, M. H. 1961. *Time for Fairy Tales*. Glenview, IL: Scott-Foresman. pp. 56-60.

The Fisherman and His Wife. 1980. Translated by R. Jarrell. New York: Farrar, Straus, Girous.

Littledale, F. 1985. *The Magic Fish*. Illustrated by W. Pels. New York: Scholastic.

"The Story of the Fisherman and His Wife." Alderson, B. 1978. *Lang's Green Fairy Book*. Illustrated by A. Maitland. New York: Viking. pp. 371-81.

Recommended for students in grades four through six.

Summary

A fisherman and his wife live in poverty in a pigsty. One day the fisherman catches a fish that can talk. The fish says he is an enchanted prince. The fisherman lets the fish swim away, but when he tells his wife about it, she makes him go back and call the fish to ask for a better place to live, such as a cottage. The fish complies, and the fisherman and his wife have a lovely little cottage that satisfies her for about two weeks. She then decides the cottage is too small and asks her husband to go find the fish and ask for a castle. No sooner has the fisherman found the fish and asked for a stone castle than his wife is standing there among lots of servants and a fine way of life. Shortly, his wife is dissatisfied with the castle and urges the fisherman to ask the flounder to make her king. That is done by the flounder and then the wife wants to be the emperor. Once she is the emperor, she decides she wants to be the Pope. These are granted by the flounder and she still is not happy: she wants to be the good Lord. The fisherman, very reluctantly goes back to the sea, which is rolling with black foam and thunder and lightening. He asks the fish for the favor, and the fish tells him to go back and find his wife waiting for him in the pigsty.

Connect

- This story will be an introduction to the plot pattern of irony (when characters bring on their own bad luck) found in children's folk literature. To help students understand irony in literature, read to them a short chapter from one of the George and Martha picture books by James Marshall. Almost any of the stories will show how characters bring on their own problems with their selfishness, greed, lying, or some other weakness. In these George and Martha stories, the two characters are lovable hippopotamuses, who always learn a lesson about interpersonal relationships. By reading one of the stories to the students before they read "The Fisherman and His Wife," the background will be set for understanding the logical consequences of "getting exactly what one deserves" and "deserving exactly what one gets."

- A banner might be posted in the class that reads: IRONY: YOU DESERVE IT!

- If multiple copies are available, give silent reading time for students to read the story independently or in pairs. Otherwise read it aloud to them.

Construct

- Following the reading of the story, dramatize the events, allowing different students to play the role of the fisherman and his wife through each of the requests. Encourage the students to use their own language rather than try to memorize the words from the story.

- After the dramatization, put students into pairs for small group questioning in which they formulate high-level questions related to this story. Group the pairs, instructing them to take turns asking and discussing their questions.

- Retell the story omitting the irony. In this retelling, the fisheman's wife will be a totally different character and will not deserve the ending as it is written in the original story.

Create

- Following dramatization and discussion of the story, students will enjoy performing this story as a **shadowtale** (VO 77) in which two students play a single role. One says what was told in the story, and the other interprets what the character was probably thinking. As in the previous dramatizations, several students may participate by allowing characters to change frequently.

The creative responses that follow may be given as additional choices for responding to this story:

- Using the ironic plot pattern, write an original story.

- Write a **copycat story** (VW 86) using the same structure but different characters and events.
- Paint a watercolor scene of a sequence of the story showing the color and storminess of the sea every time the magic flounder was called.
- Write a diary entry from the fisherman's wife after she found herself back in the pigsty.

THE CURSE OF POLYPHEMUS—GREEK EPIC

Fisher, L. 1991. *Cyclops*. New York: Holiday.
"The Curse of Polyphemus." Arbuthnot, M. H. 1961. *Time for Fairy Tales*. Glenview, IL: Scott-Foresman. pp. 257-60.
Evslin, B. 1987. *The Cyclops*. New York: Chelsea House.

This story is recommended for mature students in grades four through six.

Summary

From the Greek epic, *The Odyssey*, this story of Odysseus' encounter and curse from Polyphemus, the Cyclops and son of Poseidon, is told. Odysseus and his sailors are on their way home from the battle of Troy when they stop by a huge cave and find it inhabited by a great one-eyed monster, Polyphemus. Polyphemus holds the men captive and eats two at a time whenever he is hungry. Odysseus thinks of how he can escape and finally comes upon an idea. With the help of his remaining men, he sharpens a club to a point. When the Cyclops sits down to rest in the evening, Odysseus gives him wine from his supply and makes him sleepy. While he sleeps, the men plunge the club into the one eye of Polyphemus, blinding him. Odysseus has told Polyphemus his name is Noman, so when he calls for the help of other Cyclopes and tells them Noman is torturing him, they leave, thinking that no man is harming him. The next morning when Polyphemus opens his cave for the sheep to leave, each man is holding onto the underside of the middle of three sheep, and as they pass by the blinded Cyclops, he only feels the wool passing by. So the men from Ithaca begin to escape, but Odysseus calls back to ridicule the giant. Polyphemus, blinded and having his pride injured, calls upon his father, Poseidon, to delay these men on their journey home. His request is granted, and it is ten years before Odysseus sees his home again.

Connect

- Although the previous story of King Midas was a Greek myth, this epic hero tale from *The Odyssey* is the first introduction to the complex Greek stories. Review the information on epics from appendix B and plan to introduce the students to Homer, the Greek poet.

- An integrated study of early Greek civilization with the family structure of gods may be appropriate for mature classes. All youngsters, however, seem to enjoy the idea of a mortal man outsmarting a giant monster—especially if the monster has only one eye! This story is a natural adventure thriller that will captivate students when they are given a brief overview of the story before they read it.

- Build a **classroom reading ship** (VM 8) and fill it with pillows and stories of the Greek legends and myths. Allow students to earn time to read in the reading ship. When ready to introduce the story, gather the students around the ship and *tell*, rather than read, the story if at all possible. Dress as a traveler who has heard the story and is passing it on as truth.

Construct

- To help students construct meaning from this story, prepare to guide them through an **action map** (VM 2). Have an overlay for an overhead projector divided into 16 sections. Call on the students to sequence the action in this story. Each event shall be noted in one of the 16 sections.

    1) Odysseus left Troy with 12 ships and battles at Ismarus.
    2) They met the Lotus-eaters.
    3) They found the cave of Polyphemus.
    4) They made a fire and ate.
    5) Polyphemus returned home and ate two sailors.
    6) The next morning, he ate two more.
    7) Odysseus made a pointed club.
    8) Cyclops returned home and drank wine offered by Odysseus.
    9) Cyclops slept.
    10) Odysseus punched his eye out.
    11) Odysseus told him he was Noman.
    12) Calls for help were ignored.
    13) In the morning, each man exited the cave under three sheep, but Polyphemus only felt the sheep.
    14) From his ship, Odysseus called back to harrass the Cyclops.
    15) Polyphemus called on his father, Poseidon, to cause trouble for the sailors.

16) They traveled for ten years before reaching home.

■ Dramatize various parts of the story in small groups. Make sure all get a turn.

Create

■ The 16 segments of the action map may be divided among the students who, in groups or pairs, draw the actions described in the segments. These actions may be drawn on large pages of newsprint and the words written under the pictures to tell the story. The pages may be bound into an "epic book."

How It Happened Theme

HOW THE COYOTE DANCED WITH THE BLACKBIRDS— NATIVE AMERICAN EXPLANATORY STORY

"How the Coyote Danced with the Blackbirds." Saltman, J. 1985. *The Riverside Anthology of Children's Literature.* Boston: Houghton Mifflin. pp. 525-26.

Related stories that could be substituted

"The Tortoise and the Eagle." Santore, C. 1988. *Aesop's Fables.* New York: Jellybean Press. p. 33.

Bierhorst, J. 1987. *Doctor Coyote: A Native American Aesop's Fable.* New York: Macmillan.

"The Tortoise and the Osprey." Elliot, G. 1987. *Where the Leopard Passes; A Book of African Folk Tales.* Illustrated by S. Hawkins. New York: Scholastic. pp. 120-26.

Stevens, J. 1993. *Coyote Steals the Blanket.* New York: Holiday House.

This story is recommended for students in fourth through sixth grades.

Summary

"How the Coyote Danced with the Blackbirds" is a "how it happened" pourquoi tale from the Zuñi Tribe of North America. The story of how the coyote wants to fly and is aided by the blackbirds, only to become so obnoxious that he is betrayed by them, explains the wisps of black curls on the legs and tail of the coyote today.

Connect

- Prior to reading these stories, find a couple of simple explanatory myths to tell to the students. Examples are "Why the Bear Has a Stubby Tail" (he used it for a fishing line and the lake froze over) or Rudyard Kipling's story in the *Jungle Stories* about why the elephant has a long trunk. These explanatory myths are called "pourquoi" tales, meaning "why" in French. More information on animal explanatory stories is found in appendix B.
- Remind students of the previous story of Pecos Bill and the coyotes from the Strange Change unit. Connect the habitat and personalities of the coyotes in the tall tale so students will use that story as a base for comprehension as they hear the explanatory story. In this story, they will discover why the coyote has black fringes of hair on his legs and tail.
- Prepare an overlay for the overhead projector on which the song of the blackbirds (given in the story) is shown. Read the song to the students and set the background for the dance of the blackbirds in Zuñi territory in New Mexico. Allow some time for students to chant the song as the blackbirds might have done. Following the chant, read the story to the students.

Construct

- Prepare two **character webs** (VW 84) on charts in the classroom. Ask the students to think about a comparison of the coyotes in this story and in the Pecos Bill story. Begin with one coyote and web a description while a student serves as the recorder of ideas. Then move to the coyote in the other story, and a different student may record this description. Go back and forth until the coyotes are compared and through the comparison, this story has been discussed. Following the group collaboration on these character webs, ask students in groups of four or five to web the character of the blackbirds, collectively. Further discussion among the students will follow with this activity.
- Some **probes** (VO 72) that may be appropriate are:
    What is the first indication you have in this story that all will not turn out well? What else in the story gives you signals to impending problems? Why do you think the author told or wrote the story this way? Do you believe the blackbirds were initially sincere in their efforts? Why or why not? Did they change during the story? Why do you think so? Why do you think the author made the blackbirds turn against the coyote? Did the coyote bring on his own troubles? How?

Create

Responses to this story will be varied if students are encouraged to create from their art and music backgrounds. Some possible responses are:

- Re-enact the blackbirds' dance. Watching birds that are locally indigenous and planning a seasonal celebration for them comparable to the blackbirds' festivities are possible outgrowths.
- Create a tune to accompany the words to the blackbirds' dance. Students may also want to create words and music for a celebration of their own.
- Make masks to create the facial expressions of characters at various points in the story. These masks may be displayed in sequence in the room to depict the feelings of the characters as the story progresses.
- Having a storytelling collaboration for explanatory stories is a good review for this subgenre. Using a skein of yarn with knots painted different colors, have students begin pulling yarn and passing it to the next child. As a student receives a knot of a designated color, it will be his or her turn to add to a story started by the teacher. Suggestions for story starters:

  Why the skunk smells bad.
  Why the moon waxes and wanes.
  Why snowflakes are always different shapes.
  Why trolls are scary.

- Writing in the **lit log** (VW 92) with unguided responses is recommended frequently since stories speak to different individuals in various ways and opportunities to respond privately will be valued.

THE LITTLE SNOWGIRL—RUSSIAN FOLKTALE

Croll, C. 1989. *The Little Snowgirl.* New York: Putnam.

Littledale, F. 1989. *Snow Child.* New York: Scholastic.

"Snegourka, the Snow Maiden." Haviland, V. 1985. *Favorite Fairy Tales Told around the World.* Illustrated by S. Schindler. Boston: Little, Brown. pp.251-56.

"Snowflake." Haviland, V. 1961. *Favorite Fairy Tales Told in Russia.* Illustrated by H. Danska. Boston: Little, Brown. pp. 43-52.

Recommended for students in grades four to six.

Summary

"The Little Snowgirl," a Russian folktale, is the story of a snow-baby who comes to life and answers an old couple's dreams of having a child. Wanting her to be like other children, her parents allow her to play as a real child. When she wants to sleep outside, her parents feel cruel and bring their sleeping baby in to the warmth where she melts. Then a real life child appears in her place. In some versions, "Snowflake," for example, she does not become real but is lost forever.

Connect

- Before reading "The Little Snowgirl," remind the students of a theme often found in folk literature of parents wishing to have children. This theme was found in the first story in this unit, "Peter Bull," and is prominent in this story also.

- Prepare the students for reading a **tragic plot pattern** (when the character's tragedy is not his or her own fault) by reminding them of the ironic **plot pattern** and the banner that indicated the character deserved his or her problems. The students will remember that the coyote in the last story was not an innocent victim, nor was the fisherman's wife. Contrary to that pattern is the tragic pattern in which the character is an innocent victim.

- Hand out tissues to the students as a symbol of the sadness that is a part of tragedies.

- If possible place a cup of snow or a cube of ice in a clear glass near the furnace or a sunny window, but do not explain why you have placed it there. The melting that will occur is also symbolic of this story, and students will recognize that as the story is read.

Read the story aloud to the class.

Construct

- As this is a sensitive story, discussions will be more intense if in small groups. Group students for **communication circles** (VO 61) in which open discussions will take place. If students are comfortable with each other and have had experiences with literary discussion groups, sincere communication will occur.

- Some **probes** (VO 72) that may be used if communication is not spontaneous follow:

  Imagine how the parents felt when they received Little Snowgirl. What kind of parents were they? Did they worry about Snowgirl when she was out with the other children? How do you know? How do you think this story came about? Does it remind you of other stories you know? How do they compare to this one? Have you ever known a family in which a child needed special treatment? How did the parents handle these situations? How did the children act?

Create

■ Following the communication circles activity, students may write in their **lit logs** (VW 92).

Other experiences for students to respond to this story include the following suggestions:

■ Examine the characteristics of a tragedy and determine why Snowgirl qualifies as one. Write this story with an ironic plot and see how it differs.
■ Write another story with a tragic plot.
■ Integrate this story with a study of changes in matter.
■ Write journal entries about scientific experiments involving changes from liquid to solids and vice versa.
■ Write an advertisement for:
  a child such as Snowgirl;
  friends for Snowgirl.
■ Make a bulletin board titled "How it Happened ..." to show creations and changes. Drawings, writings, and descriptions of science experiments may be placed on the board by the students.
■ Cut snowflakes from white paper.
■ Compose a ballad that the mother and father of Snowgirl may have sung when she was born, and another they could have sung when she melted, and another when a real child appeared.
■ Sing the ballad for the class.
■ Students may see change from liquid to solid by making their own cup of ice cream in a zip-lock bag. In a small zip-lock bag, combine ½ cup milk, 2 tablespoons sugar, 1 teaspoon vanilla and close the bag tightly. Insert the bag into a gallon size zip-lock bag and add crushed ice and 2 tablespoons ice cream salt. Students shake their own bags until the liquid turns solid, and then they have their own container of ice cream.

THE HALF CHICK (MEDIO POLLITO)—SPANISH FOLKTALE

"The Half Chick." Arbuthnot, M. H. 1961. *Time for Fairy Tales.* Glenview, IL: Scott-Foresman. pp. 131-33.

"The Half Chick." Alderson, B. 1978. *Lang's Green Fairy Book*. Illustrated by A. Maitland. New York: Viking. pp. 16-22.

"The Half Chick." Arbuthnot, M. H. 1961. *The Arbuthnot Anthology of Children's Literature*. Chicago: Scott-Foresman. p. 264-66.

"The Half Chick." Haviland, V. 1963. *Favorite Fairy Tales Told in Spain*. Illustrated by B. Cooney. Boston: Little, Brown. pp. 36-49.

"The Half Chick." Sutherland, Z., and M. C. Livingston. 1984. *The Scott-Foresman Anthology of Children's Literature*. Glenview, IL: Scott-Foresman. pp. 252-54.

Recommended for students in grades four to six.

Summary

In this Spanish folktale, a rebellious half chick is born with one leg, one wing, one eye, half a head, and half a body. His mother calls him Medio Pollito, meaning half chick. Being a spoiled chick, he leaves home and meets a stream of water, a fire, a tree, and the wind, each of which asks him for help, and he refuses. Later when he arrives in town, he is snatched up and put in a stew pot for the king's dinner. He cries to no avail to the water, the fire, the tree, and the wind for help, but when he is almost burned to a cinder, he is thrown to the highest church steeple in town and there he still stands, perched on one leg and looking out of one eye.

Connect

- Bring to class a metal weathervane (**realia VA 46**), in the form of a rooster if possible. Show it to the class and ask for suggestions on how the rooster became the symbol of the weathervane.
- Prepare a **character web** (VW 84) showing students' preconceived ideas on the generic character of roosters: self-confident (hence use of term "cocky" for one who is conceited), independent, thinks highly of himself, a fighter.
- Explain that this folktale is from Spain and the little rooster's name is Medio Pollito, which means half chick.
- Give **think aloud** time (VO 81) for groups of two to three students to consider why the rooster in this story was named "Half Chick." Share ideas that have come from this thinking time and allow discussion on the processes students used to come to their conclusions.
- This story is particularly good for a read aloud, so **readers' theater** (VO 73) is an excellent choice for sharing this story. Preparations include allowing the readers time to read the story silently before reading to the whole class. Some work may be necessary with the readers to emphasize the need for expression in their reading. This story may be divided into segments or

divided among characters and narrators to give many students opportunities to read.

Construct

- The students who were not involved in readers' theater may be given roles from this story for a dramatization. Roles include Mother Hen, Medio Pollito, the stream, the fire, the wind, and the king's cook.
- Following the dramatization of the story, discussion may evolve around these **probes** (VO 72):

    Why would you consider this story ironic? Is there any tragedy in the story? Would you consider it more one than the other? Why? What made Medio Pollito's temperament as it was? Was the ending justified? Why or why not? Speculate on the life of the person who first told or wrote this tale. Was it a man or a woman? Why? What experiences had the author had to allow him or her to tell or write this story? What is there in this story that relates to modern day life?

Create

- Since this story is delightful for all ages, students may cooperatively make a **storybox** (VM 29) to share with other classes or to leave in the media center. Divide story into sections and have students draw pictures and write text for their story segments. Then tape all the pictures together and roll them around a dowel to place in the storybox.

    Other creative responses that may be selected by students are:

- responding to the story in personal **lit logs** (VW 92)
- making clay models of Medio Pollito
- building a **diorama** (VA 38) of Madrid and the church where Medio Pollito finally stood
- developing an explanatory story that will tell why:
    polar bears are at the North Pole
    kangaroos are in Australia
    elephants have good memories
    dogs are people's best friends
- Compare this folktale, which is also an explanatory tale, to the story that explained why the coyote has black wisps of hair.

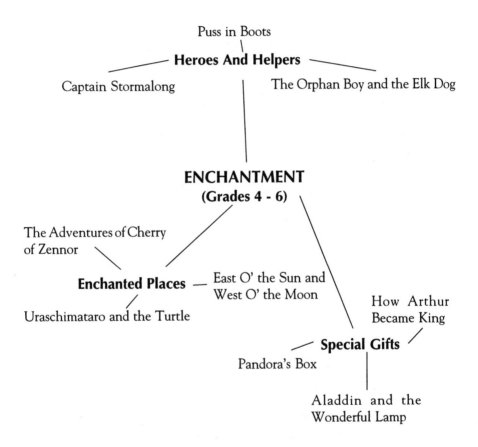

Puss in Boots

Heroes And Helpers

Captain Stormalong   The Orphan Boy and the Elk Dog

ENCHANTMENT
(Grades 4 - 6)

The Adventures of Cherry
of Zennor

Enchanted Places — East O' the Sun and
West O' the Moon   How Arthur
Uraschimataro and the Turtle   Became King

Special Gifts
Pandora's Box

Aladdin and the
Wonderful Lamp

CHAPTER
seven
❉ ❉ ❉ ❉ ❉ ❉ ❉ ❉

Enchantment Unit
Grades 4-6

LITERARY OUTCOMES

The first theme in this unit, Heroes and Helpers, provides a great contrast among tall tales, wonder tales (fairy tales), and legends. The characteristics of each subgenre are easy to identify and compare. The characters are strong and quickly admired in these stories. Character and setting studies are natural literary outcomes while connections to social studies and science are abundant.

From underground fairy lands, to an enchanted fairy land under the sea, the three fairy tales in the second theme, Enchanted Places, portray human protagonists who fall in love with fairies or enchanted people and follow them to their homes. These motifs are typical of the fairy tale subgenre. Students may be familiar with two of the tales, but in both cases, the tales will give the reader some surprises.

From an enchanted box, a wonderful lamp with a genie, to the ability to remove a sword from a rock, each protagonist in the three tales of the third theme have indeed received special gifts. All of the tales in this theme are very popular and familiar to most students. While the protagonists are chosen to receive the special gifts, they must use them wisely and are worthwhile role models for the readers.

Literary outcomes for this theme include:

- a recognition of the literary elements found in outstanding tall tales, fairy tales, folktales, novelle, legends, and myths
- an understanding of protagonists who must prove themselves before they are accepted and honored by their people
- an awareness of protagonists who must use their special gifts wisely, sparingly, and for worthwhile causes
- an awareness of enchanted settings and the unimportance of time in fairy land
- notation of the storytellers' use of descriptive language to develop suspenseful adventures and to portray settings

INTEGRATED CURRICULUM STRATEGIES

Suggestions for the integration of these stories with other curriculum areas are listed here:

- a recognition of the importance of mythology in contemporary life, i.e., names of objects, space travel, etc.
- an awareness of the differences between the scientific world and the mythological world
- a recognition of medieval times and comparison to contemporary life
- an awareness of primitive humans' explanation of environmental, sociological, and psychological phenomena
- recognition that human needs are similar in all cultural or regional groups
- recognition of the values of the cultural groups portrayed in the tales to their realistic lifestyles
- study of the shipping industry of today and in the past
- study of whaling and its environmental impact
- study of the early lifestyles and cultures of Japan, Greece, Europe, Arabia, and Native Americans
- connections to American history are abundant

Heroes And Helpers Theme

CAPTAIN STORMALONG—AMERICAN TALL TALE

"Captain Stormalong: Five Fathoms Tall." Stoutenburg, A. 1960. *American Tall Tales.* New York: Viking. pp. 37-50.

Felton, H. W. 1968. *True Tall Tales of Stormalong: Sailor of the Seven Seas.* Englewood Cliffs, NJ: Prentice-Hall.

Malcolmson, A., and D. J. McCormick. 1952. *Mr. Stormalong.* Boston: Houghton Mifflin.

"Old Stormalong, the Deep-Water Sailman." Botkin, B. A. 1949. *The Treasury of American Folklore.* New York: Crown. pp. 185-92.

Shay, F. 1930. *Here's Audacity! American Legendary Heroes.* New York: Macaulay. pp. 17-31.

"Stormalong." Carmer, C. 1949. *America Sings.* New York: Alfred A. Knopf. pp. 30-34.

"Stormalong." Osborne, M. P. 1991. *American Tall Tales.* Engravings by M. McCurdy. New York: Alfred A. Knopf. pp. 37-44.

Recommended for students in fourth through sixth grades.

Summary

Alfred Bulltop Stormalong is brought by the storks (or he brings the storks who drop him off) in a storm to the shore in New England. He is so big that his parents use a whale boat for a cradle and anchor it just offshore because there is not any other place large enough for it. When they want to wake up the freckle-faced, curly-haired boy (who could walk at birth and had a full set of teeth), they blow a foghorn. For breakfast the baby eats large quantities of whale milk, clam chowder, johnny cake, maple syrup, fish, lobster, salt port, baked beans, and brown bread. As Stormalong grows older, he helps his parents on their farm, but his heart is at sea. Many seafaring tales are told about this able bodied sailor, as he sails on the *Silver Maid*. Finally, he sails on his own clipper ship, the *Courser*, whose wheel is so large that it takes 33 regular sailors to whirl it, while Stormy can move it with one finger. The mast is high enough to scrape the sun and graze the moon. His adventures take him from the North Sea to the Caribbean and finally to rest, perhaps at Cape Cod.

Connect

- Display one banner each day in the literature center bulletin board. Some examples include: "Who fought a Kraken? What was the biggest clipper ship ever built? Who built it? Who was a successful potato farmer? Why are the cliffs of Dover white? Why did a clipper chip captain run a race with a steamship?" Entice the students with the banners, but do not tell the tale. Encourage them to find out what the banners mean.
- If the students are familiar with other tall tales, brainstorm what they know about the subgenre and record their responses on a **literary ladder** (VM 16). This ladder should be tall and wide.
- Ask the students: *If you were going to tell a tall tale about what you ate for breakfast, what would you say?* At this point let the students prepare a menu for a tall tale breakfast.
- Wear an outfit representing a sailor's uniform, and give a book talk using exaggeration found in tall tales. (See summary.)
- Place "seafaring language" arranged on the **word wall** (VM 34) shaped like a tall ship: "frigate," "brigantine," "sloop," "keel," "fathoms," "seafaring," "schooner," "mast," "mizzenmast," "bowsprit," "cleaver," "figure-of-eight knot," "rigging."

Construct

Read the story either through a teacher read aloud or by grouping students to read an incident of the text. This is a long story that naturally divides into two parts. Encourage groups to generate probes. Each group will present their rendering of the tale to the rest of the class along with probes for discussion.

- To extend the discussion, suggested **probes** (VO 72) are:
    Describe your most vivid memory of the story? What advice would you give Stormalong about his adventures?
- These questions may be used as starters for writing in the **lit log** (VW 92).
- This is an opportune time to integrate literature and social studies, especially with lessons on the American Revolution, J. P. Jones and the *Bon Homme Richard*, and the whaling industry.

Create

- Write a **what if? incident** (VW 102)based on an adventure from the tale. Change the plot or actions of Stormalong.

- Share the new incidents with others. Illustrate them and place in a bound book.
- Discuss Stormalong's movements. Pinpoint (with a colored marker) on a map the locations mentioned in the tale.
- Draw a sketch of the *Courser* (using the proper dimensions). Draw a sketch of the *Liverpool Packet*. Place on the board and make comparisons of the ships.
- Display pictures of today's ships. Discuss differences, e.g.:

  Was the Courser *as big as a battleship? How would it compare to an aircraft carrier?*
- Present a **chain-the-tale** (VO 55) with one or more tall tales.
- Sea chanteys are included in several variations of "Stormalong." (See p. 34, Carmer, *America Sings*, for a Stormalong song.) With the help of the music teacher, sing songs and write original chanteys.
- Locate other tall tales. Place information and sketches of each character on appropriately shaped paper, e.g., an ax for Paul Bunyan or a keel boat for Mike Fink. Display in classroom or school media center.
- Prepare a tall tale map. Use a large map of the United States and identify the various places the characters lived and traveled. Trace each character's travels using different colored markers or yarn. Add tall tale character information from above to the maps. Display in the media center with books about the characters.
- Prepare and present to others a **subgenre commercial** (VW 99).

THE MASTER CAT, OR PUSS IN BOOTS—FRENCH FAIRY TALE

"The Master Cat, or Puss in Boots." Perrault, C. 1981. *Classics of Children's Literature*. Edited by J. W. Griffith, and C. H. Frey. New York: Macmillan. pp. 17-19.

Goodall, J. 1990. *Puss in Boots*. New York: McElderry.

"Puss in Boots." Lang, A. 1965 (reissue). *Blue Fairy Book*. New York: Dover. pp. 141-47.

Perrault, C. 1989. *Puss in Boots*. Translated by M. Arthur and illustrated by F. Marcellino. New York: Farrar, Strauss.

Rockwell, A. 1988. *Puss in Boots and Other Stories*. New York: Macmillian. pp. 80-82.

"The Master Cat or Puss in Boots." Sutherland, Z., and M. C. Livingston. 1984. *Scott-Foresman Anthology of Children's Literature*. Glenview, IL: Scott-Foresman. pp. 204-06.

Recommended for students in fifth grade and above.

Summary

The youngest son of a miller is disappointed when his only inheritance is a cat. He does not suspect that the cat is so wise and cunning! Through a series of events using deception, threats, cleverness, and cunning behavior, the cat gains fortune and marriage to a princess for his master. As a result the master and cat live a life of idleness and pleasure.

This popular classical "wonder tale" portrays the worthwhile theme, "things aren't always what you think," as shown by the antics of a marvelous, talking cat . . . a favorite animal of children of all ages.

Connect

Prior to reading the story, try some of the following strategies to pique students' interest.

- Display a **realia** table (VA 46). Place on it a cloth bag with a handle long enough to go over a head, a small pair of boots, and a stuffed cat.
- Place a banner above the realia table stating "MASTER CAT TO THE RESCUE!" Place a note in the stuffed cat's paw reading: "Give me a bag and boots, and I'll bring home the loot!" Leave the realia on display for one or two days before using the tale.
- Discuss cats and their special abilities. Give the students time to talk about the way their cats play or purr.
- Note the MASTER CAT banner, and say: *This the hero of our tale...* (Do not use the title "Puss in Boots" at this time.) Call attention to the note and talk about "loot." Give a book talk, such as:

   As you can well imagine, our hero Master Cat isn't your ordinary, home-grown cat. He has a special talent and many abilities to help his master. After all he brings riches, wealth, and happiness to his master and luxury to himself! How he does this is told in a "Wonder Tale" recorded by Charles Perrault in the late 1600s. When I tell you that this is a wonder tale, what do you think?
- Record responses of what children think a wonder tale is in a **cluster** (VM 9) around the words "Master Cat." Give the title and read the tale to the students.
- Place various books containing the tale in the literature center. Compare the texts and illustrations of picture books. The Caldecott winner *Puss in Boots* retold by M. Arthur with illustrations by F. Marcellino and J. Goodall's *Puss in Boots* are both wonderful picture books to use. The Goodall book is a wordless text and is excellent to use when retelling the tale.

Construct

- Ask the students: *What would you do if you inherited a cat with such special talents as the Master Cat?* From this question, a spontaneous retelling may occur.
- Begin a **character attribute chart** (VM 6). Add characters as they appear in the story.
- **Probes** (VO 72) may help students construct meaning from the tale, for example:

    How does the princess feel about the Marquis de Carabas? When did you suspect her real feelings? Wonder if she would feel the same way if he were still a miller's son? Why? Do you think the characters got their "just rewards"? Why?

Create

- Prepare a **readers' theater script** (VO 73). Encourage students to practice their oral expression before the reading.
- Write a first person television report from the perspective of the people who met the cat.
- Write diary entries for the princess after meeting Master Cat and the Marquis de Carabas.
- Have partners converse in writing via a **partner journal** (VW 96) expressing several reactions to the tale.
- Make a **shadow box** (VA 49) of favorite incidents.
- Write a letter to an advice column from the marquis. Explain who he is and ask specific questions, such as, how should royalty behave in court? treat servants? to run a castle? treat a princess and keep her father happy? Another group can answer the questions.
- **Chain-the-tale** (VO 55) and present it using this method to another group, class, or the school.
- **Fax the facts** (VW 88) from one castle to another, giving the facts about what happened to get rid of the ogre; how the servants feel now that the Marquis de Carabas married the princess; and predict future events.
- Make a **pop-up-book** (VM 20) containing the incidents from the tale. Read it to younger children. Display in the school media center with other books of the tale.
- Prepare a **Venn diagram** (VM 33) comparing the special attributes of the Master Cat and your cat (or another cat in literature).

THE ORPHAN BOY AND THE ELK DOG—NATIVE AMERICAN LEGEND

"The Orphan Boy and the Elk Dog." Yolen, J. 1986. *Favorite Folktales from around the World*. New York: Pantheon. pp. 220-27.

"The Orphan Boy and the Elk Dog." Erdoes, R., and A. Ortiz. 1984. *American Indian Myths and Legends*. New York: Pantheon Books. pp. 53-60.

Related Books

Goble, P. 1982. *The Gift of the Sacred Dog*. New York: Bradbury.

Goble, P. 1978. *The Girl Who Loved Wild Horses*. New York: Bradbury.

Recommended for students in fourth through sixth grades.

Summary

A rejected, orphan boy, Long Arrow, is given a second chance for survival and proves to his adopted grandfather that he is bright and can do something great. Realizing that he is to become chief of the tribe, he proves to his people that he is courageous by traveling 36 days to the bottom of the Great Mystery Lake. When Long Arrow listens carefully to the teachings of the spirit child and the truly Great One, he brings the "Pono-Kamita-Elk Dogs" (horses) to the Blackfoot tribe for the first time. After that he earns the right to be an honored chief of the tribe.

This tale contains many Blackfoot traditions. The young warrior overcomes many obstacles, but because he is generous and brave, he earns the right to be their leader. The theme, "strive for a goal until you reach it," is shown in this Native American legend.

Connect

Prior to reading the story, help students connect to the story using some of the following strategies.

- Display Native American **realia** (VM 46), e.g., tools, utensils, dress, or other objects of everyday life of early Native Americans. Talk about the realia, discussing how and why Native Americans used them.
- Display a variety of fiction and nonfiction materials about the everyday life of early Native Americans. Entice students to find out why and how the objects on the realia table were used.
- Discuss legends. For example:

A legend is a tale, told as fact, about a national hero who made a great contribution to a cultural group. The hero may have lived, but the storyteller typically embellished his or her deeds and accomplishments. This tale has a super hero who is bigger than life.

■ Give a book talk, and if possible bring a rainbow-colored belt, a black robe, and a piece of new rope:

A rainbow-colored quelled belt and a black medicine robe are very important to Long Arrow (an orphan Blackfoot Indian boy) who was treated as an outcast by his tribe because he could not hear, talk, and respond as other boys his age. But he was determined to belong to the tribe and to do something great. When the tribe decided to leave him behind, he had to run very fast to catch up with them; this was no easy task for a starving boy. As he was running very fast a wormlike substance came out of his ears, and he realized he could hear birds sing and the rushing waters of a stream—his hearing was restored! The kindly chief, Good Running, found him on the trail and adopted him. After that he knew that to become chief he must prove his worth. As we read "The Orphan Boy and the Elk Dog" think about how the belt and robe helped Long Arrow.

■ Display a **word wall** (VM 34) containing unique language, such as: "mangy"; "remnants"; "a dugout"; "lodges"; "rawhide bags"; "travois"; "buckskin outfit"; "moccasins"; "Pono-Kamita—Elk Dogs"; "purify with sweet-smelling cedar smoke"; "lance with heavy spear point"; "buckskin robe"; "kingfisher"; "sacred vermilion paint"; "chokecherries"; "tipi"; "medicine shields"; "porcupine quills"; "footsloggers."

■ Have students write responses to the tale in **lit logs** (VW 92).

Construct

■ If **probes** (VO 72) are needed for the discussion, the following suggestions are made:

Why did the tribe treat the "orphan boy" as they did? What was the "wormlike substance" that came out of his ears? Could this really happen? What was Long Arrow's goal? Why did the grandfather want Long Arrow to first learn to be a man? How could the child become a kingfisher? Why was Long Arrow able to reach his goal? (He listened carefully and followed directions.) *What did the storyteller mean when he said, "The young man felt himself soaring through the air as a bird does, and experienced happiness greater even than the joy he had felt when Good Running had adopted him as a grandson"? What are "Pono-Kamita, the Elk Dogs"? What words did the storyteller use to give you clues about them ("galloping and gamboling," "neighing and nickering")? Why was it important for Long Arrow to follow the truly Great One's directions? Why was the tribe glad to see him? Why didn't the boy return when Long Arrow took the tribe back to the Great*

Mystery Lake? Why didn't Long Arrow just dive into the lake like he had before? Did you think Long Arrow was a good chief? Why? Why not?

■ Prepare a **character attribute chart** (VM 6). Describe Long Arrow first, then Grandfather Good Running, and the Great One. To further probe, ask: *How did the Native Americans get their names? Are the names appropriate?*

Create

■ Invite students to sit around an imaginary campfire and discuss the story. Give each student an index card. Ask them to write (or sketch) their favorite part of the tale. Ask students to share their cards as the story is discussed. Take a survey and tally the number of favorite parts.

■ Divide class into "cooperative literacy groups." Give each group a copy of another legend. After reading the legend, have groups complete a **literary ladder** (VM 16) identifying the elements of a legend as shown in the tales read.

■ Research Native American symbols and have students draw some of the symbols. Place symbols on the literary bulletin board.

■ Using the **scratchboard technique** (VA 47), prepare a mural of scenes under the Great Mystery Lake showing Long Arrow's determination and bravery.

■ Compare tale to Goble's book *The Girl Who Loved Wild Horses.*

■ Prepare a **Venn diagram** (VM 33) comparing Goble's book and the legend.

■ Write **newspaper reports** (VW 95) by the members of the tribe describing Long Arrow's gift to them and how the tribe will use the animals.

■ Predict the future of the tribe five years from the end of the legend.

■ Discuss legends from other cultures. Ask students to select a favorite legend. Give each a 9" x 9" block of material. Ask each to draw (using appropriate pens) a picture representing the legend. Sew the blocks together to make a Story Quilt. Each block could include the name of the legend and the cultural group.

■ Write a legend about a contemporary event. (Students could refer to the literary ladder for the legend format.)

Enchanted Places Theme

THE ADVENTURE OF CHERRY OF ZENNOR—ENGLISH FAIRY TALE

"The Adventure of Cherry of Zennor." Hunt, J. 1971. *Popular Romances of the West of England*. Tale 47. London: Hotten. pp. 120-26.

"The Adventure of Cherry of Zennor." Briggs, K. M. A. 1970-1971. *Dictionary of British Fairy Tales*. London: Routledge & Kegan Paul. pp. 219-20.

Protter, E., and N. Protter. 1966. *Celtic Folk and Fairy Tales*. Illustrated by C. Keeping. New York: Duell, Sloan & Pearce.

Recommended for students in fifth grade and above.

Summary

Cherry finds out that sometimes it is best to leave things alone rather than to meddle. After following the handsome master to his lovely home to care for his child, Cherry experiences a love she has never known before. Her life is perfect, except for the mysterious old grandmother, Aunt Prudence, and the strange directions she gives Cherry to care for the boy. Cherry is directed to keep her eyes closed all night long, despite the noises she might hear. Early in the morning, she is to take the boy to a spring, wash him, and anoint his eyes with an ointment. The ointment is in a crystal box in a cleft of the rock. She is never to touch the ointment to her own eyes. She has an attentive master, who does not hesitate to kiss her when she does something right; she has a disciplined child, but something is wrong. Where is she? Why is everything so beautiful? What does the ointment do to one's eyes? Why can't she go into all of the house? Then to Cherry's dismay, she finds the answers to her questions—just by placing one drop of ointment into her eyes.

The theme "follow directions or suffer the consequences" is clearly shown in this fairy tale, set in fairyland, and inhabited with fairy folks, half people and half fairies. Several motifs are found in this story: mortals as servants in fairyland; fairies made visible by ointment; taboo behavior such as mortals using fairy bath water, soap, or ointment while bathing a fairy child or touching water in a fairyland lake; mortals expelled from fairyland after committing taboo behavior; and the supernatural lapse of time in fairyland.

Connect

- During the reading, have students close their eyes and imagine themselves in the setting of the story. After you are done, ask the students to open their eyes and sketch what they saw in their "mind's eye" during the reading.
- Have children write a description of the fairyland they visualized.
- Display pictures and descriptions on a literature bulletin board titled "Our Enchanted Places."
- Display a **word wall** (VM 34) containing unique language, such as: "bewitched"; "old hag"; "shot through her heart 'like a gimblet'"; "disconcerted"; "tarried"; "wouldn't cum any furder for the wurld"; "land of Small People"; "conjurors"; "like a coffin on six legs"; "stone-people"; "crum"; "playing on the coffin"; "moor"; "never afterwards right in her head."
- Let students respond to tale in **lit logs** (VW 92).

Construct

- Wearing a fairyland costume, such as a net stole, give a book talk.
- Have students write one question to discuss with a partner. Following the discussion, ask students to place their questions in a basket. Attach the basket to a bulletin board for others to read and think about.
- If needed, use **probes** (VO 72) such as the following:

  Was Cherry lucky after she disobeyed Aunt Prudence? Do you think she ever learned to accept her fate? What did Cherry mean when she said she would get "service" close to home? What clues does the storyteller give us about what is to happen to Cherry when she meets the master for the first time? How do you feel about Cherry? about the master?

- Begin a **Venn diagram** (VM 33) comparing the personalities of Cherry and the master.

Create

- Ask students to predict what might happen in an enchanted place. Collect the predictions and place them in the **prediction pitcher** (VM 23) to be read later.

  You can also have students:

- Improvise several favorite incidents from the tale.
- Write a **what if? incident** (VW 102) based on an adventure from the tale. Change the plot or actions of a character. Share the new stories with others, and place them in an **accordion book** (VM 1).
- Make a **diorama** (VA 38) or a **shadow box** (VA 49) of the enchanted place.

- Make an **enchanted creature** (VA 40). Display the creatures and all the artwork from this unit in the school media center along with books and titles of tales with enchanted places.
- Write a diary entry from Cherry describing her adventures in fairyland.
- **Cluster** (VM 9) a description of "fairyland." Discuss fairyland as described in folk literature, in Disneyland, in the media, i.e, "Is fairyland as 'perfect' as we might have thought?"

URASCHIMATARO AND THE TURTLE—JAPANESE FAIRY TALE

"Uraschimataro and the Turtle." Lang, A. 1967(reissue). *Pink Fairy Tale Book.* New York: Dover. pp. 25-32.
Matsutani, M. 1969. *Fisherman under the Sea.* New York: Parent's Press.
"Uraschima." Cole, J. 1982. *Best-Loved Folktales of the World.* Illustrated by J. K. Schwarz. Garden City, NY: Doubleday. pp. 521-23.
Yashima, T. 1967. *Seashore Story.* New York: Viking.

Recommended for students in fourth grade and above.

Summary

One day while hauling in his fishing net, Uraschimataro, a young Japanese fisherman, finds a small turtle. He returns it to the sea after the turtle promises to help him later in life. Many years later the turtle saves the fisherman from drowning. Uraschimataro decides to travel on the turtle's large back to her home, the palace of Ringu. At this palace of the sea god, the turtle is Otohime, the Sea Princess. Uraschimataro and Otohime fall madly in love and live happily for many years. However, Uraschimataro grows lonely to see his beloved parents and promises to return to the princess after a brief visit back home. The heartbroken princess bids him farewell and gives him a tiny golden box telling him not to open it until he returns to her. His return home is not as he has envisioned, especially after he opens the box.

This Japanese fairy tale reflects the Japanese lifestyle and values as shown in the theme "love of parents can be strong." The enchanted fairyland under the sea is descriptively portrayed. Typical motifs are creatures disguised as enchanted maids, princesses, princes, and warriors; an enchanted box never to be opened; human love for the enchanted is not always enough. The differences of time in enchanted worlds and our world are all shown in this traditional tale.

Connect

■ Display information books about underwater life. Find out what students know about the topic. Record this information on a chart titled "UNDER THE SEA." Show pictures from the information books and encourage students to find new information to add to the chart. There will be two columns on the chart. Title the left column "REAL" and place factual information about undersea life. Title the right column "ENCHANTED" and place information gained from reading and discussing folk literature.

■ Before or after reading the tale, read Yashima's *Seashore Story* and Matsutani's *Fisherman under the Sea*. Both books are re-tellings of this popular traditional tale. Yashima's book contains expressionistic illustrations to help students visualize the enchanted seaworld.

■ Display and discuss realia (VM 46) found in the tale, e.g., a turtle, a small gold box, a mermaid (representing an enchanted sea creature), and an hour-glass (representing the passing of time).

■ Use a book talk such as the following:

Today we know a great deal about under sea life because we have scientists who photograph under the sea and write about their experiences. In the very early days, women and men spent time observing the sea and daydreaming about what the sea world looked like and who lived there. They imagined sea creatures with human forms—half-men, half-fish "merman"; and half-women, half-fish "mermaids." They envisioned enchanted human forms living as their rulers did, in awesome castles and palaces. Storytellers wove these dreams into new tales and poems often placing mortals interacting with enchanted creatures. Many events represented real experiences, but through "enchanted" objects, settings, and characters, the storytellers told "enchanted oral tales" that were modified and eventually recorded in writing. Our tale today is a very old Japanese fairy tale. There are several familiar motifs included in this tale.

Construct

■ **Probes** (VO 72) may be used following student's spontaneous responses during discussion, for example:

What did you think when Uraschimataro threw the little turtle back in the sea? Were you surprised when the turtle saved him later? How did Uraschimataro and the princess spend their time at the palace? What do you know about the other characters? What did you think when the storyteller said that Uraschimataro knew only later how long he stayed with the princess? When Uraschimataro returned home, why had everything changed? If you had been a person at the village, what would you have told Uraschimataro to do? Would you have believed him?

- Give students shell-shaped pieces of paper to record motifs they recognize in the tale. Display motifs on the bulletin board titled "Enchanted Sea Motifs."

Create

- Find tales from other countries with enchanted undersea settings. Compare and contrast pictures and content. Return to the under the sea chart, and elicit student responses.
- Prepare a **visual display** (VA 52) of the palace of Ringu.
- Have children make **enchanted origami creatures** (VA 40) that might be found in the palace.
- Place information books, folk literature tales, under-the-sea chart, realia, the visual display, and enchanted creatures produced by the students in the literature center.

Suggest some of the following strategies.

- Write an eyewitness report describing life on the bottom of the sea.
- Present a group improvisation representing what Uraschimataro and the princess did at the Palace of Ringu.
- Research the Japanese theater. Prepare this tale and present it in Japanese theater style.
- Compare and contrast Asian art style with Western art. Ed Young's *Lon Po Po* is a good example of Asian art style. Display and discuss illustrations. Compare Asian illustrations with picture books set in the United States.
- Prepare a **golden love box** (VM 41) for mothers, grandmothers, parents, siblings, friends, etc.
- Collect poetry about friendship and love. Organize the poems into a poetry collection, place them in the golden love box, and give it to a friend or family member.
- Discuss Asian verse forms, e.g., **haiku** (VW 90); **haikon** (VW 89); **senryu** (VW 98); **tanka** (VW 100). Select a verse form and write about real or enchanted sea creatures.
- Place verses on rice paper or thin paper. Roll the paper in scrolls. Display verses with sea display.

EAST O' THE SUN AND WEST O' THE MOON— NORWEGIAN FOLKTALE

"East o' the Sun and West o' the Moon." Sutherland, Z., and M. H. Arbuthnot. 1984. *Scott-Foresman Anthology of Children's Literature*. Glenview, IL: Scott-Foresman. pp. 236-41.

"East of the Sun and West of the Moon." Cole, J. 1982. *Best-Loved Folktales of the World*. Illustrated by J. K. Schwarz. Garden City, NY: Doubleday. pp. 287-95.

"East o' the Sun and West o' the Moon." Asbojornsen, P. C., and J. Moe. 1988 (reissue). *Popular Tales from the Norse*. Translated by Sir G. W. Dasent. Edinburgh: David Douglas. pp. 22-35.

Lynch, P. J. 1992. *East O' the Sun and West O' the Moon*. New York: Candlewick.

Mayer, M. 1980. *East of the Sun & West of the Moon*. New York: Alladin.

Related Stories

"Cupid and Psyche Legends." Clouston, W. A. 1968. *Popular Tales and Fictions: Their Migrations and Transformations*. Vol. 1. Detroit: Singing Tree Press. pp. 205-14, 469-70.

"East of the Sun and West of the Moon." Thompson, S. 1969. *100 Folktales*. Tale #26. Bloomington, IN: Indiana University Press. pp. 113-21.

"White-Bear-King-Valemon." 1988 (reissue). *Popular Tales from the Norse*. Translated by Sir G. W. Dasent. Edinburgh: David Douglas. p. 150.

"Whitebear Whittington." Hearne, B. 1993. *The Oryx Multicultural Folktale Series: Beauties and Beasts*. Phoenix, AZ: The Oryx Press. pp.76-83. This collection also contains a variant of "East of the Sun and West of the Moon" as well as 25 other tales of transformation.

Recommended for students in fourth through sixth grades.

Summary

A bear offers a poor farmer great wealth in return for his youngest daughter. The farmer talks his daughter into the match, and she rides on the bear's back to his lovely castle. She enjoys the bear's company but soon discovers that after she goes to bed, someone goes to bed in the next room. In time the girl becomes homesick, and the kind bear gives her permission to return home, if she follows his promise not to talk to her mother alone. At home she breaks her promise and tells her mother about the strange happenings when she goes to bed. As the bear has predicted, the mother gives her a candle to light after the bear goes to sleep to see what is happening. She does and discovers that he is a very handsome prince. While looking at him she accidently drops three spots of tallow on him. He awakens and tells her that he is enchanted by his troll stepmother and must, because she broke her promise, now return to the castle which stands East O' the Sun and West O' the Moon and marry a princess with a nose three ells long. The girl vows to follow him and through the help of three hags and the four winds she finds the castle. Now she must find the prince, break the stepmother's enchantment, and accomplish a task to marry the prince.

This famous Norwegian tale has at least 50 written variations found in European and Scandinavian folktales. The theme is "true love is eternal and will survive at all cost." Students will recognize motifs such as an animal bridegroom and a human bride; an enchanted spell that can only be broken by true love; and beauty is in the eyes of the beholder. The tale is similar to "Beauty and the Beast." (See reference to *Beauties and Beasts*, Oryx Press, for more variants of this tale.)

Connect

- Display and discuss **realia** (VM 46) related to the story, for example: a golden apple, a golden carding-comb, and a golden spinningwheel.
- Give a book talk similar to the following:

  This very old Norwegian folktale tells about a young girl who, because of a broken promise, must travel many miles to strange and enchanted places to find her handsome prince. Fortunately she is helped by three different hags and the East, West, South, and North winds. Each help her in her quest in different ways. How can a golden apple, a golden carding-comb, and a golden spinningwheel help her find her true love and break the enchanted spell placed on him by the troll stepmother?

- Display a **word wall** (VM 34) containing unique language, for instance: "troll," "a nose three ells long," "crag," "carding-comb," "hag."
- Let students respond to the tale in a **lit log** (VW 92).

Construct

- Discuss events in the tale. **Probes** (VO 72) such as these may be helpful in the discussion:

  Why wasn't the girl afraid of the White Bear? What happened when the bear "threw off his beast shape at night"? Wonder why the prince told her that she would make them both unlucky if she broke his promise? Could you keep this promise if you were talking to your mother? How long is "a nose three ells long"? How did the hags and the wind know who she was? Why was it so important for her to find the prince? Why was she able to wash out the spots in his shirt when all the others could not?

- Prepare a **literary circle** (VM 15) illustrating incidents from the story.

Create

- Have the children "interview" the "hags" and "winds." Find out why they helped the girl find her true love. This interview could be written or presented orally.
- Discuss similarities and differences between this tale and the movie *Beauty and the Beast*. Ask: *Which version do you prefer? Why?*
- Help children prepare a **Venn diagram** (VM 33) comparing and contrasting this tale and "Beauty and the Beast."
- Have the class design a mural depicting the various incidents in the tale or scenes of the bear's castle, the troll's castle, and the castle after the prince and girl were married.
- Prepare a video book talk of the tale. Use the mural, and present it on the school television.
- Divide the tale into major incidents and let children use the **scratchboard technique** (VA 47) to illustrate each incident.
- Have students make a **wordless text** (VO 35) to share with others.
- Read other tales from *East o' the Sun and West o' the Moon* (see bibliography). Compare elements found in the tales, i.e., trolls, enchantment, etc.
- Conduct a **folk literature treasure hunt** (VO 67) in the media center for other variants.
- Organize students in "literary cooperative groups" and have each group write another variation of the tale combining elements from the picture books and other variants.

Special Gifts Theme

HOW ARTHUR BECAME KING—ENGLISH LEGEND

"How Arthur Became King." Nelson, M. A. 1971. *A Comparative Anthology of Children's Literature*. New York: Holt, Rinehart & Winston. pp. 132-35.

Lanier, S. 1989. *The Boy's King Arthur*. New York: Scribner.
Lister, R. 1990. *The Legend of King Arthur*. Illustrated by A. Baker. New York: Doubleday.
Pyle., H. 1990. *King Arthur and the Magic Sword*. New York: Dial.
Talbott, H. 1991. *The Sword in the Stone*. New York: Morrow.

Recommended for students in fifth grade and above.

Summary

This popular legend tells of the birth and early life of Arthur, who is given at birth to Merlin, the mighty magician. On his death bed King Uther Pendragon proclaims Arthur his heir-apparent. Merlin realizes that the child's chances of survival are slim. Therefore, he leaves Arthur in the care of Sir Ector and his wife who raise him as their own. Many years later Merlin and the archbishop of Canterbury call all the noblemen and women together at St. Paul's Cathedral in London to pray. Outside the church is a large marble stone, and in the middle of it is an anvil of steel a foot high. Stuck in this anvil is a beautiful sword with a naked blade. Written in gold about the sword is "WHOSO PULLETH THIS SWORD OUT OF THIS STONE AND ANVIL IS RIGHTLY KING OF ALL ENGLAND." The tale describes Arthur pulling the sword out of the stone and the events leading up to his eventual coronation as king of England and Wales.

Perhaps an English chieftain lived in the sixth century who was the historical figure around whom the Arthurian legend developed. In the twelfth century Geoffrey of Monmouth discussed his parentage and career in his book, *Latin History of the Kings of Britain*. German and French versions appeared during this same century. The French version added the courtly romance theme to the warrior's adventures. Sir Thomas Malory combined these sources when writing his *Morte d'Arthur* (1469) and added the cycle dealing with man's search for the Christ-like life. The Arthurian Cycle is often classified as an epic, because it has an epic tone and length. Malory's version, written in prose, is classified as legend. Many tales are not appropriate for elementary age students, but this tale and the following ones are suitable and popular with 10- to 16-year-old students: "The Winning of the Sword Excalibur," "The Winning of a Queen," "The Story of Merlin," "Sir Lancelot," "Sir Gawain," "Sir Galahad's Search for the Holy Grail," and "The Passing of Arthur."

Connect

- Cover a heavy box with suitable contact paper and place a sword (many letter openers are in this shape) in it that can be removed.
- Prepare and display a banner with the words found on the sword.
- This story could be the initial tale for a unit of medieval times. Castles, early kings, and their lifestyles may be studied. Books of fiction, fantasy, biography, and information books, portraying the times, would also be appropriate to use.
- Display visuals and other **realia** (VM 46) of the period in the literature center, e.g., castles, armor, swords, ladies' dress, etc.
- Introduce the topic by asking students to examine the realia and predict the setting of the tale. Give students information about the tale and heroes. If the students name a hero found in legends or epics who lived before 1600, record the name on a bulletin board.
- Have students conduct a **folk literature treasure hunt** (VO 67). They can locate other Arthurian tales or ballads and find information about the characters in the media center.
- Prepare a collection of Arthurian legends in a bound book. Cover the book with old parchment-looking paper, and place in literature center.
- Give a book talk, including information from the summary of the story. Pose these **probes** (VO 72) just prior to reading the story:
  Will the young man live to be king? If he does, will the people believe he is king and accept him as their ruler?

Construct

- Place the following question on a large piece of poster board for student discussion in small groups prior to large group interaction: "WHAT DOES THIS STORY REMIND YOU OF?" Accept students' answers; ask them to tell this story to their parents and find out if it reminds their parents of any history during their lives. Return to the story the next day with information from the students' parents. Show the video of the musical, *Camelot*. Talk about the comparisons made to John Kennedy's White House and Camelot. Research information on the production of *Camelot*. If possible, write to a person who was responsible for producing *Camelot* and ask for more information.
- If **probes** (VO 72) are needed to further discussion, consider these suggestions:
  How could we find out if Uther Pendragon and his son Arthur were really kings of England? Why did Merlin make sure the king's deathbed proclamation was followed? Could an event such as this happen today? What did a sword

represent in that day? Do we have something today that is comparable? Do you think Arthur knew why the sword was there? Did Sir Ector know who Arthur really was? Were you surprised at the nobility's treatment of Arthur? Why do you think that the commoners proclaimed Arthur king before the nobility? What kind of king do you think he became? What do we really know about Arthur?

Create

Have the children try some of the following strategies.

- Write a letter from Arthur to his foster father, Sir Ector, asking why he didn't tell him about his birth. Include in the letter Arthur's feelings about growing up in the family thinking he was Sir Ector's son.
- **Role play** (VW 74) a conversation Sir Ector, his wife, his son, and Arthur might have had, expressing their feelings about the situation.
- Write first person television accounts from fictional knights and their ladies, reporting what happened at St. Paul's courtyard when Arthur pulled the sword out of the stone. Have each of these reports on different days, e.g., the Twelfth Day, Candlemas, Easter, and the Feast of Pentecost.
- Prepare a research project about the "real" King Arthur; the Round Table; Merlin the Court Magician, his position and duties, and why King Uther left Arthur in his care. Display the project in literature center.
- Prepare a mural representing several incidents in the tale or scenery of the marketplace or great hall in the palace.
- Conduct an interview between Merlin and the archbishop after Arthur pulled the sword out of the stone; explain the role they played from the time Arthur was born. Present the interview before the mural or scenery.
- Prepare a **pop-up-book** (VM 20) showing the major incidents of the legend. After enjoying in class, share with younger children and place in the school media center.
- Prepare a **literary ladder** (VM 16) on a shield-shaped visual. Display as the focal point of the literature center. Add other information about the subgenre on the shield. Display other student visuals and papers.

References

"Camelot." Musical by F. Loewe and A. J. Lerner, 1960. From T. H. White's *The Once and Future King*. Movie and video available.

PANDORA'S BOX—GREEK MYTH

"Pandora's Box." Alexander, B. 1947. *Famous Myths of the Golden Age.* New York: Random House. pp. 5-6.

"Pandora's Box." D'Aulaire, I., and E. D'Aulaire. 1962. *D'Aulaires' Book of Greek Myths.* New York: Doubleday. pp. 74-75.

"Pandora's Box." Low, A. 1985. *Macmillan Book of Greek Gods and Heroes.* New York: Macmillan. pp. 26-29.

"Pandora's Box." 1986. (Videorecording.) Los Angeles: Embassy Home.

"Pandora's Box." Williams, M. 1992. *Greek Myths for Young Children.* New York: Candlewick.

Weil, L. 1986. *Pandora's Box.* New York: Atheneum.

Related References

Caduto, M. J., and J. Bruchac. 1991. *Native American Stories.* Golden, CO: Fulcrum.

D'Aulaire, I., and E. D'Aulaire. 1962. *D'Aulaires' Book of Greek Myths.* New York: Doubleday.

Hamilton, V. 1988. *In the Beginning: Creation Stories from around the World.* Illustrated by B. Moser. New York: Harcourt.

Norse Gods and Giants. 1967. New York: Doubleday.

Recommended for students in fourth and fifth grades.

Summary

Jupiter calls on all the gods and goddesses to help him make the first woman. From Venus she receives beauty; Apollo gives her music; Minerva provides wisdom and sewing ability; and Mercury gives her some human failings, in particular, curiosity. After she is finished, the gods name her Pandora, "the gift of all the gods." They send her to earth to be the wife of Epimetheus, a Titan who helped make man. Jupiter also gives her a carved, ivory chest and tells her to keep it by her side, but never to open it. Pandora is a good wife, but her curiosity gets the best of her, and one day she opens the box. Out jumps wicked winged things, but because she immediately closes the box, the one thing all humans need is left inside the box, and that is hope.

This short myth is an excellent introduction to mythology since many gods and goddesses are briefly introduced. The theme, "don't let curiosity get the best of you," is obvious. Set at Mount Olympus and on Earth the myth clearly identifies undesirable human frailties that all possess, but it ends on a positive note, pointing out that "hope" remained in the box.

Connect

- In the literature center display a box covered with iridescent net or paper. Encourage students' curiosity about the box by asking **probes** (VO 72), such as:

  Have you seen a box like this before? What could be in it? What was in it before I placed it here?

- Use a **K.W.L. chart** (VM 14) titled "Pandora." Place four columns on the chart. Title the left column, "What I Know about Pandora"; title the next column, "What Others Know about Pandora"; title the third column, "What I Want to Know about Pandora"; and title the last column, "What I Have Learned about Pandora." Group students in triads and have them write responses in the first column. Then have them interview several adults. Ask the adults what they know about Pandora. Record results of the interview in the second column. Ask the triads to decide what they want to know about Pandora in the third column and share their responses. Finally, in the last column, have them write what they learned after reading the story.

- Have students write predictions about Pandora. Place the predictions in the box.

- Discuss the names of gods and goddesses and how these names are used today. Prepare, with students, a **character attribute chart** (VM 6) comparing the names of Greek, Roman, and Scandinavian Gods and what they represent. Discuss Epimetheus (a Titan, from a gigantic race, who inhabited the Earth before man and who with his brother, Prometheus, made man).

- Discuss the elements of myths. (See appendix B.) Give students yellow or gold paper shaped like coins. Ask them to write literary characteristics of myths on the "gold coins," and attach the coins to the iridescent box.

Construct

- Hang a sign from the ceiling that reads: "Mount Olympus." Place students under the sign. Ask each to share predictions. Use these predictions as the basis for discussing the story. Collect predictions, after reading myth, distribute predictions to other students to read and compare predictions to the actual story.

- After reading the story, discuss important elements of the story, using the following **probes** (VO 72) if needed:

  How is Pandora different from Jupiter or Venus? Why did Jupiter give Pandora a box to keep with her all time? Could you keep a box without opening it? Describe

Pandora's actions. Is it really Pandora's fault that we have greed, envy, colds, measles? Why do you think the storyteller said, "If Hope had escaped with the rest, the world would have been worse off today"? What do people mean when they say "curiosity killed the cat"? Is this myth real?

Create

■ Give students very ugly, terrible looking, repulsive paper. Ask them to write a description of the most horrible "tiny, ugly winged creature" that could escape from the box.

■ Give students beautiful paper. Ask them to write a description about the most important positive attributes to stay with hope. Encourage them to justify their choice. Ask students to place their responses in Pandora's Box. Individual students will open the box, select a response, and read and discuss it.

■ Prepare a collection of mythology expressions used today in business, literature, and media, and place the language on a mythology **word wall** (VM 34).

■ Let students write reactions to myths in their **lit logs** (VW 92).

■ If a mythology unit begins with this tale, encourage students to collect, read, and share myths representing various cultural and regional groups.

■ **Cluster** (VM 9) information about myths around the terms: Greek, Roman, Norse, and Native American myths. (Greek and Roman myths are not always separated in the literature, but because the names of the gods are different they could be organized according to the names used; other clusters could be related to the role of the specific gods and goddesses, i.e., "creation myths," "animal myths," etc. See appendix B for additional information.

■ Have students identify and sketch mythological creatures, e.g., unicorns, satyrs, phoenix, and others on large sheets of paper. Have them place interesting information about the creature under the sketches and cite sources for information.

■ Let students select a favorite myth. Have them copy the myth and draw an original illustration to place in a bound book titled, "Our Classroom Mythology Collection."

■ Divide the students into triads, and give them the following scenario: *Assume that Pandora is your best friend.* Have each group improvise a conversation between Pandora and the participants discussing the box given to her by her father and whether she should disobey her father and look inside the box. One person should assume the role of Pandora, and the other two should be friends.

- Write and present a myth commercial. Videotape the commercial. Present commercial on the morning television programming at the school. Place in media center. Request media specialist to show tapes to other classes.

ALADDIN AND THE WONDERFUL LAMP—ARABIAN NOVELLA

"Aladdin and the Wonderful Lamp" from *The Arabian Nights*. Cole, J. 1982. *Best-Loved Folktales of the World*. Illustrated by J. K. Schwarz. Garden City, NY: Doubleday. pp. 467-77.

"Aladdin and the Wonderful Lamp. " Sutherland, Z., and M. C. Livingston. 1984. *The Scott-Foresman Anthology of Children's Literature*. Glenview, IL: Scott-Foresman. pp. 295-301.

Carrick, C. 1989. *Alladin and the Wonderful Lamp*. Illustrated by D. Carrick. New York: Scholastic.

Lang, A. 1991 (reissue). *Reader's Digest Arabian Nights*. Pleasantville, NY: Readers Digest. pp. 199-214.

Recommended for students in fifth grade and above.

Summary

Aladdin, an idle son of a poor tailor, is given a ring by a famous African magician. The magician tricks Aladdin into a cave. While in the cave, Aladdin rescues an old lamp. The ring helps Aladdin escape from the cave. Aladdin and his family soon realize the value of the lamp. Aladdin falls in love with the sultan's daughter and with the help of his mother and the genie in the lamp, he marries the princess. While living in the palace "built" by the genie, a slave gives the old lamp away to the magician's younger mean brother, in trade for a new one. With the help of the ring, the clever Aladdin rescues his wife and palace and lives happily ever after.

This popular novella reflects a traditional oriental folk background. Telling of Aladdin, along with the adventures of Sinbad, and the flying carpet, and Ali Baba and his 40 thieves, Scheherazade enthralled the king of Persia with adventures for 1,001 nights. A written fragment of the tales was penned in Arabic shortly after A.D. 800. For generations the stories were passed in the coffee houses and marketplaces (they were not considered polite stories) and finally in 1704 a Frenchman, Antoine Gallard, translated 300 tales from a Syrian manuscript written in Egyptian. Fortunately, Gallard was a skillful storyteller, and his tales became so popular that they were translated into many languages of the world, including many oriental languages. Novelle are intended to entertain adults; they tend to be long with complete plots and contain mature content.

Connect

- Display a **word wall** (VM 34) containing unique language, such as: "piteously," "Persia," "lamenting," "hideous genie," "chink," "idle dream," "scimitar," "thither," "pious," "roc egg," "wretch."
- Give a book talk along the lines of the following:
  I went to a flea market over the weekend. I was stopped by a strange looking man who told me that he wanted to give me a ring and this lamp. He told me I could rub the ring and lamp at the same time to discover a secret. He told me that he couldn't give them to just anyone; if the ring and lamp fell into the wrong hands, the world would be in trouble. Since I had an honest face, he felt that he could trust me. I was skeptical at first, but he insisted that I take them. I put them away, intending to bring them to school and make my wish here. You know how impatient I am. Late Sunday night, I just had to rub them and say, "Oh ring and lamp reveal your secret to me." As I was rubbing the lamp, I turned it over and there inside the lamp was a book and a note. The note said, "Open the book to find out about Sinbad the Sailor, Ali Baba and his 40 thieves, and especially about Aladdin who used the ring and lamp to help him reach his goal. These stories were originally told by a young girl named Scheherazade to the king of Persia for 1,001 nights, and the stories saved her life. They were passed from one generation to another in coffee houses and marketplaces. They were then written in this book." I opened the book and found that it was a first edition, 1709, written by Antoine Galland. Here in the classroom today are a ring, a lamp, and a collection of stories.
- Read the title, "Aladdin and the Wonderful Lamp." Organize students in buddy teams, and distribute copies of the tale to each group. After reading, show videotape and compare the tale to the movie.
- Let students write comparisions or reactions to this novella in their **lit logs** (VW 92).

Construct

- Ask students what they would wish for if they had a magic ring or lamp. **Cluster** (VM 9) wishes into categories, such as wealth, happiness, others' benefits, etc.
- Place an old piece of carpet on the floor, and ask a student to sit on "the flying carpet." This person assumes the role of Aladdin and makes comments about

the wishes expressed by class members. The comments will be based on the student's knowedge of Aladdin's personality.

■ Interview "Aladdin." Have different students assume the role of Aladdin to answer questions such as:

Did you act cleverly when the stranger visted you and your mother? Why was your mother afraid of the lamp? Tell us about the sultan and the vizier and their plan. Where did the genie come from? Did you really think the genie would deliver so much? Were you amazed to find out how the people helped you? How did you know who the false Fatima really was? How did you change during the story?

Create

■ Have students paint some of the wishes requested earlier. They should write a rationale explaining why the wish should be granted.

■ Have students prepare a **readers' theater script** (VO 73) for the story and present a dramatic reading of the script to another class.

■ Let students sketch various incidents in the story. Use these sketches as a background for the bulletin board, or hall wall, to advertise the tale (or various stories from the *Arabian Nights*).

■ Write a **newspaper report** (VW 95) from the vizier's point of view reporting Aladdin's trickery to wed the princess. Other reports could be written by "anonymous reporters" inside Aladdin's palace.

■ Have students write a summary for different selections from *The Arabian Nights* (see summaries of tales for model). Share summaries and compare individual stories, i.e., characters, problems, conflicts, and solutions.

■ Record information from above on **character and plot chart** (VM 7).

■ Identify the attributes of novelle and record on a **literary ladder** (VM 16). Cut the chart into the shape of the magic lamp, a genie, or other symbols typical of the tale.

■ Have class write letters to the media specialist, public librarians, and school administration requesting additional copies of the novella for their respective libraries. Ask them to justify the request.

■ Let students write letters to the School Curriculum Committee (or appropriate personnel) stating why all 5th and 6th grade students should read stories from *The Arabian Nights*.

■ **Brainstorm** (VO 53) the meaning of "roc egg" and have children sketch it. Prepare a story **mobile** (VA 44) with the "roc egg" as the initial object. Make papier-mâché "roc eggs." Make a "roc egg" tree.

■ Ask students: "How would you present this novella to other students?"

■ Let students prepare a **storytelling festival** (VO 78) using a variety of *Tales from the Arabian Nights*.

Tyll Ulenspiegel

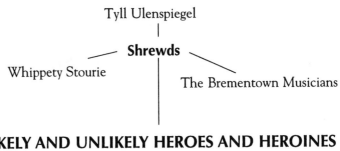

Shrewds

Whippety Stourie

The Brementown Musicians

LIKELY AND UNLIKELY HEROES AND HEROINES
(Grades 4-6)

Jack and the Robbers

Dick Whittington
& His Cat

Noodleheads, Silly Clever Manka
Heroes, And Heroines

The Three Sillies

Heroes, Heroines,
John Henry   **and Friends**

Sedna

CHAPTER
eight

Likely and Unlikely Heroes and Heroines Unit
Grades 4-6

LITERARY OUTCOMES

Through these nine stories, designed to focus on the nontraditional hero or heroine, students will examine their own definitions of heroic motivations, actions, and deeds. The seriousness of heroic standards is balanced with the humor and lightheartedness of good-natured characters whose heroism may be easily overlooked or miscalculated.

Some heroes and heroines are simply shrewd enough to survive, while others provide leadership and dedication to an ideal; there are others whose heroism may be questioned as they seem to accidentally trip upon good fortune. These stories will provide an abundant source of critical thinking and discussion for students.

The literary element of characterization must be developed as heroes and heroines are explored. Additionally, the element of theme is easily studied with these stories. Similar themes may be compared, as are characters and subgenres.

Through these stories, students may continue their comparison of cultures through folktales from diverse countries and peoples. They will meet another English legend, Dick Whittington, and reinforce the idea that legends are based on figures who are believed to have lived. Through the Eskimo myth, "Sedna," students will meet a female heroine whose sad and tragic life gave way to an explanation for sea creatures' beginnings. The African-American ballad in this unit tells a story of a hero's sacrifice.

The unit concludes with three examples of the jest. From three cultures come the humor that may remain in the minds and lives of the students for a lifetime.

INTEGRATED CURRICULUM STRATEGIES

These areas may lead to further curriculum integration:

- animals as pets
- supply and demand in economics
- musical instruments
- Appalachia and the eastern U.S. mountains
- Germany, England, and Western Europe
- current status of Eastern European countries
- Eskimo traditions
- railroads and their history
- humor
- noodlehead actions throughout the world (politics)
- standards in the workplace; workman's compensation; OSHA

Shrewds Theme

WHIPPETY STOURIE—SCOTTISH FOLKTALE

"Whippety Stourie." Arbuthnot, M. H. 1961. *Time for Fairy Tales*. Glenview, IL: Scott-Foresman. pp. 31-32.

"The Three Spinners." Manheim, R. 1981. *Rare Treasures from Grimm: 15 Little Known Tales*. Illustrated by E. Blegrad. Garden City, NY: Doubleday. pp. 35-38.

Related Stories

"Rumpelstiltskin." Arbuthnot, M. H. 1952. *Time for Fairy Tales*. Glenview, IL: Scott-Foresman. pp. 60-62.

"Rumpelstiltskin." Haviland, V. 1985. *Favorite Fairy Tales Told around the World*. Illustrated by S. Schindler. Boston: Little, Brown. pp. 91-96.

"Rumpelstiltskin." Opie, I., and P. Opie. 1992 (reissue). *The Classic Fairy Tales*. New York: Oxford. pp. 183-84.

Sage, A. 1991. *Rumpelstiltskin.* Illustrated by G. Spirin. New York: Dial for Young Readers.

"Tom Tit Tot." Arbuthnot, M. H. 1952. *Time for Fairy Tales.* Glenview, IL: Scott-Foresman. pp. 21-23.

"Tom Tit Tot." Williams-Ellis, A. *Tales from the Enchanted World.* Great Britain: Hodder & Stoughton. pp. 185-95.

Zelinsky, P. 1986. *Rumpelstiltskin.* New York: Dutton.

Recommended for students in fourth through sixth grades.

Summary

This Scottish tale will appeal to the sense of humor of intermediate age students. A slight romance tale, this story is of a man who insists his wife spin 12 hanks of thread a day or "it will be the worst" for her. After some time of not being able to perform this task, she is left by herself when he goes on a trip, warning her that if she has not spun 100 hanks of thread by his return, he will find another wife.

She goes out to the countryside and meets six wee ladies, all with lopsided mouths, one of whom is spinning madly and singing that her name is Whippety Stourie. The six wee ladies vow to help the woman with her problem.

When her husband returns, she invites the ladies for dinner. Finally, after much conversation, he asks how they happened to have lopsided mouths. They tell him it is from spin-spin-spinning all day long. He immediately has the spinning wheel burned and never again asks his wife to spin.

Connect

- Begin this unit by asking students to define "hero" and "heroine" and to give examples. With the students, develop a list of **hero/heroine criteria** (VW 91) for use as each character is evaluated for the status.

- Provide a **hero/heroine bulletin board** (VM 12) on which students may place hero/heroine stories, pictures, descriptions, and other memorabilia following the credentialing of the character by a student. One side of the board should be titled "UNLIKELY" and the other side, "LIKELY." Characters may be placed on one side or the other after the **credentialing process** (VO 64) is complete.

- Introduce the students to six tiny finger puppets who are said to be Whippety Stourie (on one hand) and her friends (on the other hand). They should each have a lopsided mouth. Because this feature of the little ladies in prominent in the story, it should be mentioned, but discussion about the lopsided mouths may be delayed until after the story is read.

Suggest to the students that they will recognize other stories that are similar in that a character in the story needs help and the little ladies offer their assistance. Someone may wish to nominate Whippety Stourie and the ladies for the status of heroine after the story is finished.

Note that this story is from Scotland and encourage the students to listen for evidence of the Scottish origin.

Read the story to the students.

Construct

- Students will likely remember "Rumpelstiltskin" and "Tom Tit Tot" and be anxious to make comparisons. Several comparisons are obvious: 1) the lady with a problem; 2) who causes her problem; 3) what the problem is; 4) who helps solve the problem; 5) how that solution becomes a larger problem in some of the stories.
- Any of these differences may be developed visually by the students with a **comparison chart** (VW 85). The chart shown below compares the rewards requested by the helpers in all three stories (Rumpelstiltskin, Tom Tit Tot, and Whippety Stourie and her friends).

Whippety Stourie	Rumpelstiltskin	Tom Tit Tot
Invitation to dinner	Guess his name or give him her child	Guess his name or she would belong to him

- Divide the class into literary discussion groups to further discuss motivation behind the deeds of the so-called helpers in these stories.
- Some **probes** (VO 72) to help the students focus on this area include the following:

   If you were measuring the assistance given to the lady in this story by Whippety Stourie, on a scale of one to five (five is high), where would you place a mark? Why? What do you think was the most valuable help given her? Why did the little ladies wish to come to dinner? What might have happened if they had not been invited? Do you think the lady might have been reluctant to invite them? Why? Would you classify Whippety Stourie and her friends as heroines? How do they meet the criteria for heroes and heroines?

- Another topic for discussion might be the relationship between spinning ("constant spin-spin-spinning") and the lopsided mouths of the little ladies.

Students who are not familiar with a spinning wheel may profit from a picture of one and some speculation on how spinning could cause the ladies to have lopsided mouths.

- Further research projects on jobs and how they affect physical features might be interesting for some students as a follow-up to gain more meaning and insight into this story. (If students are unclear on how activities performed in a job affect the physical body, a realistic analogy might be the knot that develops on the middle finger after writing extensively. Most of them will have had this experience and can relate to the example.)

Create

Responses to this story may include both shared responses as well as individual choices. Some options include the following suggestions:

- Dramatization of this story may occur as a group of students plan the production with finger puppets and create additional puppets for the added characters.
- Let students respond in the **lit logs** (VW 92) on some of the areas discussed in small groups. Written responses might include:
  What might have happened if the lady had been frightened of or shunned the six wee ladies because of their physical appearance?
- Researching Scottish folklore will produce other stories in which "wee folk" or "fairies" play strong roles. Some students will be interested in finding out more about the "wee folk," drawing pictures, and making posters.
- **Copy cat stories** (VW 86) may follow with students using the little old ladies or other wee folk as a pattern for their story.

TYLL ULENSPIEGEL—GERMAN JEST

Bell, A. 1990. *The Merry Pranks of Till Eulenspiegel*. Illustrated by L. Zwerger. Saxonville, MA: Picture Book Studio.

Jagendorf, M. A. 1938. *Tyll Ulenspiegel's Merry Pranks*. New York: Vanguard Press.

"Tyll Ulenspiegel, The Tale of a Merry Dance." Rugoff, M. 1949. *A Harvest of World Folk Tales*. New York: The Viking Press. pp. 375-77.

(Note: The spelling of Tyll varies with different publications.)

Related Story

Nickl, P. 1992. *The Wonderful Travels and Adventures of Baron Münchhausen.*
Translated by E. Taylor. New York: North-South.

(Another shrewd character with adventures similar to Tyll's.)

This story is recommended for students in grades four through six.

Summary

In this jest from Germany, Tyll demonstrates his wit and mischievousness, which delights youngsters. Tyll stretches a rope across the river from tree to tree, calls for Sunday afternoon passersby to notice him while he prances on the rope in the air, and then collects coins for his payment. He then announces to the villagers that he will perform a greater feat the next Sunday. Others in the village are also mischievous and they clip the rope, so that on the next Sunday as he walks the rope, it breaks and he falls into the river. Climbing out, he is good-natured in challenging them to come next Sunday and watch him dance with all their shoes at the same time. He agrees to give them his earnings if he cannot do that.

When the next Sunday comes, he wears a leather apron in which he deposits all their shoes. He dances on the ropes with their shoes in the apron pockets. They are not happy that he doesn't share his money with them, but he argues that he has danced with their shoes, not in them, just as he has promised.

Connect

- An introduction to the subgenre of jests will be appropriate before reading this story. Jests, also called "schwanks," are humorous anecdotes, supposedly told with a grain of truth, but with very deliberate humor. These stories are told so that everyone will laugh along with the character and the funny episodes.
- Place a large banner in the room that reads "COME, WATCH TYLL ULENSPIEGEL PERFORM." Prepare the students for a performance by telling them about a juggler and tight rope walker, who spent his whole life "walking tightropes" and "keeping his head above water." Warn them, also, that he is very clever, and they will do well to keep an eye on him.
- The students will remember the trickster characters in other stories. In those stories, the tricksters were animals, but in this story, the character is a man. After the story, they will determine whether he is considered a trickster or a hero—or perhaps both.

- Read several of the episodes to the students (see additional references). The story, referenced above, in which he juggles shoes while on the tightrope, may be retyped and transferred onto an overlay for the overhead projector.
- **Chorally read** (VO 59) the story together.

Construct

- After reading the story, ask each student to draw or sketch a picture of what Tyll might have looked like. These **mind's eye images** (VA 43) may be shared to broaden understanding of the story. After displaying the pictures on a line (to resemble a tightrope), students need opportunities to study each other's drawings and ask questions.
- There may be a structured "Tyll tour" for students to study each drawing to get an idea of Tyll's personality and character.
- The tour may be followed by a **round table discussion** (VO 75). These discussions may include some of the following areas:

    Justify your drawing of Tyll in terms of what you know about his actions and what he was able to do. (In other words, when you drew his picture, did you consider that he must have been athletic to walk a tightrope and to juggle?)

    From the stories of Tyll that you have heard or read, what kind of personality did he have? On what do you base your answers?

    Was he a hero? Why or why not?

    To whom might he have been a hero? How could that have happened?

    Why do you suppose this story was told? Was it told to entertain? Is it an entertaining story? What parts are the best?

    What is meant in the story by the words, "I'm going to tread a tightrope all my life!" (In the story of his baptism, he is said to have "learned to keep his head above water.") Are these puns (statements in which the double meanings make them humorous) crucial to the humor in the story? Why or why not?

Create

- Collect other Tyll stories, retell, or originate adventures for him. Have the retold and newly created stories typed and mounted on a bulletin board for all to share.
- Have an oral **jest for fun** (VO 69) in which students are able to create and tell short, funny stories about their friends and family. These stories will be written and previewed by the teacher or teams of students before being told to the class. Through the tellings of these stories, students will begin to recognize jests and their place in literature. Students may help in the planning of the event by preparing refreshments and inviting guests.

- Students may be interested in creating more humor with additional puns. A picture album may be placed in the room with the suggestion that when anyone hears, reads, or creates a pun, that it be recorded in the album, which will be named "Pun Fun." Students may read or add to the album independently.

THE BREMENTOWN MUSICIANS—GERMAN FOLKTALE

Wilhelm, H. 1992. *The Bremen Town Musicians*. New York: Scholastic.

"Brementown Musicians." Hutchison, V. 1992. *Chimney Corner Stories, Tales for Little Children*. Illustrated by L. Lenski. Hamden, CT: Shoestring Press. pp. 107-16.

"The Bremen Town Musicians." Sutherland Z., and M. L. Cohen. 1984. *The Scott Foresman Anthology of Children's Literature*. Glenview, IL: Scott-Foresman. pp. 188-90.

Easton, S. 1991. *The Bremen Town Musicians*. Illustrated by M. Corcoran. New York: Andrews & McMeel.

Evans, E. 1990. *Bremen Town Musicians*. Illustrated by J. Boddy. New York: Unicorn.

"The Four Musicians." Arbuthnot, M. H. 1961. *Scott-Foresman Anthology of Children's Literature*. Glenview, IL: Scott-Foresman, pp. 37-38.

Page, P. 1991. *The Traveling Musicians of Bremen*. Illustrated by K. Denton. New York: Little, Brown.

Palacer, J. 1988. *The Brementown Musicians*. Saxonville, MA: Picture Book Studio.

Stevens, J. 1992. *Brementown Musicians*. New York: Haliday House.

Watts, B. 1992. *The Bremen Town Musicians*. Illustrated by A. Bell. New York: North-South Books.

This story will be enjoyed by students from fourth through sixth grades.

Summary

Another story from the Grimms' collection, this fun story shows how four animals, themselves turned out in the world, scare away robbers with their own style of music. The animals are a cat, a rooster, a dog, and a donkey.

Connect

- Before reading the story, construct posterboard replicas of a cat, a rooster, a dog, and a donkey and glue magnet strips to the back of each. Place the visuals across the top of the chalkboard and draw columns for each. Ask the students to give information on the sounds made by each animal and record their responses under each picture. Divide the class into four sections and give each section an animal sound to make.
- On a given signal, allow all animals to make their sounds. These sounds then may be orchestrated with a tune or rhythm.
- Tape-record this "animal concert" and play it for youngsters just prior to reading the story.
- To set the stage for understanding the feelings of each of these animals, **probe** (VO 72) with questions related to how it feels to be alone and scared, for example:
  How would it feel to be alone and not have friends or family who cared for you?
- After discussion, permit brief role playing of scared, lonely, or lost feelings.
- Have students read aloud "The Four Musicians" in the manner that follows under the "Construct" subheading.

Construct

- Divide a copy of the story into paragraphs, giving every two students one or two paragraphs. Ask each buddy team to read the paragraphs silently and to think about where the paragraph fits into the sequence. Then ask the team who has the introduction to read it to the class. The students will then read the appropriate paragraphs to complete the story sequence.
- Group the class into literary discussion groups of four to six students. Possible discussion questions follow and may be written on an overlay or chalkboard or given orally:
  Why were these animals scared and lonely? Why did they join together? How were they able to scare the bank robbers, not just once, but twice? Why did the animals suspect that bank robbers were in the house? If you had been there, what would you have thought was happening? How do you suppose the owners of the animals might have felt when they discovered they were gone? How do you suppose the animals felt to be together? Why do you think this story was told? Were there any heroes in this story? Whom would you nominate and why?

Create

- Students of all ages will enjoy **role playing** (VO 74) this story, because it is action filled. Students may be assigned various roles and the story may be replayed with the various interpretations of those who are playing the roles.
- All students may participate if the story is broken into three sections:
    1) the animals leaving home and meeting each other (4-8 students may be involved if each animal and its master is depicted);
    2) the first encounter when the animals come upon the robbers' house and scare them away (4-8 students as the animals and any number of robbers may be used in this episode);
    3) the second encounter when the robbers reappear at the house and are frightened a second time. (again 4-8 or more students may play these roles).
- Music may be included by adding the "animal concert," previously experienced, to the role playing. The concert may vary if you choose to add nontraditional music (i.e., rubber-bands around notebooks, homemade drums, pencils striking).
- Considering that the animals were looking for a safe, quiet place to sleep at night, each student may select one animal and make it a bed with a **checkbook box diorama** (VA 39). Further development of animal habitats may be included with this project. A "robbers' house" might also be constructed by some of the students from cardboard and construction paper and then dioramas may be displayed around the house.

Heroes, Heroines, and Friends Theme

DICK WHITTINGTON AND HIS CAT—ENGLISH LEGEND

"Dick Whittington and His Cat." Arbuthnot, M. H. 1961. *Time for Fairy Tales.* Glenview, IL: Scott-Foresman. pp. 27-31.

Brown, M. 1950. *Dick Whittington and His Cat.* New York: Scribner's.

"Dick Whittington and His Cat." Haviland, V. 1985. *Favorite Fairy Tales Told around the World*. Illustrated by S. Schindler. Boston: Little, Brown. pp. 51-62.

"Dick Whittington and His Cat." Saltman, J. 1985. *The Riverside Anthology of Children's Literature*. Boston: Houghton Mifflin Company.

"Whittington." Crossley-Holland, K. 1985. *Folktales of the British Isles*. Illustrated by H. Firmin. New York: Pantheon. pp. 291-96.

This story is recommended for students in grades four through six.

Summary

In this English legend, a poor boy, named Dick Whittington, seeks his fortune in London, meeting various people who both help and hinder his plight. While being taken in by a kind man, he sleeps in a rat infested room, and so he purchases a cat to rid his room of mice. When the gentleman in whose home Dick lives prepares to send out a ship, Dick is given a chance to venture something on the ship for future profit. As he has nothing but the cat, he reluctantly allows his cat to go on the ship. While he suffers through hardships at home, the cat is ridding a country of its mice and receiving rewards for Dick. Dick hears the church bells ring and predicts that he will be the mayor of London, so he is able to put to good use the rewards from his cat's endeavors. After marrying, he leads a successful life as sheriff and mayor, and is knighted by Henry V. Until the year 1780, his figure is supposedly carved in stone over a prison which he built.

Connect

- Refer to the **hero/heroine bulletin board** (VW 91) (created before reading "Whippety Stourie" at the beginning of this unit) on which pictures and articles are attached. Announce that the candidates for hero/heroine so far in this unit have been varied, ranging from wee little folk, to animals, to humorous tricksters, so it is time to turn to someone who may have really lived and is now known to us through a legend: Dick Whittington—and his cat!
- Invite some open **thought-splashing** (VO 82) on ways that a man and his cat might become heroes. The students' thoughts may be recorded on a chart.
- The setting of the story will be established as London, during the fifteenth century. Prepare a background setting display of London at that time, or share the information orally.

■ Depending on the version of the story that is accessible, determine whether students can read silently, in pairs, or if the story should be read aloud to them. For older students with strong reading ability, individual silent reading is recommended. If multiple texts of Marcia Brown's Dick Whittington are available, students will enjoy the woodcut illustrations as they read.

Construct

■ Following the reading of the story, draw up a **cause and effect story frame** (VM 4) to have the children fill out. Students will probably identify some of the following:

CAUSE	EFFECT
He was born into a poor family.	He was hungry and had few clothes.
He asked a wagoner to walk by the wagon.	He was able to go to London.
He begged for money in London.	He was given a job by a farmer.
He lay down at the door of a rich merchant.	He was spotted by a cook who gave him a hard time. He was also spotted by the merchant who offered him a place to live.
He was tormented by rats where he slept.	He bought a cat.
The master had a ship ready. He asked Dick to donate his cat to the journey.	Dick donated his cat.
The cat killed the rats on the ship and in the king's palace.	The king of the country bought the goods and the cat and paid a high price for all.
Dick, unaware of his cat's adventures, ran away and sat on a rock, tired and hungry.	He heard a bell toll a prediction that he would be the mayor of London.
The ship's captain brought payment to the rich merchant and to Dick for the cat.	Dick became aware of his wealth.
Dick bought clothes and cleaned himself to become a fine gentleman.	He courted and married the rich merchant's daughter.
As mayor of London, he built a prison at Newgate.	Legend says that his figure and his cat's were carved over the prison.

■ Have children consider the following questions, and track their responses by a show of hands:
  Who was the real hero in this story? Why?

Create

■ Students who see Marcia Brown's Dick Whittington will be fascinated by the woodcut illustrations. Some opportunities to experience woodcuts or printing techniques include the following suggestions.

■ Basic **potato printing** (VA 45) will allow students to imitate the woodcuts of Dick and the cat.

■ Stories may be generated by taking one or several of the causes from the chart made earlier and developing different effects.

■ Debates may be planned around some of these issues:

Dick was accidentally lucky to have his cat make a fortune for him. Even if fortune did land in his lap, Dick had to work to meet his goals, and he did that well. The rich merchant was the real hero because ...

■ Literary letters may be written by students regarding the following subjects:

A letter from Dick to his family, explaining his problems and his good fortune.

A letter from the cat back to Dick after he was purchased by the king of Barbary.

A letter from Dick to the king of Barbary telling him of the cat's favorite foods and playthings.

A letter from Dick to his subjects in London, thanking them for their support after the election.

Dick's political platform.

The notice from Henry V indicating that Dick will be knighted.

Dick's thank you address at the opening of the prison at Newgate and the unveiling of the carving of Dick and the cat.

A loveletter from Dick to the merchant's daughter.

SEDNA—ESKIMO MYTH

"The Sedna Legend." Saltman, J. 1985. The Riverside Anthology of Children's Literature. Boston: Houghton Mifflin Company. pp. 535-36.

McDermott, B. B. 1975. Sedna, An Eskimo Myth. New York: Viking Press.

Similar Stories

De Armond, D. 1990. The Boy Who Found the Light: Eskimo Folktales. San Francisco: Sierra Books.

Ginsburg, M. 1974. The Proud Maiden, Tungak, and the Sun, A Russian Eskimo Tale. Illustrated by F. Galanin. New York: Macmillan.

"The Story of Nuliajuk, Mother of the Sea, Ruler of All Beasts, the Most Dangerous and Terrible of All Spirits, to Whom Nothing is Impossible."

Field, E. 1973. *Eskimo Songs and Stories*. Illustrated by Kiakshuk and Pudlo (No first names). New York: Dell. pp. 46-48.

This story is complex and will require a mature reader to fully appreciate it. Therefore, it is recommended for students in grades five and six.

Summary

An Eskimo creation story, this is a tale of Sedna, who is courted by many young men and refuses to marry any of them until she meets a handsome young hunter from a faraway land. She finally agrees to go to his home, but when they are sailing in his kayak, he transforms into a spirit bird with the wings of a loon. She is unhappy as the spirit bird has been deceitful, and when her father visits her a year later, she leaves with him. While on their way home, the loon follows them and plunges into the sea, enraging the sea gods. The seas rise in a storm and to save himself, Sedna's father pushes her from the kayak. When she surfaces and tries to hold onto the boat's side, he stabs her hands over and over. As her blood congeals in the water, sea animals are created. Finally, Sedna sinks to the bottom of the sea with the animals created from her blood. Her father arrives home at his igloo, but Sedna sends her sea animals to retrieve him. To this day, they both live at the bottom of the sea with the sea animals. Sedna is bitter and resentful and only reluctantly gives up an animal to a hunter.

Connect

- Understanding of this story will be enhanced by a background setting display which may consist of an overview of water birds and sea animals, such as:
    loons
    walruses
    seals
    whales
- Remind the students of stories they have read that explain why or how certain things happen. Explain that origin stories are often called myths, and that the story to be read is sometimes called a legend and is sometimes referred to as an Eskimo myth that tells of the creation of the sea animals, such as walruses, seals, and whales.
- Prepare overlays for the overhead projector that represent Sedna, a beautiful Eskimo girl, her father, a handsome young hunter, the loon, or spirit bird who was disguised as the hunter, seals, walruses, whales. These transparency characters will add realism to the story as it is read or told. The solemn mood of the story may be extended through playing soft instrumental music, tapes

of ocean waves from sounds of nature, or the call of the loon as a background to the story.

Construct

This story is appropriate for mature students, so the construction of meaning will focus on more abstract, higher-level thinking.

■ Prepare cards on which these words are written:
  DECEPTION
  BETRAYAL
  DESERTION
  REVENGE
  DEATH
  SACRIFICE

■ Use these "theme cards" with small groups who will discuss how the theme on the card is developed in this story. Other stories with the same theme might be compared.

■ Some discussion **probes** (VO 72) for each group are the following:
  Give examples of incidents in the story that lead you to perceive this theme. How is this theme carried out uniquely in an Eskimo story as opposed to how it might be carried out in a story from another culture? What emotions are evoked by this story and the theme?

■ Seek independent nominations from this story for heroes/heroines to be credentialed for the bulletin board created earlier. (See "Whippety Stourie.")

Create

■ Together with the class create a ballad that Sedna might have sung as 1) she ran away with her young hunter; 2) saw him transformed into loon; 3) spent her cold days and nights with the birds; 4) escaped with her father; 5) was thrown from the kayak by her father; 6) the sea animals were being born from her blood (and in some versions from her fingers); 7) to how she feels living at the bottom of the ocean, controlling the release or protection of the sea animals to and from hunters.

■ Perform the ballad for another class after it has been completed and rehearsed.

■ Paint a mural, depicting the scenes of remembrance in the story. Printing may be a medium which some students would like to use. Linoleum printing is a sophisticated version of the **potato printing** (VA 45) mentioned earlier and would make a good medium choice. Show students Beverly McDermott's *Sedna, An Eskimo Myth*, which is illustrated with prints of indigo and violet.

- Create a bulletin board to accompany an environmental unit on Alaskan wildlife. Research projects may include information on the sea, land, and air creatures; their habitats; and their environmental status.
- A collection of bird calls on tape at a **listening post** (VO 70) may be of interest to many students.

References to bird calls:
Borror, D. 1988. *Florida Bird Songs.* (Sound recording and illustrated book.) Illustrated by M. Giltz. Mineola, NY: Dover.

Sheen, M. 1991. *Messages from the Birds.* Alexandria, VA: PBS Video.

Walton, R., and R. Lawson. 1991. *Backyard Birdsong: Eastern and Central Northa America: A Guide to Bird Song Identification.* Boston: Houghton Mifflin.

JOHN HENRY—AFRICAN-AMERICAN BALLAD

"John Henry Races the Steam Drill." Walker, P. R. 1993. *Big Men, Big Country.* Illustrated by J. Bernardin. San Diego: Harcourt, Brace and Jovanovich. pp. 55-61.

Bowman, J. C. 1942. *John Henry.* Illustrated by R. LaGrove. Chicago: Albert Whitman, Co.

Gianni, G. 1988. *John Henry.* New York: Kipling.

"John Henry." Osborne, M. 1991. *American Tall Tales.* Illustrated by M. McCurdy. New York: Alfred A. Knopf. pp. 87-95.

"John Henry." Ross, N. P. (*Time* ed.), and E. K. Thompson. (*LIFE* ed.) 1961. *The Life Treasury of American Folklore.* New York: Time, Inc. p. 168.

"John Henry." Young, R., and J. Young. 1993. *African American Folktales for Young Readers.* Little Rock: August House. pp. 124-29.

Keats, E. J. *John Henry: An American Legend.* 1965. New York: Pantheon.

Rogers, C. 1992. *John Henry.* (Video.) Illustrated by B. Jackson. Westport, CT: Rabbit Ears.

Sanfield, S. 1986. *A Natural Man: The True Story of John Henry.* Illustrated by P. Thornton. Boston: D. R. Godine.

This story is recommended for students in grades four through six.

Summary

This ballad from the 1800s in the American South fascinates students as it tells the story of a man who was not only a hero among his peers, but who competed in a contest against a machine—and won the contest, but lost his life.

John Henry is the name given the "steel-driving man" who laid railroad tracks throughout the South. Legend indicates that such a man did exist (although he may have had another name) and that the duel between the steam engine drill and John Henry's powerful arms took place either in West Virginia or Alabama in the late 1800s.

Connect

- Background on how rails were laid in the 1800s may be developed by showing pictures of railroad tracks, setting up a miniature railroad track, or videotaping local tracks to show in the classroom. Students need a concept of why steel posts were driven into the rocks by the railroad companies. They may relate to highway construction going on in their own neighborhoods and how power drills are used to break through rocks in order to level the land for the highways. They will understand that the same challenges faced today by highway construction crews were there when the railroad construction companies began building. And the resources, in those days, were significantly fewer. In fact, men did the work, rather than machines.
- Students may read the narrative silently while listening to the text of the ballad being read aloud to them.

Construct

- Following the reading and listening of the story, ask students to share their images of John Henry with a partner. Ask the partner to try to imagine John Henry by the descriptors used. Switch roles and the other partner will describe while the listening partner will imagine John Henry. This activity clarifies students' thinking and gives them an opportunity to express in descriptive language what they picture in their minds.
- Break group up into literary discussion groups of four to six students. If **probes** (VO 72) are needed try the following:

    Why was John Henry considered a "king" among railroad workers? How do you think this story came about? Who do you think told it first? Speculate on why this story was told in ballad form. What other ballads of heroes do you know? What was the significance of man dueling a machine? Do you know of other examples of such happenings? What would a contemporary story be about if a man competed against a machine? Do you think John Henry would have thought the price was worth what he paid for the victory? Why or why not?

Create

- Nominate John Henry for "hero." Pass out **sentence strips** (VM 27) on which "railroad track" lines have been drawn with markers. Ask students to write reasons that John Henry meets or does not meet the criteria for hero.
- The strips may be placed around his name on the hero bulletin board. Once a decision has been made on his status as hero, vote on whether he is a "Likely" or "Unlikely" candidate for hero.
- John Henry is described as one "who had to be best on the job." Students may write in their **lit logs** (VW 92) what it might mean to them to "be best on the job."
- Listen to a recording of the story in ballad form. Learn to sing this ballad or the old favorite, "I've Been Working on the Railroad." Find other railroad songs or choral readings and orchestrate a repertoire of railroad related songs and verses for the class to perform.
- Using pieces of railroad track from a miniature train set, recreate the setting of the story. Make John Henry with his big hammer from clay, construction paper, or cardboard and place it near the tracks. Complete the display with various copies of the book or story.

Noodleheads, Silly Heroes, and Heroines Theme

JACK AND THE ROBBERS—AMERICAN FOLKTALE VARIANT

"Jack and the Robbers." Arbuthnot, M. H. 1961. *Time for Fairy Tales.* Glenview, IL: Scott-Foresman, pp. 194-96.

Chase, Richard. 1943. *The Jack Tales.* Illustrated by B. Williams. Boston: Houghton Mifflin. pp. 40-46.

Other Jack Tales

Chase, R., J. Compton., and K. Compton. 1993. *Jack the Giant Chaser: An Appalachian Tale.* New York: Haliday House.

Dodson, B. 1979. *Lazy Jack.* New York: Troll.

Garner, A. 1992. *Jack and the Beanstalk.* Illustrated by J. Heller. New York: Doubleday.

Haley, G. 1988. *Jack and the Fire Dragon.* New York: Crown.

"Jack and the Beanstalk." Opie, I., and D. Opie. 1992. *The Classic Fairy Tales.* New York: Oxford. pp. 162-63.

"Jack and the Giant Killer." Opie, I., and D. Opie. 1992. *The Classic Fairy Tales.* New York: Oxford. pp. 47-50.

"Jack and the Green Lady." Garner, A. 1984. *Alan Garner's Book of British Fairytales.* Illustrated by D. Collard. New York: Delacorte. pp. 17-24.

"Jack and the Robbers." Sutherland, Z., and M. C. Livingston. 1984. *The Scott-Foresman Anthology of Children's Literature.* Glenview, IL: Scott-Foresman. pp. 358-61.

Leeds, B. 1990. *Fairy Tale Rap: "Jack and the Beanstalk" & Other Stories.* Illustrated by C. Hamilton. New York: Miramonte Press.

This story is recommended for students in grades three through six.

Summary

This American variant of an old European "Lazy Jack" tale is very similar to "The Brementown Musicians" and will be easily recognized. Jack is the boy who, after getting a "tanning" from his Daddy, takes off down the road to find his fortune. He runs into an assortment of animals (ox, donkey, dog, cat, and rooster) that are in danger of being killed. Jack invites them to come along. They come upon a house for the night where robbers have been living, and exactly as the Brementown Musicians, these characters scare off the robbers. In the end, it is mentioned that Jack is back home with his family.

Connect

- This story is a definite change from the emotionally heavy stories of the last theme. Noodleheads, silly people, and simpletons represent another form of jest, or humorous anecdote. To begin the Jack story, the students may be reminded of their old friend, Tyll Ulenspiegel and his escapades.
- Display one of the students' drawings of Tyll on the chalkboard and write these words underneath: "Clever, Takes Initiative." To the side of this information on Tyll, write "Jack and the Beanstalk." Solicit from students

their perceptions of words to use to describe Jack as you have described Tyll. If they do not readily remember "Jack and the Beanstalk," remind them that he sold his mother's cow for a handful of beans and that another name for some of the Jack stories is "Lazy Jack." With that background, compare Jack to Tyll. Note the term, "simpleton," as being one that is used to refer to Jack.

Construct

- Read the story to the students in the Appalachian dialect if possible. There are several audiocassettes also available of the "Jack Tales." (Local bookstores have copies of various storytellers' versions of the Jack Tales. The tapes of Jackie Torrence are particularly entertaining.)
- Before beginning the story, group students into teams of four to five, and give each student five index cards to record five of the most important points in the story. Allow a few minutes after the reading for students to think about the important parts and to get their thoughts on paper. Their cards, **mirror cards** (VM 17), will represent what they believe to be most significant in the story, but the group must also reach consensus on the five most important points in the story. Negotiation on these points will bring considerable discussion in the groups.

This story is a good one for this activity because it is very similar to another one they have recently read. Having already discussed and role played "The Brementown Musicians," they have a working familiarity with the story.

Create

Research on other jests, noodlehead stories, or specific Lazy Jack stories may provide a foundation for additional activities in the classroom. Some suggestions:

- Set up a **listening post** (VO 70) for individual opportunities to hear tapes of Jack stories.
- Plan a **storytelling festival** (VO 78) in which students become familiar with folktales—especially humorous stories. Practice telling them, and then tell them to an audience. The art of storytelling may be directly taught, followed by students practicing in pairs. The festival may be a classroom or grade-level activity.
- After hearing additional Jack tales (see Chase in references), students may wish to prepare **file folder pop ups** (VM 20) to depict some of Jack's activities. These pop ups may be displayed on shelves in the library to attract others to the Jack stories.

- These adventures of Lazy Jack may also be portrayed on a mural made with a **crayon etching** (VA 37) technique. Several stories may be told on such a drawing.

THE THREE SILLIES—ENGLISH JEST

Hewitt, K. 1986. *The Three Sillies*. San Diego: Harcourt, Brace and Jovanovich.
"The Three Sillies." Williams-Ellis, A. 1960. *Fairytales from the British Isles*. New York: Frederick Warne & Co. pp. 249-54.
Zemach, H. 1963. *The Three Sillies*. Illustrated by M. Zemach. New York: Holt, Rinehart & Winston.
Rockwell, A. 1979. *The Three Sillies and Ten Other Stories to Read Aloud*. New York: Crowell.

This story is recommended for students in grades four through six.

Summary

In this absurd noodlehead story, a young man is having dinner with his girlfriend and her parents when the girl goes to the cellar to get something to drink. She doesn't return, her mother goes to find her, and then her daddy goes to find both of them; after a while, the young man goes to the cellar to find them crying over a ridiculous thought that the girl had. The man laughs at them and tells them if he can find three sillier people than the three of them, he will return and marry her. So he travels through the country looking for sillies. He finds them and returns to marry the silly girl.

Connect

- Before the students arrive for class, hang a sign over the door on the inside of the classroom that reads "CHUCKLE ZONE." Point to the sign and indicate to the students that they will be chuckling before this story is over.
- Begin the preparation for this story by asking students to think of the silliest things they have ever heard of people doing. Write their ideas on a chart or an overhead projector overlay.
- They have already met several characters from jests and humorous anecdotes. Remind them of these characters (Tyll Ulenspiegel and Lazy Jack) and tell them that in the next story, the characters are not shrewds, as Tyll was, or dull, as Jack was, but they do things that are just plain SILLY!
- If possible, have multiple copies for students to read silently, otherwise, read it aloud to them.

Construct

- Give the students an opportunity to think of one question they would ask the original teller of this story. The questions may be written on index cards and shared orally for discussion of the story. Later the cards may be placed on a table near a collection of similar stories or of different versions of the same story.
- Divide the class into four groups for dramatizations:
  1) silly family at dinner time
  2) the lady and her cow
  3) the man and his trousers
  4) the villagers and the moon

Give students 15 minutes to prepare a dramatization of the story as read. Students may use their own language, but they should dramatize the original story.

- Present dramatizations to the class.

Create

- Following the dramatizations of the original story, give the same groups an opportunity to create a **modern adaptation** (VW 94) of the story and dramatize it as a group after it is written.

Other individual responses may include the following:

- Have students write an original "silly" story—either **copy cat** (VW 86) form or completely innovative.
- One technique for inventing stories, along with reinforcing story structure, is for students to write their stories using a **character-but-then-so frame** (VO 56). A little time will be required to explain how to use the frames and to draw examples from the students. Once they understand the structure of the story frame, they will find it easy to retell old stories or write new ones.
- Students may write or draw a **travelogue** (VW 101) from the perspective of the young man who met the sillies.

CLEVER MANKA—CZECHOSLOVAKIAN JEST

"Clever Manka." Sutherland, Z., and M. C. Livingston. 1984. *The Scott-Foresman Anthology of Children's Literature*. Glenview, IL: Scott-Foresman. pp. 274-77.

"Clever Manka." Arbuthnot, M. H. 1961. *The Arbuthnot Anthology.* Glenview, IL: Scott-Foresman. pp. 280-82.

"Clever Manka." Arbuthnot, M. H. 1961. *Time for Fairy Tales.* Glenview, IL: Scott-Foresman. pp. 147-49.

Minard, R. 1975. *Womenfolk and Fairy Tales.* Illustrated by S. Klein. Boston: Houghton Mifflin. pp. 77-82.

Variants

"Clever Mollie." Young, R., and J. Young. 1993. *African American Folktales for Young Readers.* Little Rock: August House. pp. 101-02.

Sherman, J. 1993. *Rachel, the Clever, and Other Jewish Folktales.* Little Rock: August House. pp. 44-48.

This story is recommended for students in grades four through six.

Summary

In this Czechoslovakian* humorous jest, the clever Manka wins the burgomaster as her husband by providing ingenious answers to his riddles. He asks her to come to see him not by day, nor by night, neither riding nor walking, neither dressed nor undressed. She comes before daybreak but after the darkness of night has passed, with one leg on a goat and one on the ground, wrapped in a fishnet which makes her neither dressed nor undressed. They live happily until her cleverness becomes intimidating to him. When she embarrasses him by helping someone show him how he is wrong, he asks her to leave their home but tells her she can take one thing with her that she treasures. She makes him a wonderful dinner and when he goes to sleep, she ties him up and takes him to her father's cottage. He is the one thing she treasures enough to take with her. He laughs, and they go back home together.

Connect

■ Announce to the class that there will be nominations through the week for the winner of the **cleverest character contest** (VO 60). Guide the students as they develop criteria for a clever character. List the criteria on a chart and ask a group of students to develop nomination forms and ballots for voting.

---

*The sources list this as a Czechoslovakian tale, and we were unable to determine whether it is actually a Czech or a Slovak tale. In all truth, it is a tale indigenous to the region, crossing changing international borders.

- Students have had exposure to jests and to humorous stories throughout this unit, so this one will not be a surprise. Introduce them to the character named Clever Manka. Review with them the term "burgomaster" and its meaning as a chief magistrate of a municipality, similar to our mayor.
- This story is one that is easily sequenced and could be shared with a **cooperative reading activity** (C.R.A.) (VO 63). After students have read sections of the story silently in pairs or small groups, ask for the story to be sequenced and reread aloud.

Construct

- Give each pair or group of students some pieces of fabric, construction paper, odds and ends for collage making and ask them to make something that is symbolic of Manka. Share the symbols as a way of discussing the story.
- Display the following **probe** (VO 72) on the chalkboard for small group discussion for five minutes:

  What made Manka clever?
- After discussing the question with the entire class, delve into Manka's character traits with a **character continuum** (VW 83) using some of these character dichotomies: Brave-Coward; Smart-Dull; Fun-Serious; Shrewd-Victim. Let students place their Manka symbols on continuum lines drawn on a bulletin board or add magnetic strips to the symbols and draw the continuum lines on the chalkboard with colored chalk, placing the symbols at appropriate spots on each line. As pairs or small groups place their symbols on the continuum, have them share their reasoning for their decisions.

Create

- Have students plan and create graphics to compare the characters in this unit: Manka, Tyll, Jack, the characters in the Sillies, Dick, Whippety, Brementown Musicians, Sedna, and John Henry. Some options may be: **Venn diagrams** (VM 33), **character attribute charts** (VM 7), **character continuums** (VW 83), or **literary report cards** (VO 57). Other ideas may come from the students. A block of time will be needed for students to plan, create, and share their graphics.
- The hero/heroine bulletin board (VM 12), started with "Whippety Stourie," will be completed with this story and with the final determination of which characters will make it to the board as heroes/heroines and of those, which ones will be dubbed "Likely" or "Unlikely."
- The final activity will be a voting for the cleverest character contest. Students may select one character for nomination, make a poster advertising that character's ability to meet the criteria (already developed). A forum on

cleverness will allow students to select a candidate, support that candidate by gathering data on the character's qualifications, make posters, and present a persuasive speech at the forum to convince classmates to vote for a given character as the most clever character met in this unit.

■ Share the results of the voting on a bar graph displayed in the room. Students may construct the graph from the voting results to practice graphing.

APPENDIX A

❀ ❀ ❀ ❀ ❀ ❀ ❀ ❀ ❀

Literary Response Modes

Responses to literature in the classroom are made in many forms. They may be natural, spontaneous reactions to a story; they may be private and totally unrecognized by another person; or they may be prompted by a teacher or another student. In the classroom, responses often extend the enjoyment of the story. They help students react and respond to literature. They may arise from thoughts stimulated by another.

Teachers need to provide opportunities for students to experience and respond to literature.

The responses suggested in this text are varied. They may be self-selected by a student or guided by a teacher. For the purpose of providing a balance between visual and verbal modes we have categorized them across four dimensions, which often overlap. These dimensions are:

VISUAL MANIPULATIVE (VM in unit narrative)
VISUAL ARTISTIC (VA in unit narrative)
VERBAL ORAL (VO in unit narrative)
VERBAL WRITTEN (VW in unit narrative)

To help locate specific responses, we have also numbered them within this four-part organization.

VISUAL MANIPULATIVE (VM)

1.   **ACCORDION BOOK:** This book is made from a long strip of heavy paper, folded, accordion fashion, to make the pages for the book. The events of the tale are placed in order on each folded page. When the book is completed, it can be folded, then gently pulled apart.

2.   **ACTION MAP:** Have students map the actions in a story by listing action sequences on charts or overlays. Pictures may be drawn to accompany the labeled actions later. (Example: see actions listed on page 109 from "Polyphemus.")

3.   **BOARD GAME:** Using poster board, children may create their own board games. The usual format is to have a set of squares meandering over the face of the board, with the first square on the left side indicating a beginning point for the player and the last square on the right as the end of the game. Along the way, there are bits of advice and tasks for the player whose token lands on various squares. There may be cards to draw upon landing on a certain square. The cards may be the source for moving forward or moving back, and these moves may be determined by how a child answers a question on the card. Content, story structure, skills, and strategies may be reviewed or practiced with the cards. If children have not played many board games, teachers will need to have some games available and play them several times before expecting children to make their own.

4.   **CAUSE AND EFFECT STORY FRAME:** Prepare a frame on a chart, overlay, or on individual worksheets for the students.
     Causes and effects in the story will be remembered and listed in this manner:

CAUSE:	EFFECT:
(SPECIFIC EVENT)	(SPECIFIC RESULT)

     This activity is more effective if done as a group immediately following the reading of a story.

5.   **CHALK, TALK, AND WALK:** By using this strategy, the teacher is able to reach those children who learn best by seeing (chalk), hearing (talk), and doing (walk). The activity should provide for the content to be shown visually or auditorially in some way, and then to provide an opportunity for children to physically experience the content. For example, when children write, they are chalking; when they speak about a story, they are obviously talking; and when they act out a role or have a physical activity, they are walking. An example is found on p. 77 in "James and the Vine Puller."

6.   **CHARACTER ATTRIBUTE CHART:** The purpose of this response is to give the children an opportunity to identify and place on a visual the personality traits, actions, and behaviors of the characters found in a story. The chart can consist of one character, or a listing of two or more characters, eliciting their attributes, and a final column comparing characters. List the attributes at the top of the chart (in columns) and the names of the characters down the left side. (See examples, "Five Queer Brothers" p. 53 and "The Tailor and the Giant" p. 62)

7.   **CHARACTER AND PLOT CHART:** Discuss with students the characterization, i.e., growth of the characters who are either static (staying the same) or dynamic (growing); and the descriptions of characters, i.e., flat (stereotyped) or

round (well-developed). Prepare a chart with "Characterization," "Problem," and "Solution" on the top columns. Down the left side list the names of the major characters. Prepare column designations. Elicit brief statements describing the growth and description of each character, the problem each faced, and how the character solved the conflict. (See example chart, "Thumbling," *Overcoming Odds Unit*, p. 68).

8. **CLASSROOM READING SHIP:** Using a cardboard refrigerator box, cut and form the sides of a ship. Place pillows inside on the floor and allow reading in the ship as an earned privilege. The building of the ship could be a class project, or the shell could be built by the teacher and then students could research and paint the outside to resemble the ship of a given era.

9. **CLUSTER:** This visual organizer elicits students' prior knowledge about a particular topic. The name of the topic is placed in the center, and the descriptions of the topic are clustered together around the topic.

10. **FILE FOLDER GAMES:** These games are made by the teacher to reinforce concepts or strategies previously taught. The games are made on file folders and may be laminated for durability. A pocket attached to the outside cover will hold dice, cards, playing pieces, or whatever is needed for the game. (See Board Games for more ideas.)

11. **FLANNEL BOARD and OBJECTS:** A board is covered with flannel or felt material and used as a background for flannel or felt objects (pieces of fabric, pellon, light-weight paper) that are cut to represent characters or the setting of the story. The story may be told to the children using the flannel board. Later, it may be placed in a learning center for children to manipulate independently or in small groups as they retell the story.

12. **HERO/HEROINE BULLETIN BOARD:** This bulletin board may remain in the class throughout the year reflecting characters from various ages and genres. Students will decide who has a place on the board through various procedures. (See **VO 64 Credentialing Process** p. 180).

13. **HOOK 'N LOOP BOARD:** Have children prepare artwork representing the tale or verse on squares of pellon, felt, or sandpaper. They may use water-based paints, markers, or crayons. Glue velcro squares or circles on the artwork. Prepare a board with felt or pellon backgrounds and matching velcro squares. Have the children place their visuals in the appropriate order of narrative. Later the artwork can be used for other sequencing games.

14. **KNOW, WANT TO KNOW, HAVE LEARNED (K.W.L.):** The purpose of this visual organizer is to determine what students know about a subject, what they would like to find out, and finally, what they learned. It is often used to begin the study of a literary selection, topic, or unit and can be used with any of the units in this book. The organizer has three columns, "What I Know," "What I Want to Learn," and "What I Learned." Students chart under the "Know" everything they know about the subject during a brainstorming session. Then they begin listing what they "Want" to know in the second column. After the study is completed they

go back to the chart and list what they have learned and look at their "Want to Know" list to evaluate their progress.

15. **LITERARY CIRCLE:** The purpose of this response is to give the children an opportunity to identify the events in a tale or verse. Prepare a large circle on a chart or background, e.g., oil cloth, felt, etc. Place each incident on a separate visual (appropriate to the background), and place the incident in sequential order clockwise around the circle, beginning at the top and returning to the top for the conclusion of the literary selection.

16. **LITERARY LADDER:** This is a visual representing the characteristics (attributes) of folk literature in general or a specific subgenre. Put the name of the genre or subgenre on top of the ladder. On strips of poster board (or other lightweight cardboard) write attributes (characteristics) of the genre or subgenre the children have observed while reading, hearing, or seeing several tales and verses. Attach the strips to the ladder with pipe cleaner, yarn, etc. Appendix B contains descriptions of each subgenre. **ALTERNATIVE:** Write attributes on a chart shaped like a castle or other content found in the tales and verses that the children are comparing.

17. **MIRROR CARDS:** Students should try to mirror the important points in the story. Have each student write five points on index cards. Let the group negotiate until only five major points remain. At that time, they will share both their five points and their reasons for them being the most important. Try to have the class agree on the five most important points.

18. **MOTIF COMPARISON CHART:** Students or adult should identify motifs (smallest recognizable element existing independently as a complete story), such as transformation, magic objects, marvels, other world journeys, wise and unwise conduct, cleverness, reversal of fortune, rewards and punishments, etc. After the motifs are identified in two or more tales, have the students compare and contrast them. Record responses on a chart. Place motifs down the left side of the chart. List titles of tales or poems at the top of the column. See "Cinderella" stories, p. 35.

19. **PICTURE STORY CIRCLE:** Divide the class into the number of groups representing the number of incidents. Each group selects one event. The group should sketch the action in the incident on the paper and write a brief description of the event. When the groups are finished, the sketches will be placed in the proper story sequence on a large paper circle. Place the title on the circle and display it on the literary bulletin board.

20. **POP-UP-BOOK (STORIES):** This is a form of book binding. Using a file folder, cut a slit across the fold 1/2 inch by three inches. Push the cut slit inside out so that it protrudes on the inside of the folder. Then pictures of characters, objects, settings, or actions may be attached to the slit. The folders may be displayed to tell parts of the story. To close the file folder for storage, fold the item attached to the slit.

21. **POSTER BOARD REPLICAS:** Using poster board, cut out replicas of characters, paint or color them, and add magnetic tape to the backs for displaying on the

chalkboard. These replicas may also be manipulated by the students to retell the story from the chalkboard.

22. **PREDICTION CHART:** Prepare a chart with two columns at the top, "What I Think Will Happen" and "What Actually Happened." Before reading, place major events down the side of the chart, and allow the children to predict what will happen. After reading actual events, record what happened.

23. **PREDICTION PITCHER:** Use a plastic water pitcher as a container for the students' written predictions. Making predictions adds to the mystery and excitement of the tales.

24. **PUN FUN:** A picture album that contains puns. Encourage students to read and add to it. Place it on a table for independent use.

25. **REAL AND ENCHANTMENT CHART:** On the left side of the chart list major events, elicited from children. At the top of a chart label one column "Real" and another "Enchantment." Separate the columns and events. Ask children to identify real and make-believe incidents and check responses in appropriate cells (columns) on the chart. If applicable, notations could be included in the cells. See "Uraschimataro and the Turtle" (Enchantment, p. 131).

26. **SEMANTIC MAP:** This graphic represents vocabulary found in the selection. The map provides students with an opportunity to elicit their prior information about the vocabulary. The map can be started when the selection is introduced and continued throughout the reading of the selection. For example, when using a phrase, such as "big as a thumb," write the phrase on the chalkboard and brainstorm other ideas related to size, phrases, and other words that might enhance the understanding of the story. All terms should be written around the central thought as a semantic network. See "Thumbling," p. 66.

27. **SENTENCE STRIPS:** Tagboard strips are cut and prepared for distribution to students who should write questions or probes about the theme, plot, or characters in the tale. The strips may be used for sequencing plot, to elicit responses from others, or for display on a thematic bulletin board.

28. **SHOW-ME CARDS:** These cards are made by cutting one sheet of construction paper in half across the short side. Fold up one half inch on the long side and staple each side. A show-me card will provide a pocket for showing or displaying words, numbers, or pictures. See "The Elves and the Shoemaker," p. 24.

29. **STORYBOX:** This visual aid is used for retelling stories. The events of the story are drawn on a long strip of paper or sheets taped together. The top of the first page is taped to a dowel and the end of the bottom page is attached to another dowel. The dowels form rollers that are inserted into holes in a cardboard box. Cut a square from the cardboard box to show the pictures.

30. **STORYTELLING BONE:** This prop is used to encourage storytelling among the children. Build the bone with papier-mâché over a wire base shaped like a large bone. Make it large enough to paint symbols of several stories on it. It will later be passed around the storytelling circle for tellers to hold while telling a story. Example: "The Bear Says North," p. 42.

31. **STORYTELLING HAT:** A hat may be used to designate storytelling time. Sometimes storytellers will attach objects to strings and hang them from the hat. Children may select an object about which a story will be told.

32. **TALE-A-TIMELINE:** In groups have the children sequence the tale and sketch incidents on several sheets of continuous fold computer paper. Title the timeline, laminate it, and display it in the hall, pod, or school media center.

33. **VENN DIAGRAM:** This visual graphic is used for comparisons. Two circles overlay each other. The independent sections of each circle represent how the two ideas or objects to be compared are different. The overlapping sections represent ways they are alike.

34. **WORD WALL:** The purpose of the word wall is to visually saturate children with interesting or unusual language found in the tale or verse. The words are written on a chart or a sheet of paper. The paper is given to the student who can pronounce (or define or use in a sentence, etc.) the words. Then the visual is placed on a wall (that might be in the shape of something related to the tale). Place the word wall in a central location of the classroom. The title of the tale is placed at the top of the wall.

35. **WORDLESS TEXT:** This is a picture book that tells a story without words. These books promote oral language, logical sequencing, and critical thinking as children organize thoughts and genuinely view visual information. Children "read" the visuals to interpret the narrative. After reading many wordless texts, have the children make an original wordless text. When children draw their own wordless texts in cooperative groups, talking, thinking, and planning occur. For young children, teachers may have to structure this experience with whole group discussion and planning, but for second and third graders who are accustomed to working in cooperative groups, the task may be completed with minimal teacher direction.

VISUAL ARTISTIC (VA)

36. **BANNER:** Cut a piece of Kraft Paper or burlap material 12" x 24". Fringe the bottom of the material. Place the material on a hanger or dowel rod (with a string for hanging). Attach visuals representing the folk literature selection, to celebrate, to alert, or to inform. These banners may also be made with computers and appropriate software.

37. **CRAYON ETCHING:** This art technique is done by drawing a scene with heavy crayon and then painting the entire page with black or blue tempera paint. The paint adheres to the unwaxed portion of the picture and makes a background for the drawing.

38. **DIORAMA:** Objects are placed inside a box to represent, in a three-dimensional visual perspective, a particular scene portrayed in a literary selection.

39. **DIORAMA—CHECKBOOK BOX:** This diorama is made from the box in which checkbooks are mailed to bank customers. By covering them with contact or construction paper, they may be decorated to represent parts or a whole story.

They are particularly popular for stories that have beds, such as Goldilock's bed or Red Riding Hood's Grandmother's bed.

40. **ENCHANTED CREATURES:** Let students design and make enchanted creatures from paper, feathers, material, sequins, or whatever might make them enchanted, but not realistic. The creatures may have the partial shape of real animals, birds, or humans, but with obvious changes to make them enchanted. If children know how, they can make the creatures using origami.

41. **GOLDEN LOVE BOX:** This is a small empty box wrapped in golden paper. Attach a poem about friendship and love to the box.

42. **GOLDEN SCRATCHBOARD:** Color the entire background of a picture with a heavy layer of gold crayon. Paint over it with tempera paints with blue at the top, green at the bottom, and various colors in between. When the paint is dry, scratch a design with a toothpick or sharp pointed object. The design will show golden edges as an outline.

43. **MIND'S EYE IMAGES:** When students hear a story without illustrations they will create a picture of the character and the events in their mind's eye. These pictures may be sketched, drawn, or otherwise illustrated and shared among the class. Impressions will be varied and through sharing, students may become aware of parts of the story that were not clear to them.

44. **MOBILES:** Provide appropriate materials for a mobile, e.g., paper, felt, net, fishing cord, yarn or dental floss, and sticks or hangers. Direct children to write the title of the tale and attach it to the top of the mobile. Complete the mobile by attaching other story incidents to the title. ALTERNATIVE: Have children select a favorite character from the tale. Direct them to make a silhouette (by cutting, drawing, sketching, etc.) of the character and attach to the title on the mobile. Other characters may be constructed and attached to the silhouette of the favorite character to complete the mobile.

45. **POTATO PRINTING:** Cut a potato in half and carve a design with a blunt knife. The design on the potato is then dipped into a shallow dish or tray containing tempera paint. The potato is then placed against a sheet of paper and the design will be "printed." Negative or positive designs are possible depending on whether the design is dug out of the potato or the background is carved out, leaving the design protruding.

46. **REALIA:** A collection of real objects representing elements, objects, and characters found in a selection. They are displayed for the purpose of creating interest prior to the reading of the selection. The display and materials may be expanded by the children after the initial reading.

47. **SCRATCHBOARD TECHNIQUE:** This artistic technique is similar to etching. The entire paper is colored with heavy crayon. Then, the drawing paper is covered with smooth layers of paint. When the paint is dry, the top layer is scraped with a sharp instrument. The underneath layer is exposed to form a picture related to the story.

48. **SKETCH AN IDEA:** After listening to a story, students should sketch an idea or character from the story and share with members of a small group. Discussion will

occur as each student receives feedback on how his or her perceptions are aligned with those of the other students. Various media—pencils, colored pencils, markers, charcoal, etc.—may be used.

49. **SHADOW BOX:** This is a three-dimensional visual presentation of a particular scene from a selection. The visual is placed inside a box (with a removable lid). The inside of the box is painted to represent the background of the selected scene. Objects are arranged in front of the scene. Paper, sticks, or sand may be used for the three-dimensional perspective. Most of the box lid is cut away and replaced with a colored cellophane paper. The lid is placed on the box and the viewer can look down into the box. Also, a small peep hole can be placed at one end of the box and a viewer can look into the hole. There are alternate ways to get the light into the box, such as a flashlight. Innovation is the key to this strategy.

50. **STORY QUILT:** Give students 9″ x 9″ squares of muslin cloth. Have the students draw, with fabric markers, favorite scenes from a tale. The title of the tale and the students' names should be included on the squares. The squares should be sewn together, lined with another piece of cloth, and quilted as desired. A bright border would make the quilt attractive.

51. **WANTED POSTER:** Have students use the proper format to advertise for a missing person. Characters found in a particular selection will be used for the poster. ("Five Queer Brothers," p. 53.)

52. **VISUAL DISPLAY:** Reserve a place in the room where student art products related to folk literature may be displayed. A mural display behind the visuals will focus attention to them. Visuals may also be hung from the ceilings.

VERBAL ORAL (VO)

53. **BRAINSTORMING BOARD:** A tablet of newsprint is used to record ideas elicited from brainstorming. After completing the brainstorming session, remove paper and display it to be used later for oral or written language productions. Encourage partners, triads, and/or small groups to use boards when they are interpreting selections and planning personal language productions.

54. **BUDDY BUZZ:** When children talk together in pairs at a designated time, it is called "buddy buzz." The "buddies" should be predetermined, so that as soon as the signal is given for talking quietly (buzzing), they may begin. Sometimes a question may be given for buddies to talk about, but often the time is unstructured for free responses.

55. **CHAIN-THE-TALE:** Group students to prepare a role play of (or orally retell) a specified incident. A student or teacher will begin the tale, holding a long rope or thick yarn. When he or she stops telling the tale, the students who are responsible for role playing the next incident of the tale will present the event, holding on to the rope. Each group continues in the same manner. The audience will decide if the groups presented the incidents in the proper sequence. The strategy can be repeated with different participants.

56. **CHARACTER-BUT-THEN-SO FRAME:** This technique for replicating stories allows students to see the character's initiative, followed by a problem (but), followed by a solution (then), followed by a resolution (so). For example, The man (character) wanted to marry the girl,(but) her family was so silly that he wanted to find people sillier than they were. (Then) he searched and found three sillies who were sillier than his girlfriend and her family, and (so) he came back and they were married.

57. **CHARACTER REPORT CARD:** Determine criteria for giving grades and give story characters a report card. For example, Red Riding Hood might be graded on critical thinking and bravery. Criteria for critical thinking might be listed as:

   1) asks questions to determine real identities
   2) listens to the voice to determine if it is an imposter
   3) asks questions but does not sense danger
   4) accepts what she is told without question

   The grading scale could be:

   1) A   3) C
   2) B   4) D and she may get eaten!

58. **CHARACTER TAG:** A 6" x 6" poster board name tag made with a ribbon hanger designates a character in a story. Each tag is given to a separate child who wears the tag around his or her neck. Various activities may follow as children portray their characters.

59. **CHORALLY READ:** Teacher and students read aloud together. Sometimes they will be reading from an overlay on an overhead projector, or they may be reading from multiple texts or big books.

60. **CLEVEREST CHARACTER CONTEST:** Students may nominate and then vote on a character who is the cleverest among folk story characters. Criteria for "cleverness" should be developed by the students. Some possible criteria include:
   outsmarted others
   had answers to riddles and questions
   was considered smart and clever
   had unusual answers (See "Clever Manka," p. 168.)

61. **COMMUNICATION CIRCLES:** In these circles, students may express any feelings or thoughts as long as they follow these rules:

   1) Everyone contributes to the discussion.
   2) What is said is honest (thought to be true) and fair.
   3) What is said is connected in some way to what was previously said.
   4) Participants respect each other's rights and speak one at a time.

62. **COMPARE THE VARIANTS:** Have students locate different variants of a tale and compare them with the tale presented. The comparisons should focus on similarities and differences in plot development, characters, names of characters, events, behavior of characters, conclusion, language used, and settings.

63. **COOPERATIVE READING ACTIVITY (C.R.A.):** In this activity, the teacher prepares a copy of the story. Then the story is cut apart and given to groups of children to read aloud to the class. After each section is read, the class will place the sections in proper sequence of the story. After the sequence has been determined, the story should be reread aloud.

64. **CREDENTIALING PROCESS:** When a student wishes to nominate a hero or heroine from folklore, he or she must gather evidence that the character meets given criteria. Once the evidence is gathered it may be presented to the class, and a vote will take place to decide if the person is to be placed on the Hero/Heroine Bulletin Board. Additional discussion, listing of criteria and voting will be necessary for determining whether the candidate is a "likely" or "unlikely" hero or heroine.

65. **DRAMATIZING ACTION WORDS:** Have children act out the meaning of the words. For example, in "The Billy Goats Gruff" story, children may not understand the meaning of "tripping" and "tramping" until they see someone demonstrating the actions for those words.

66. **EVERY PUPIL RESPONSE (EPR):** With this activity, every child has a responsibility and upon signals from the teacher will respond. Although children are responding collectively, the type of EPR will allow the teacher to recognize individual progress. Some typical EPRs are:
   - children hold thumbs up or thumbs down on a given signal in response to a question (thumbs up is "yes"; thumbs down is "no")
   - smiley or frowny face circles on tongue depressors to indicate perception of feelings
   - slates or cards on which answers may be written and displayed at appropriate times.

67. **FOLK LITERATURE TREASURE HUNT:** Have the students look for different variants of the same tale. Consult the media specialist for assistance. Share the variants with others in the class.

68. **IMAGINARY CAMPFIRE:** Make a safe, but inviting campfire in the classroom using these simple props: a basket with a tall handle, a flashlight, and a yellow plastic garbage can liner. Place the flashlight inside the basket and turn the liner over the basket handle and down around the basket. Crunch it a little. When the light is on and the room is darkened slightly, the basket appears to be a campfire.

69. **JEST FOR FUN:** This event should be planned several days before it occurs. Students will know that at this "jest" event, they will be able to tell funny stories about each other. Rules need to be strictly developed and enforced to prevent hurt feelings or embarrassment.

70. **LISTENING POST:** A cassette recorder connected to a set of several headphones provides the technology for a listening post. A sign hanging over the center, perhaps displaying a picture of ears, will indicate the purpose of this area to children. Stories, poems, riddles, and rhymes may be prerecorded for children's independent listening. Children may also record their own pieces of literature,

either those found in books or those composed by themselves. The text of each piece should be available for listeners to read along as they listen.

71. **LITERARY COOPERATIVE GROUPS:** Small groups of students are formed to respond to or interpret a literary selection previously read by the group. The group may prepare a **creation** to represent their response or interpretation of a literary work. The group may decide on an appropriate visual or verbal approach to introduce a literary selection to another group.

72. **PROBES:** Probes invite children to share their personal "transactions" to the tale showing children that their personal reactions are valued by the adult. (See chapter two.) Probes usually elicit open-ended responses to the content or literary elements, i.e., plot, characterization, setting, theme, or literary form portrayed in a selection. Probes elicit **inferential involvement,** and when applicable, **evaluative** in-depth understandings of the text. Literal (factual) questions are used if it is apparent that the children do not understand concepts, information, or the author's use of literary elements in the tale or verse. By using **probes** frequently in literary discussion groups, students develop a template for thinking about stories.

73. **READERS' THEATER SCRIPT:** Have two or more readers orally present a literary selection. A dramatic script should be developed directly from a selection. The script is then read by a narrator and other readers who assume the role of various characters found in the selection.

74. **ROLE PLAY:** Students assume the role of a character and improvise their actions in a particular situation. The students use their own words to express the feelings of characters (while being "in character" and consistent with the original story), but without memorizing any lines from the story.

75. **ROUND TABLE DISCUSSION:** Students form circles or sit around a table, maintaining eye contact with everyone. A topic is opened for discussion and students go around the table expressing their views or presenting information. The discussion may be continued for as long as new information or valuable interactions are present.

76. **SAY WHAT I SAW:** After drawing pictures of a story, other children in the small group describe the pictures drawn by their peers. In doing so, children are "saying what others have seen."

77. **SHADOWTALE:** With two students playing each role, one paraphrases the text, and immediately following the words from the paraphrase, the other person playing the same role "shadows" by saying what the character may have been *really* thinking.

78. **STORYTELLING FESTIVAL:** Students learn the fundamentals of the art of storytelling and plan an afternoon or a Saturday event for telling stories to families, friends, or another class or grade level.

79. **SURVEY:** Under the guidance of a teacher, the children develop a list of questions to ask a group of people. They decide what questions to ask and whom they should ask. They also decide how to record the answers. Have them bring all responses back to class for a composite view of the responses. The responses may be charted or graphed for visual information.

80. **THEME CARDS:** These are cards on which underlying themes from stories may be written. The cards may be displayed for total class discussion of how the theme is shown in the story, or groups of students may receive individual cards for discussion and later group sharing.

81. **THINK ALOUD:** This technique is based on showing children how adults solve problems. Teachers verbalize what they think about as they approach a problem (meaning of character's action or implied meaning of language) and how they find a solution to the problem.

82. **THOUGHT-SPLASHING:** Thoughts are splashed into a pool of acceptance as students allow their minds to run freely with imaginative ideas. Thought-splashing with older students may occur as they individually draft their thoughts for a few minutes and then share them orally; with younger students, the entire process may be in oral form.

VERBAL WRITTEN (VW)

83. **CHARACTER CONTINUUM:** Character traits may be identified and clarified through placing a character on continuum of various dichotomies. Some contrasts for exploration include:

X	X
SMART	DULL

X	X
OPTIMISTIC	PESSIMISTIC

84. **CHARACTER WEBS:** Place the name of the character in the center of the paper within a circle. Draw lines encircling the center, spider web fashion, as students volunteer information on the character being webbed. For example, on the first layer of the web describe the character; the second layer might refer to the character's actions and the third layer to the emotions and integrity of the character.

85. **COMPARISON CHART:** On a chart or chalkboard, compare literary subgenres, elements, or content. Place titles of selections on the top and the comparison items are written down the side. Checks can be used to indicate similarities of content within each title.

86. **COPY CAT WRITING:** Compose another line, story, song, or poem, with just a few changes in words or rhythm.

87. **DESCRIPTIVE NAME TAGS:** Have students create a new name for an object or persons in a selection based on specific characteristics. This activity may originate with a study of Native Americans whose names were often descriptive, such as "Sitting Bull" or "Running Bear." Students should write the name on their name tag and illustrate it. Students could write a statement supporting the justification of their name choice. Students must be sensitive, select positive names, and avoid using stereotypical names.

88. **FAX-THE-FACTS:** Have student "send" faxes from one group of children to another. Each fax represents one incident. The fax will expand information about a tale or subgenre. Future predictions could be written at the conclusion of the tale. The faxes could be placed in a binder and placed with a copy of the tale in the media center.

89. **HAIKON:** This Japanese verse form follows the same rules as Haiku: three lines, 5-7-5 syllable counts, and is based on nature. Haikon is drawn around a picture that describes the content of the verse.

90. **HAIKU:** Traditional Japanese poetry about nature. The verses are written in 17 syllables and three lines, i.e., line one contains 5 syllables; line two, 7 syllables; and line three, 5 syllables.

91. **HERO/HEROINE CRITERIA:** Students will list what makes a hero or heroine. Their lists will be different based on their ages and their perceptions of the concept. Allow for consensus building, perhaps by voting, if there are conflicts on the criteria. Then write a **character sketch** for each hero or heroine.

92. **LITERATURE RESPONSE LOG (LIT LOG):** Students write their structured or spontaneous reflections or reactions to a literary selection in a notebook or booklet. **Structured** writing is motivated by teacher-initiated probes. **Spontaneous** writing reflects the child's personal "transactions" to the text. (See chapter 2.) Students also record questions they have about the text or unusual or unknown language. A log is intended for a child to write to himself or herself as the sole audience. Although teachers often read the logs as a way of evaluating the impact a story has on a child, the logs are not graded.

93. **MAGAZINE STORY:** Students should study, compare, and contrast content, format, and organization of magazine articles. Then have them write a magazine story about an event in the literary selection or write an original event predicting what happened at the conclusion of the selection.

94. **MODERN ADAPTATION:** Students adapt an old story with modern language and actions. The story may be presented in written or dramatized form to other students.

95. **NEWS REPORT:** News items will be studied, compared, and contrasted to determine the content, style of writing, and format used by news reporters. Students then write news reports related to a particular literary selection. The report may become a part of a newspaper devoted to a particular selection, unit, or topic.

96. **PARTNER JOURNAL:** Two students write a journal. The students write reflections, ideas, and questions to a partner. The other partner replies and adds personal comments.

97. **PLAY-IT-AGAIN SCRIPT:** Photocopy the tale and give it to the students. Have them look at each incident and characters, then modify some or all of the text and rewrite it. The students could be instructed to keep certain elements of the tale intact, e.g., the theme, major characters, etc., or the tale can be completely different. Then write the incidents in script format and present them orally to others.

98. **SENRYU:** Japanese poetry that uses 17 syllables like Haiku, but the content of the verse is not limited to nature. The verses may be about any *single* idea the author desires to express. The 17 syllables are divided into three lines, line one, 5 syllables; line two, 7 syllables; and line three, 5 syllables.

99. **SUBGENRE COMMERCIAL:** The purpose of this response is to write and present an enticing commercial to convince others that they should read a particular tale or verse from a given subgenre. Visuals or props would be helpful. Students may be encouraged to be extremely creative, "wild," or outlandish in the content of their commercials, as long as the focus is on "selling" the selection. (See appendix B.)

100. **TANKA:** This Japanese verse form is about nature and the seasons of the year. It is divided into 31 syllables divided into five lines containing 5-7-5-7-7 syllables in each of the five lines.

101. **TRAVELOGUE:** This response product may be written or drawn and may include geographical notes on where the character traveled; whom he or she met; and what adventures he or she had; tourist attractions along the way; and his or her recommendations for inns, restaurants, and side trips.

102. **WHAT IF? INCIDENTS:** Students should replace one important event in a plot, and imagine another compatible event. In groups or pairs they may discuss what might happen if the event was replaced with the second one. Individually or in groups they write and share predictions with others. The predictions may be compared and discussed for consistency of other events and character behavior.

103. **WRITE CONVERSATIONS BETWEEN CHARACTERS:** Have students write conversations that could transpire between characters in a selection. The ideas and dialogue must be authentic to the individual characters. Students should be grouped to represent the number of characters involved in the selected incident.

104. **WRITERS' WORKSHOP:** This is a block of time designated daily for "authoring" self-selected pieces of work. During the workshop, students write, draft, edit, proofread, and share works from various styles and genres.

APPENDIX B

❊ ❊ ❊ ❊ ❊ ❊ ❊ ❊

Subgenres of Folk Literature

Folklorists representing different disciplines have studied folk literature for diverse reasons and with their own particular methods of analysis. Their positions have produced differences, not only in definitions of subgenres, but in examples of stories that represent various types of folk literature. The tales blend together easily, and it is common for one story to resemble a fairy tale while another version, a variant of the same tale, may have characteristics of myths or animal tales. For this reason, we have accepted the conclusion that a strict division of the various selections is almost impossible.

Even with the ambiguities of precise classifications and descriptions of folk literature, we have identified the basic characteristics of 15 subgenres that appear to be generally accepted by the various disciplines interested in folklore.[1]

Folk literature subgenres may be clustered in poetry or prose classifications representing the literary form in which they were originally produced. In this appendix, we will discuss five subgenres typically found in poetry form: 1) nursery rhymes; 2) childhood rhymes; 3) ballads; 4) folk songs; and 5) epics. Ten prose narrative subgenres will be classified under the broad rubric of "folktales": 1) myths; 2) legends, including 3) tall tales; and tales which include 4) folktales, 5) fairy tales, and 6) novelle; 7) jests, schwanks, and humorous anecdotes; and animal tales including 8) explanatory tales, 9) trickster tales, and 10) fables.

Since many tales and verses from folk literature were composed by unknown authors centuries ago and were transformed with each telling by the culture, the setting, and the experiences of the audience, we believe that it is important for teachers and librarians to be knowledgeable about the background of the literature. In this section we present a chart for each subgenre. Included in the chart is a "definition" of the subgenre; a column listing "language," denoting linguistic characteristics of the subgenre; a "story" column providing information of the structure and literary elements of the type of literature; and the last column, "context," providing information on the origin of the subgenre and some of its uses and audiences—past and present.

The information in this section is meant primarily for the adult, but it is hoped that it might also be used by students in some cases. For example, the charts can be used for reference when introducing a subgenre to students. The charts also provide information for the students as they become familiar with the structures of various subgenres and begin to compare and contrast the different categories and variants of folk literature. Although there are typical ages for which interest peaks in various genres, students continue to enjoy the literary study of a subgenre or several variants of the same tale long after the initial interest in the tales and verses have passed. For such activities, the background information provided in this section may be used by students and teachers.

Poetry Forms in Folk Literature

NURSERY RHYMES

Nursery rhymes are short traditional verses represented by lullabies, rhymes, and memory games adults sing or play with children primarily for entertainment.[2]

LANGUAGE	STORY	CONTEXT
Characteristics:	**Characters:**	**Origins:**
■ chants	■ animate and inanimate	■ many appeared in early
■ dialogue	■ real and fantastic	inexpensive books,
■ may be nonsensical	**Plots:**	accessible to ordinary
■ riddles	■ childlike experiences	"folk"

LANGUAGE (continued)	STORY (continued)	CONTEXT (continued)
Characteristics:	**Characters:**	**Origins:**
■ simple, short, narrative poetic form ■ tongue-twisters ■ use of rhymes, rhythm, repetition, alliteration	■ common and fantastic happenings ■ loving care **Setting:** ■ in palaces ■ some set in common, everyday places	■ often classified as "Mother Goose" ■ some from old hymns, ballads, or prayers ■ some represent political satire **Uses/Audiences:** ■ encourage physical movement ■ manipulate language ■ mothers croon lullabies to infants and toddlers ■ playful attention to young ones ■ some used to teach manners and proper behavior ■ some used to "teach" secular topics ■ stored in memory and passed to next generation ■ used for language purposes; rhyming, repetition, poetry ■ usually a child's initial exposure to literature

EXAMPLES:
Rock-a-bye Baby (Lullaby)
Now I Lay Me Down to Sleep (Prayer)
Little Nancy Etticoat (Riddle)
This Little Piggy (Physical Activity)
A Diller, A Dollar (Mother Goose)
One, Two, Buckle My Shoe (Teaching chant)

CHILDHOOD RHYMES

Childhood rhymes are sidewalk and jump-rope chants, riddles, tongue-twisters, and witty verses children sing and say to each other through childhood. The rhymes are similar to nursery rhymes, but are transmitted from child to child, rather than from adult to child.

LANGUAGE	STORY	CONTEXT
Characteristics:	**Characters:**	**Origins:**
■ chants	■ children	■ many are centuries old
■ easy to remember	■ ridiculed adults	■ recited by children to
■ may be nonsensical	**Plots:**	children
■ riddles	■ chants	**Uses/Audiences:**
■ short poetic form	■ games	■ accompany games
■ tongue-twisters	■ jokes	■ fun with language
■ use of rhymes, rhythm,	■ riddles	■ meant solely for the
repetition, alliteration	■ usually not apparent	ears of children
	Setting:	■ used as challenges
	■ timeless	from one child to
	■ unknown	another
Examples:		
Step on a Crack (Break Your Mother's Back) (Chant)		
I Am a ( ) Key (Game)		
One Potato, Two Potatoes (Choosing Chant)		
How Much Wood Would a Woodchuck Chuck? (Tongue-twister)		
Cinderella, Dressed in Yellow (Jump-rope rhyme)		

BALLADS

Ballads are narrative songs, more concerned with the story than the lyrics or the music. The songs are meant to be sung and are often accompanied with instrumental music.[3] "Folk Ballads" were transmitted orally, e.g., traditional hunting, working, and marching songs, carols, chants, spirituals, and serenades.

LANGUAGE	STORY	CONTEXT
Characteristics:	**Characters:**	**Origins:**
■ dialogue	■ real world	■ "Folk Ballads"
■ meanings of words are	**Characters:**	transmitted orally:
vital	■ "folk" heroes	traditional hunting,
■ narrative	■ not well developed	working, marching
■ repetition and refrains	■ represent historical	songs, carols,
often included	periods, societal	chants, spirituals,
■ tone is objective and	patriotism and values	serenades
impersonal	**Plots:**	■ "Literary Ballads"
■ verses contain	■ assume audience	originated in written
couplets, four-line	knows hero and some	form:
stanzas or quatrains	adventures	
	■ dramatic	

STORY (continued)	CONTEXT (continued)

Characters:
■ focus on a single event in life of well-known personality
■ full of action
■ story may begin in the middle of an event
	Origins:
	  composed by literary-conscious poets
	  influenced by "folk ballads"[4]
	  by 16th century preserved in "broadsides" or "chapbooks"
	■ originally meant to entertain adults, thus adult themes, content included
	■ product of Middle Ages
	Uses/Audiences:
	■ adventures have universal appeal for students over 8 years
	■ found in all levels of society, but taken over by "folk"
	■ meant for entertainment
	■ performed by semi- and professional performers
	■ represent communal form of expression
	■ songs trigger emotions and strong feelings

Examples of Ballads: Barbara Allen Robin Hood John Henry The Old Chisholm Trail Get Up and Bar the Door Sweet Betsy of Pike The Raggle, Taggle Gypsies	

FOLK SONGS

If the heritage of a people is found in its folklore, then the "soul of a people was expressed in their folk songs."[5] Folk songs are perpetuated by oral tradition and are more functional than ballads. They focus on the music and the lyrics rather than telling a story.

LANGUAGE	STORY	CONTEXT
Characteristics:	**Characters:**	**Origins:**
■ governed by recurrent contrasts of stress or length consistent from line to line	■ less important since lyrics stressed, not story	■ may have been written originally, but perpetuated orally, even today
■ lyrical	■ may be unknown	**Uses/Audiences:**
■ often rhythm and meter controlled by number of syllables	**Characters:** ■ daily life characters	■ enjoyed by all ages
■ repetitive refrains	■ flat and static	■ sung by all levels of society and every
■ short stanzas of 1 to 4 lines	■ represent daily tasks or work	country worldwide
	Plots:	■ used for entertainment
	■ represent incidents of daily experiences, sometimes physical or courage	■ used to make daily tasks more acceptable
	■ short episodes	
	■ underdeveloped	
Examples: Happy Birthday Sourwood Mountain Big Rock Candy Mountain Down in the Valley My Old Kentucky Home Suwanee River		

EPICS

One of the oldest forms of poetry, epics portray the heroic actions of historical or traditional persons in high positions. Epics represent historical development of a nation or culture. They portray a nation's conception of its past and its aspirations, and glorify and perpetuate ideals valued by a society. The word "epic" originally meant "oral" and reflects the early mode of performance.[6]

LANGUAGE	STORY	CONTEXT
Characteristics:	**Characters:**	**Origins:**
■ descriptive passages	■ broad in scope, in nations, world, or universe	■ eventually written by poets
■ grandiose language		■ material from ancient cultures, but not barbaric or savage societies
■ long greetings	■ real places	
■ may include lofty speeches by hero	■ set in ancient, unknown time	
■ sophisticated structure and expressions		

LANGUAGE (continued)	STORY (continued)	CONTEXT (continued)
Characteristics:	**Characters:**	**Origins:**
■ use of rhyme, alliteration, assonance, repetition	■ protagonists possess valor and superhuman courage	■ material originally sung or told
	■ segments of national hero's life	■ narratives preserved episodes perpetuating national pride
	Plots:	■ passed from one generation to another
	■ adult themes	**Uses/Audiences:**
	■ ends abruptly, without adequate conclusion	■ audience expected to know about hero's adventures
	■ flashbacks used	
	■ hero accomplishes impossible often with assistance of supernatural beings	■ early audiences, "folk" from all levels of society
	■ incidents begin in middle of event, usually tell only three events about hero's life	■ modern audiences, mature adolescents and adults interested in adventure tales
	■ long narrative poem shows hero's struggle over evil forces	
	■ violent events	

Examples:
Gilgamesh, 3,000 B.C. (Sumerian, believed to be first story ever written)[7]
Ramayana (India)
Beowulf (oldest English epic recorded A.D. 1000)
The Iliad, Odyssey (credited to Greek poet, Homer, several hundred years after Trojan
 War, around 1200 B.C.)
Milton's Paradise Lost
Spenser's Faerie Queene
Nibelungenlied (German)

Prose Narratives

Three major folklore prose narrative forms are myths, legends, and tales.[8]

MYTHS

Myths are defined as symbolic tales "presented as having actually occurred in a previous age, explaining the cosmological and supernatural traditions of a people, their gods, heroes, cultural traits and religious beliefs."[9]

LANGUAGE	STORY	CONTEXT
Characteristics: ■ limited use of dialogue ■ names of characters and setting changes from one culture to another ■ sophisticated language ■ symbolic and abstract terms rely on figurative language and imagery to portray mood, events, set in another world	**Characters:** ■ depends on culture or origin ■ often in regions inhabited by characters **Characters:** ■ deities, demons, and some humans ■ flat, static personalities ■ possess supernatural powers **Plots:** ■ complex, often pit humans against gods, gods against gods ■ incidents linked by characters ■ limited descriptions of events ■ severe punishments	**Origins:** ■ most cultures have myths to explain natural phenomena, origins, customs, or human relationships, i.e., mysteries of natural sciences, psychology, and religion ■ must have religious base, otherwise, are folktales ■ possibly oldest type of traditional tale **Uses/Audiences:** ■ because of gods' unusual names, religious overtones, and language used, many "creation myths" are above the linguistic, cognitive, and affective level of most children under 9 years ■ "pourquoi tales," explain natural happenings or characteristics of man or beast, understood and enjoyed by children 8 years and above ■ religion to some in past ■ studied today for literature and culture

Examples:
Midas and the Golden Touch (Greek myth)
Icarus and Daedalus (Greek myth)
How Thor Found His Hammer (Norse myth)
Why the Woodpecker Has a Red Head (pourquoi)

LEGENDS

Legends are prose narratives, told as truth, intermingled with traditional material, about a person, place, or incident.[10]

LANGUAGE	STORY	CONTEXT
Characteristics:	**Characters:**	**Origins:**
■ local legends told in unpolished "folk" talk of setting	■ definite time and place identified with real people or events	■ found all regions of world
■ narrated as true report from one who knows	■ feeling for time and passage of time	■ many oral transmissions, later written
■ told as if teller knows something "uncanny"	**Characters:**	■ Saint's Legends written by clergy
■ told as truth, sound believable	■ may be based on actual persons or composites of real people	■ same tale may exist as legend, tall tale, ballad, e.g., Robin Hood
	■ often heroes endowed with fictional traits and adventures	**Uses/Audiences:**
	■ Saint's Legends depict holy people of past	■ originally told to adults
	Plots:	■ primary age children enjoy simple re-tellings of hero adventures
	■ conflict often focuses on one event in protagonist's life or setting	■ some legends contain mature content, sophisticated literary style, and cultural ideals, enjoyed and understood by students 10 and above
	■ many adult themes	

Examples:
The Song of Roland (French Legend)
Bigfoot (Contemporary Legend)
Saint George and the Dragon (Saint's Legend)
Pied Piper of Hamlin (Saga)
Lover's Leap (Local Legend)
Dick Whittington (English Legend)

TALL TALES

Tall tales are exaggerated narratives, containing boisterous characters, humorous actions, and picturesque language. They are identified with early frontier life in America.[11]

LANGUAGE	STORY	CONTEXT
Characteristics: ■ language of "folks" ■ often racy and picturesque ■ use of hyperbole, exaggeration ■ vivid details and dramatic descriptions	**Characters:** ■ detailed with realism ■ set in specific regions **Characters:** ■ boisterous actions ■ likeable protagonist who performed "impossible" feats with ease ■ may be fictionalized or historical characters, animals ■ physical strength emphasized ■ sometimes inanimate objects **Plots:** ■ dramatic, action-packed adventures ■ themes of love, courting, working, or fighting the elements of nature ■ length and complexity vary	**Origins:** ■ fragments of hero deeds from other legends mixed with original yarns ■ late 19th-century tales written to glorify occupations ■ related to "lying tales" and anecdotes of cultural heroes **Uses/Audiences:** ■ enjoyed by children 7 and above ■ entertain with straight faces while telling biggest "whoppers" possible ■ "folks" enjoy telling and listening to tales

Examples of Tall Tale Characters:
Paul Bunyan
Pecos Bill
Captain Stormalong
Mike Fink
John Henry
Johnny Appleseed
Casey Jones
Slue-Foot Sue

FOLKTALES

In English, the term "folktale" is a broad one, referring to all prose narratives passed down through the ages in oral or written form.[12] Folktales are called the "cement of society" because they embody the historic wisdom, rituals, superstitions, mores, and beliefs of the ordinary folk in a society.[13]

LANGUAGE	STORY	CONTEXT
Characteristics:	**Characters:**	**Origins:**
■ formula beginnings and conclusions	■ timeless and unknown	■ from oral and written traditions with identifiable motifs and types
■ language of storyteller: cultural names dialogue figurative language repetition rich descriptions unique terms	■ usually not important **Characters:** ■ changelings ■ commoners and royalty meet often ■ contrasting qualities (very good/bad; smart/ dull)	■ most cultures have own variant of familiar tales ■ reflect values of early cultures **Uses/Audiences:** ■ allow acceptable outlet for expression of emotions
■ short refrains, predictable phrases might be included	■ limited development ■ often three, seven, or twelve characters ■ personified animals and objects ■ poor are good; wealthy are evil ■ supernatural or magical powers **Plots:** ■ begin quickly ■ logical, predictable incidents ■ move fast to a climax and predictable conclusion ■ poetic justice provides the good their rightful rewards ■ recognizable motifs ■ short narratives ■ simple, linear plot structure, no subplots ■ specify type of conflict ■ structure often based on three or seven events	■ enjoyed by 6 to 12 year olds ■ express typical human dreams, wishes, or fantasies ■ instruct values, mores, beliefs of a society ■ may reflect values, characters, magic unacceptable to some groups, but provide insight into human relations ■ originally intended for adult audiences, children listened ■ used for entertainment
Examples: Molly Whuppie Three Billy Goats Gruff Hansel and Gretel Jack and the Beanstalk		

FAIRY TALES (MÄRCHEN)

Fairy Tales ("Märchen," see note at end of chart) are "wonder tales," stories involving magical creatures and supernatural powers. These characters become involved in the day-to-day struggles of common people.

LANGUAGE	STORY	CONTEXT
Characteristics:	**Characters:**	**Origins:**
■ language of storyteller: dialogue formula beginnings and conclusions predictable phrases repetitive phrases and refrains unique terms	■ imaginary worlds inhabited by fantasy creatures	■ about peasant folks' lives, dreams, wishes and fears.[14]
	■ not bound by the real world	■ few from pure oral traditions; most from preserved texts
	■ vague and unnamed settings	■ origins not determined, believed some remnants from 13th century B.C.[15]
■ language refers to characters' actions	**Characters:**	
■ limited details and descriptions	■ characters unnamed, called "King,""Queen," "Ugly Sister," or "Beautiful Princess," etc.	■ wonder tales from the streets, alleys, fish markets, and country life
■ short, prose narratives	■ dwarfs, gnomes, ogres, brownies, rather than fairies	**Uses/Audiences:**
	■ flat, stereotyped, i.e., protagonists, humble; females, suffer silently; simpletons, compassionate; poor, good; rich, evil, etc.	■ collected to study and preserve early language (Grimms)
		■ compiled and adapted for children (Jacobs)
	■ poor people included, e.g., woodcutters, hunters, shepards, merchants, etc.	■ especially enjoyed by pre-school through primary grades, older students enjoy some tales
	■ usually three or seven major characters	■ secular entertainment
	Plots:	■ told to entertain royalty (Perrault)
	■ begin quickly, move rapidly to a climax and predictable conclusion	
	■ limited religious overtones, no moralizing	
	■ linear development, no subplots	

STORY (continued)
Characters: ■ often three or seven events ■ protagonist frequently assisted by supernatural to achieve goals ■ represent pure fantasy more than other folktales ■ succession of motifs

Examples of Fairy Tales:
The Elves and the Shoemaker
Toads and Diamonds
Cinderella
The Fisherman and His Wife
Snow White
The Water of Life
The Magic Pot

NOTE: In 1812 the Grimm Brothers adopted the term "märchen" (from old German, "mär" means a short story) for their scholarly publication, *Kinderund-und Hausmärchen* (Fairy Tales for Children and the Home). In 1823 the book was translated and published in English as *German Popular Tales*.[16] When the English attempted to translate the German "Märchen," there was no comparable term in their language, so they chose to use the term "fairy tales" (from the old French "fairie," for the supernatural creatures who inhabited the tales of old France). Thus, the märchen, the magic tale—the fairy tale—was labeled. Actually, only a small number of such stories have to do with fairies. In folk literature, fairies are often found in tales that relate real beliefs or traditions. Even so, the term "fairy tales" has in English become universally accepted for the body of wonder tales.[17]

NOVELLE

Novelle (singular: novella) are similar in structure to fairy tales and märchen, but the fantastic element plays a lesser role. Sometimes referred to as romantic tales, the stories are set in a real world and portray a definite setting.[18]

LANGUAGE	STORY	CONTEXT
Characteristics: ■ dialogue often witty, clever	**Characters:** ■ adventure or evil fate often takes characters far from home	**Origins:** ■ mostly dependent on literary sources

LANGUAGE (continued)	STORY (continued)	CONTEXT (continued)
Characteristics:	**Characters:**	**Origins:**
■ dwell on riddle-solving ability and witty replies to tricky questions to reach desired goal ■ shrewd characters involved in verbal sparring ■ straightforward, simple prose narrative	■ real places, often linked to history ■ time is usually definite **Characters:** ■ antagonists ruthless human character, represent human motives ■ city merchants and "folk" rather than royalty ■ emphasis on typical human qualities, i.e., wit, wisdom, cleverness, trickery, endurance, etc., rather than heroism ■ heroes do not seek luck beyond human limitations ■ protagonist fights evil in form of human antagonists ■ succeed without help from magical sources ■ two-dimensional development **Plots:** ■ magic or supernatural limited ■ motifs similar to other tales ■ romance, tragedy, humor highlighted ■ stories may be part of a series ■ themes are adventurous, pathetic, and sentimental	appeared in Persian and Arabic collections, biblical, Greco-Roman, and medieval romance literature ■ origin unknown, considered ancient, first published in early 18th century.[19] ■ reflects philosophy and religious ideals of Buddhism, Islam, Judaism, and Christianity **Uses/Audience:** ■ provide insight into ancient civilizations and values ■ tales require prior knowledge and interest in setting, adventure, religion, or romance naturally appeal to persons over 10 years of age, who find content interesting and enjoy particular type of riddle solving and witty replies found in these stories ■ used for entertainment

Examples:
The Arabian Nights (Folk Tales)
Rapunzel (Fairy Tale)
Clever Manka
Cap o' Rushes (Fairy Tale)

JESTS, SCHWANKS, AND ANECDOTES

Short, humorous stories told as truth, even when they are ridiculous, are classified as jests, schwanks, and anecdotes.[20]

LANGUAGE	STORY	CONTEXT
Characteristics:	**Characters:**	**Origins:**
■ anecdotes move freely from one place to another	■ could be any place or time	■ several thousand years old
■ brief narratives	■ often in teller's environment	■ transmitted orally
■ easy to remember and retell because of humor and simple anecdotes	**Characters:**	**Uses/Audiences:**
■ humorous one-liners	■ "numbskulls," "noodleheads," "simpletons," "morons," etc.	■ all strata of society listen and tell because of humor
■ limited details	■ anthropomorphic animals	■ anecdotes are satirical, didactic and may be vulgar, obscene, or offensive to person or cultural and ethnic groups
■ use of humor, figurative language, puns, and hyperbole	■ people in everyday life, e.g., family members, members of racial, ethnic, regional, or college groups	■ entertainment for 8 years and above if selected according to appeal of topic, level of humor, ridiculee, or joke for individual
■ witty questions and answers	**Plots:**	■ social commentary
	■ appear in cycles	■ some used as satirical ridicules
	■ frequently ridicule of person, place, group	■ sometimes used as deliberate bigotry or a vehicle for lower class to speak against superiors
	■ simple, one event plot	
Examples: Little Moron Stories Knock, Knock Jokes The Boomer Fireman's Fast Sooner Hound Clever Manka		

Animal Tales

EXPLANATORY TALES (POURQUOI)

Explanatory tales are short, prose narratives explaining the origin of well-known animals and their physical attributes.

LANGUAGE	STORY	CONTEXT
Characteristics: ■ lack figurative language ■ limited descriptions ■ written in style of storyteller	**Characters:** ■ real places within culture of tale's origin ■ timeless **Characters:** ■ realistic animals in animal form and habitat ■ stereotyped characteristics, e.g., sly fox, slow turtle, etc. **Plots:** ■ fictional stories explaining the creation and attributes of animals ■ simple narratives	**Origins:** ■ found in every culture, at all levels of society ■ oral versions influenced other literary tales ■ told for thousands of years worldwide **Uses/Audiences:** ■ entertain all ages ■ explain creation, habits, characteristics of animals ■ may answer why something is the way it is
Examples: Why the Bear is Stump-Tailed Why the Tiger Has Stripes Why the Camel Has a Hump How the Coyote Danced with the Blackbirds		

TRICKSTER TALES

Trickster Tales humorously portray shrewd, cunning, or wise protagonists who may switch between animals and humans.

LANGUAGE	STORY	CONTEXT
Characteristics: ■ dialogue represents dialect of teller's region ■ persuasive language used to support trickster ■ short, humorous prose narratives	**Characters:** ■ related to the site of the origin, i.e., American versions of Brer Rabbit set in South; Anansi found in West Africa, South, and Central America ■ setting implied **Characters:** ■ may be a culture hero ■ character may switch between animal and human form ■ characters attempt to outwit one another ■ fictional animals thinly disguised with human characteristics ■ protagonist is cunning, shrewd, wise, even when tricking another ■ protagonists usually has another animal as a companion **Plots:** ■ short narratives, varied length ■ similar to pourquoi tales ■ simple structure	**Origins:** ■ found in oral and written history and literature worldwide ■ some told as caricatures of bourgeois, wealthy, those in power ■ told to elevate cleverness, stupidity of animals, and thinly disguised humans ■ very old tales ■ a storyteller's delight ■ enjoyed by those 7 and above ■ entertainment and humor

Examples:
Brer Rabbit (American South, from Africa)
Reynard the Fox (France)
Anansi the Spider (West Africa)
The Coyote (Native American)

FABLES

Fables are simple didactic tales used to teach a moral or behavior.

LANGUAGE	STORY	CONTEXT
Characteristics:	**Characters:**	**Origins:**

■ limited description
■ short, simple prose
  narratives
■ some dialogue
	■ unimportant
	■ unknown
	Characters:
	■ characters often
	  unnamed
	■ often actions and
	  dialogue of two
	  characters portray
	  "lesson" to be learned
	  from tale
	■ usually animals,
	  occasional use of
	  humans, plants, or
	  inanimate objects
	■ include a body and
	  separate line stating
	  moral of tale
	■ short, single-incident
	  narrative
		■ first told two thousand
		  years ago
		■ legendary credited to
		  Aesop, a former Greek
		  slave
		■ told in royal courts,
		  streets, homes of "folk"
		Uses/Audiences:
		■ currently used for
		  entertainment, not
		  didactic p21urposes
		■ older children
		  understand moral
		■ used for inculcation of
		  cultural values
		■ younger children enjoy
		  animal tale, if not
		  presented didactically

Examples:

Aesop's Fables, such as The Greedy Dog, The Hare and the Tortoise, The Fox and the Crow

Fables of the Bidpai from The Panchantantra, such as The Partridge and the Crow, The Tyrant Who Became a Just Ruler,

The Jataka Fables (about the lives of Buddha as animals)

LaFontaine's French Fables (taken from Aesop and the Bidpai collections)

ENDNOTES

1. A variety of sources were consulted and included in the endnotes.

2. "Certain Laws of Folklore". Opie, I., and P. Opie. 1978. *Folklore Studies in the 20th Century*. Edited by V. J. Newall. Bury St. Edmonds: St. Edmondsbury Press.

3. Cuddon, J. A. 1977. *A Dictionary of Literary Terms*. Garden City, NY: Doubleday. pp. 68, 71, 72.

4. Leach, M., and J. Fried. (eds.). 1972. *Standard Dictionary of Folklore, Mythology, and   Legend*. New York: Funk & Wagnalls. pp. 106-11.

5. Dundes, A. 1989. *Folk Matters*. Knoxville: University of Tennessee Press.

6. Ben-Amos, D. (ed.). 1976. *Folklore Genres*. Austin, TX: University of Texas Press.

7. See Cuddon, 1977, pp. 220-25 for additional information about epics—examples and approximate dates of publication.

8. Leach and Fried, 1972, pp. 1140-42.

9. Leach, M., and J. Fried. (eds). 1949. *Standard Dictionary of Folklore, Mythol-*

ogy, and Legend. New York: Funk & Wagnall. p. 778.

10. Wolfe, G. K. 1986. *Critical Terms for Science Fiction and Fantasy.* New York: Greenwood Press. p. 67.

11. Battle, K. P. 1986. *Great American Folklore.* New York: Simon & Schuster. pp. xviv-xxiv.

12. Thompson, S. 1951. *The Folktale.* New York: Dryden Press. p. 4.

13. Sutherland, Z., and M. H. Arbuthnot. 1991. *Children and Books.* New York: HarperCollins. p. 186.

14. Sale, R. 1978. *Fairy Tales and After: From Snow White to E.B. White.* Cambridge: Harvard University Press. p. 23.

15. Thompson, S. In Leach and Fried. 1949. p. 366.

16. Griffith, J. W., and C. H. Frey. 1981. *Classics of Children's Literature.* New York: Macmillan. pp. 55-56.

17. Thompson, S. In Leach and Fried 1949. p. 365.

18. Thompson, S. 1955. *Motif Index of Folk-Literature.* Bloomington, IN: Indiana University Press. pp. 30-35. Dorson, R. (ed.). 1972. *Folklore and Folklife.* Chicago: University of Chicago Press. pp. 67-68.

19. Rugoff, M. 1949. *A Harvest of World Folk Tales.* New York:Viking.

20. Thompson, 1951. p. 10.

APPENDIX C

❁ ❁ ❁ ❁ ❁ ❁ ❁ ❁

Resources

FOLK LITERATURE COLLECTIONS CITED IN INSTRUCTIONAL UNITS

Aesop. 1947. *Aesop's Fables*. Illustrated by F. Kredel. New York: Grosset & Dunlap.

Alexander, R. L. 1947. *Famous Myths of the Golden Age*. New York: Random House.

Alley, R. W. 1986. *Seven Fables of Aesop*. New York: Dodd-Mead.

Andersen, H. C. 1987 (reissue). *Andersen's Fairy Tales*. New York: Grosset & Dunlap.

Arbuthnot, M. H. 1961. *The Arbuthnot Anthology of Children's Literature*. Glenview, IL: Scott-Foresman.

Arbuthnot, M. H. 1961. *Time for Fairy Tales*. Glenview, IL: Scott-Foresman.

Arkhurst, J. C. 1964. *The Adventures of Spider*. New York: Scholastic.

Arnott, K. 1962. *African Myths and Legends*. Illustrated by J. Kiddill-Monroe. New York: Walck.

Asbojornsen, P. C., and J. Moe. 1988 (reissue). *Popular Tales from the Norse*. Translated by Sir G. W. Dasent. Edinburgh: David Douglas.

Babbitt, E. C. 1950. *Jataka Tales*. Illustrated by E. Young. New York: Appleton Century Crofts.

Book of Fables. 1963. New York: Warne.

Botkin, B. A. 1949. *The Treasury of American Folklore*. New York: Crown.

Bowman, J. C. 1937. *Pecos Bill, the Greatest Cowboy of all Time*. New York: Whitman.

Briggs, K. M. A. 1970-1971. *Dictionary of British Fairy Tales*. London: Routledge & Kegan Paul.

Butler, F. 1989 (reissue). *Sharing Literature with Children: A Thematic Anthology*. Prospect Heights, IL: Waveland.

Butler, F. 1987 *The Wide World Around*. White Plains, NY: Longman.

Caduto, M. J., and J. Bruchac. 1991. *Native American Stories*. Golden, CO: Fulcrum.

Carmer, C. 1949. *America Sings*. New York: Alfred A. Knopf.

Campbell, J. F. 1890-1893. *Popular Tales of the West Highlands*. Edinburg: Edmonston & Douglas.

Chase, R. 1956. *American Folk Tales and Songs*. New York: New American Library.

Chase, R. 1948. *Grandfather Tales*. Boston: Houghton Mifflin.

Chase, R. 1943. *The Jack Tales*. Illustrated by B. Williams. Boston: Houghton Mifflin.

Clouston, W. A. 1968. *Popular Tales and Fictions: Their Migrations and Transformations*. Detroit: Singing Tree Press.

Cole, J. 1982. *Best-Loved Folktales of the World*. Illustrated by J. K. Schwarz. Garden City, NY: Doubleday.

Cox, J. H. 1925. *Folksongs of the South*. Boston: Harvard.

Crossley-Holland, K. 1985. *Folktales of the British Isles*. Illustrated by H. Firmin. New York: Pantheon.

Cushing, F. H. 1931. *Zuni Folk Tales*. New York: Alfred A. Knopf.

De Armond, D. 1990. *The Boy Who Found the Light: Eskimo Folktales*. San Francisco: Sierra Books.

De la Mare, W. 1980 (reissue). *Tales Told Again*. Illustrated by A. Howard. London: Faber Fanfares.

De Regniers, B. S. 1966. *The Giant Book*. Illustrated by W. Cummings. New York: Atheneum.

De Roin, N. 1975. *Jataka Tales*. Boston: Houghton-Mifflin.

Dobbs, R. 1950. *Once Upon a Time: Twenty Cheerful Tales to Read and Tell*. Illustrated by F. Gag. New York: Random House.

Dolch, E. W., and M. P. Dolch. 1956. *Pueblo Stories*. Illustrated by R. Kerr. Champaign, IL: Garrard.

Elliot, G. 1987. *Where the Leopard Passes: A Book of African Folk Tales*. Illustrated S. Hawkins. New York: Scholastic.

Erdoes, R., and A. Ortiz. 1984. *American Indian Myths and Legends*. New York: Pantheon.

Fables of Fontaine. 1954. New York: Viking.

Field, E. 1973. *Eskimo Songs and Stories*. Illustrated by Kiakshuk and Pudlo. New York: Dell.

Felton, H. 1968. *True Tall Tales of Stormalong: Sailor of the Seven Seas*. Englewood Cliffs, NJ: Prentice-Hall.

Fillmore, P. 1922. *Mighty Mikko: A Book of Finnish Fairy Tales and Folk Tales*. Illustrated by J. V. Everen. New York: Harcourt.

Foster, J. R. 1955. *Great Folktales of Wit and Humor*. New York: Harper.

Gaer, J. 1955. *The Fables of India*. Illustrated by R. Monk. Boston: Little, Brown.

Gag, W. 1979 (reissue). *Tales from Grimm*. New York: Coward-McCann.

Garner, A. 1984. *Alan Garner's Book of British Fairytales*. Illustrated by D. Collard. New York: Delacorte.

Glassie, H. 1985. *Irish Folktales*. New York: Pantheon.

Griffith, J. W., and C. H. Frey. 1981. *Classics of Children's Literature*. New York: Macmillan.

Grimm, J., and W. Grimm. 1972. *The Complete Grimm's Fairy Tales*. New York: Pantheon.

Grimm, J., and W. Grimm. 1959. *Favorite Fairy Tales Told in Germany*. Retold by V. Haviland and illustrated by S. Suba. Boston: Little, Brown.

Gruenberg, S. M. 1942. *Favorite Stories Old and New*. Illustrated by K. Wiese. Garden City, NY: Doubleday.

Hamilton, V. 1988. *In the Beginning: Creation Stories from around the World*. Illustrated by B. Moser. New York: Harcourt.

Hastings, S. 1990. *Miss Mary Mac All Dressed in Black: Tongue Twisters, Jump-Rope Rhymes, and Other Children's Lore from New England*. Little Rock, AR: August House.

Hatch, M. C. 1949. *More Danish Tales*. New York: Harcourt, Brace & World.

Haviland, V. 1972. *The Fairy Tale Treasury*. Illustrated by R. Briggs. New York: Dell.

————. 1985. *Favorite Fairy Tales Told around the World*. Illustrated by S. Schindler. Boston: Little, Brown.

————. 1961. *Favorite Fairy Tales Told in Russia*. Illustrated by H. Danska. Boston: Little, Brown.

————. 1963. *Favorite Fairy Tales Told in Spain*. Illustrated by B. Cooney. Boston: Little Brown.

Hawthorne, H. 1892. *A Wonder Book for Girls and Boys*. New York: Ticknor, Reed, & Fields.

Heady, E. B. 1965. *Jambo Sungura: Tales from East Africa*. Illustrated by R. Frankenberg. New York: Norton.

Hearne, B. 1993. *The Oryx Multicultural Folktale Series: Beauties and Beasts*. Phoenix, AZ: The Oryx Press.

Hunt, J. 1971. *Popular Romances of the West of England*. New York: Bloom.

Hutchison, V. 1927. *Candlelight Stories*. Illustrated by L. Lenski. New York: Minton, Bolch.

————. 1992. *Chimney Corner Stories, Tales for Little Children*. Illustrated by L. Lenski. Hamden, CT: Shoestring Press.

Jacobs, J. (No date). *English Folk and Fairy Tales*. New York: Putnam.

————. 1894. *More English Fairy Tales*. London: David McNutt.

Jagendorf, M. A. 1938. *Tyll Ulenspiegel's Merry Pranks*. New York: Vanguard.

Kherdian, D. 1992. *Feathers and Tails*. Illustrated by N. Hogrogian. New York: Philomel.

Lanier, S. 1989 (reissue). *The Boys King Arthur*. New York: Scribner.

Lang, A. 1991 (reissue). *Arabian Nights*. Pleasantville, NY: Readers Digest.

————. 1965 (reissue). *The Blue Fairy Book*. New York: Dover.

————. 1949 (reissue). *The Green Fairy Book*. New York: Longmans, Green.

————. 1967 (reissue). *The Pink Fairy Book*. New York: Dover.

Lester, J. 1990. *Further Tales of Uncle Remus: The Misadventures of Brer Rabbit, Brer Fox, Brer Wolf, the Doodang, and Other Creatures*. New York: Dial.

————. 1987. *The Tales of Uncle Remus: The Adventures of Brer Rabbit*. New York: Dial.

Lewis, S. *One-Minute Christmas Stories*. Illustrated by J. Palmer. New York: Doubleday.

MacDonald, M. R. 1993. *The Oryx Multicultural Folktale Series: Tom Thumb*. Phoenix, AZ: The Oryx Press.

MacDonald, S., and B. Oakes. 1990. *Once Upon Another*. New York: Dial for Young Readers.

Malcolmson, A., and D. J. McCormick. 1952. *Mr. Stormalong*. Boston: Houghton Mifflin.

Manheim, R. 1981. *Rare Treasures from Grimm: 15 Little Known Tales*. Illustrated by E. Blegvad. Garden City, NY: Doubleday.

Martin, E., and L. Gal. 1984. *Tales of the Far North*. New York: Dial.

Melzack, R. 1967. *The Day Tuk Became a Hunter and Other Eskimo Stories*. New York: Dodd, Mead.

Minard, R. 1975. *Womenfolk and Fairy Tales*. Illustrated by S. Klein. Boston: Houghton Mifflin.

Mitsumasa, A. 1989. *Anno's Aesop: A Book of Fables by Aesop and Others*. New York: Orchard.

Morel, E. 1970. *Fairy Tales and Fables*. Illustrated by G. Frijikawa. New York: Grosset & Dunlap.

National Association for the Preservation and Perpetuation of Storytelling. 1991. *Best Loved Stories Told at the National Storytelling Festival*. Jonesborough, TN: NAPPS.

Nelson, M. A. 1971. *A Comparative Anthology of Children's Literature*. New York: Holt, Rinehart & Winston

Nickl, P. 1992. *The Wonderful Travels and Adventures of Baron Munchausen*. Translated by E. Taylor. New York: North-South.

Olcott, F. 1945 (reissue). *Red Indian Fairy Book*. Boston: Houghton Mifflin.

Opie, I., and P. Opie. 1992 (reissue). *The Classic Fairy Tales*. New York: Oxford.

Osborne, M. 1991. *American Tall Tales*. Illustrated by M. McCurdy. New York: Alfred A. Knopf.

Osborne, M. P. 1991. *American Tall Tales*. Engravings by M. McCurdy. New York: Alfred A. Knopf.

Perrault, C. 1967 (reissue). *Perrault's Fairy Tales*. Mineoala, NY: Dover.

Protter, E., and N. Protter. 1965. *Folk and Fairy Tales of Far-Off Lands*. New York: Duell, Sloan & Pearce.

———. 1966. *Celtic Folk & Fairy Tales*. Illustrated by C. Keeping. New York: Duell Sloan & Pearce.

Rackham, A. 1930. *The Arthur Rackham Fairy Book*. Philadelphia: Lippincott.

Richardson, F. 1972. *Great Children's Stories*. Northbrook, IL: Hubbard.

Roberts, L. 1964. *South from Hell-fer-Sartin*. Berea, KY: Council of Southern Mountains.

Rockwell, A. 1988. *Puss in Boots and Other Stories*. New York: Macmillan.

———. 1979. *The Three Sillies and Ten Other Stories to Read Aloud*. New York: Crowell.

Ross, E. S. 1958. *The Buried Treasure and other Picture Tales*. Illustrated by J. Cellini. Philadelphia: Lippincott.

Ross, N. P. 1961. *The Life Treasury of American Folklore*. New York: Time.

Rugoff, M. 1949. *A Harvest of World Folk Tales*. New York: Viking.

Saltman, J. 1985. *The Riverside Anthology of Children's Literature*. Boston: Houghton Mifflin.

Santore, C. 1988. *Aesop's Fables*. New York: Jellybean Press.

Shannon, G. 1992. *The Oryx Multicultural Folktale Series: A Knock at the Door*. Phoenix, AZ: The Oryx Press.

Shay, F. 1930. *Here's Audacity! American Legendary Heroes*. New York: Macaulay.

Sherman, J. 1993. *Rachel, the Clever, and Other Jewish Folktales*. Little Rock: August House.

Shub, E. 1971. *About Wise Men and Simpletons: Twelve Tales from Grimm*. Illustrated by N. Hogrogian. New York: Macmillan.

Sierra, J. 1992. *The Oryx Multicultural Folktale Series: Cinderella*. Phoenix, AZ: The Oryx Press.

Sierra, J., and R. Kaminski. 1991. *Multicultural Folktales: Stories to Tell Young Children*. Phoenix, AZ: The Oryx Press.

Sian-Tek, L. 1948. *More Folk Tales from China*. New York: John Day.

Spector, N. 1988. *The Complete Fables of Jean de la Fontaine*. Evanston, IL: Northwestern University.

Stoutenburg, A. 1966. *American Tall Tales*. New York: Viking.

Sutherland, Z., and M. C. Livingston. 1984. *The Scott-Foresman Anthology of Children's Literature*. Glenview, IL: Scott-Foresman.

Thompson, S. 1969. *100 Folktales*. Bloomington, IN: The University of Indiana Press.

Uchida, Y. 1977. *The Dancing Kettle and Other Japanese Folk Tales*. New York: Harcourt, Brace and Jovanovich.

Walker, P. R. 1993. *Big Men, Big Country*. Illustrated by J. Bernardin. San Diego: Harcourt, Brace and Jovanovich.

Williams-Ellis, A. 1960. *Fairy Tales from the British Isles*. Illustrated by P. B. Baynes. New York: Frederick Warne.

———. 1987. *Tales from the Enchanted World*. Illustrated by M. Kemp. Great Britain: Hodder & Stoughton.

Wilson, B. K. 1966. *Greek Fairy Tales*. Illustrated by H. Toothill. Chicago, IL: Follett.

Yei Theodora Ozaki 1903. *Japanese Fairy Tales*. New York: Burt.

Yolen, J. 1986. *Favorite Folktales from around the World*. New York: Pantheon.

———. 1992. *Street Rhymes around the World*. New York: Wordsong.

Young, R., and J. Young. 1993. *African American Folktales for Young Readers*. Little Rock: August House.

ADDITIONAL FOLK LITERATURE COLLECTIONS

Andersen, H. C. 1987 (reissue). *Andersen's Fairy Tales*. New York: Grosset & Dunlap.

Barbosa, R. A. 1993. *African Animal Tales*. Illustrated by C. Fittipaldi. Volcano, CA: Volcano Press.

Bawden, N. 1981. *William Tell*. Illustrated by P. Allamand. New York: Lothrop, Lee & Shepard.

Briggs, R. 1966. *The Mother Goose Treasury*. London: Coward.

Bryan, A. 1993 (reissue). *The Ox of the Wonderful Horns and Other African Folktales*. New York: Atheneum.

Carle, E. 1976. *Eric Carle's Storybook: Seven Tales by the Brothers Grimm*. New York: Watt.

Chaucer, G. 1988. *Canterbury Tales*. Adapted by B. Cohen and illustrated by Trina S. Hyman. New York: Lothrop, Lee & Shepard

Cohn, A. (Compiler). 1993. *From Sea to Shining Sea: A Treasury of American Folklore and Folk Songs*. Illustrated by eleven Caldecott Medal and four Caldecott Honor Book Artists. New York: Scholastic.

De Angeli, M. 1954. *The Book of Nursery and Mother Goose Rhymes*. New York: Doubleday.

De Paola, T. 1985. *Tomie de Paola's Mother Goose*. New York: Putnam.

Eisen, A. 1992. *A Treasury of Children's Literature*. Burlington, MA: Houghton Mifflin/Ariel Books.

The Friendly Beasts: A Traditional Christmas Carol. Illustrated by S. Chamberlain. Bergenfield, NJ: Dutton.

Fox, P., and F. Vecchi. 1993. *Amzat and His Brothers: Three Italian Tales*. Illustrated by E. A. McCully. New York: Orchard/Jackson.

Gatti, A. 1992. *Aesop's Fables*. Illustrated by S. Salter. Orlando, FL: Harcourt, Brace and Jovanovich/Gulliver Books.

Gerson, M. 1992. *Why the Sky Is Far Away: A Nigerian Folktale*. Illustrated by C. Golembe. New York: Joy Street/Little.

Haley, G. 1992. *Mountain Jack Tales*. New York: Dutton.

Hamilton, V. 1992. *Many Thousand Gone: African Americans from Slavery to Freedom*. New York: Alfred A. Knopf.

Headington, C. 1990. *Sweet Sleep: A Collection of Lullabies, Poems and Cradle Songs*. New York: Potter/Random House.

Hill, E. 1982. *The Nursery Rhyme Peek-a-Book*. New York: Price-Stern.

Irwin, W. 1992. *The Legend of Sleepy Hollow*. Illustrated by D. San Souci. New York: Doubleday.

Jafe, N., and S. Zeitlin. 1993. *While Standing on One Foot: Puzzle Stories and Wisdom Tales from the Jewish Tradition*. Illustrated by J. Segal. New York: Holt.

Kherdian, D. 1992. *Feathers and Tails: Animal Fables from around the World*. New York: Philomel.

Krull, K. 1992. *Gonna Sing My Head Off*. Illustrated by A. Garns. New York: Alfred A. Knopf.

Kuskin, K. 1993. *A Great Miracle Happened There: A Chanukah Story*. Illustrated by R. A. Parker. New York: HarperCollins.

Lester, J. 1989. *How Many Spots Does a Leopard Have? and Other Tales*. New York: Scholastic.

Lobel, Arnold. 1986. *The Random House Book of Mother Goose*. New York: Random House.

Marks, A. 1992. *Ring-a-Ring o' Roses and a Ding, Dong, Bell: A Book of Nursery Rhymes*. Old Tappan, NJ: Picture Book Studio.

Marshall, J. 1979. *James Marshall's Mother Goose*. New York: Farrar & Strauss.

McClintock, B. 1991. *Animal Fables from Aesop*. Boston: Godine.

Neil, P. 1991. *Fairy Tales of Eastern Europe*. Illustrated by L. Wilkes. New York: Clarion.

Opie, I. 1992. *I Saw Esau: The Schoolchild's Pocket Book*. Illustrated by M. Sendak. New York: Candlewick.

Paxton, T. 1990. *Belling the Cat, and Other Aesop's Fables*. Illustrated by R. Rayevsky. New York: Morrow Junior Books.

Pilling, A. 1993. *Realms of Gold: Myths and Legends from around the World*. Illustrated by K. M. Denton. New York: Kingfisher.

Provensen, A., and M. Provensen. 1976. *The Mother Goose Book*. New York: Random House.

Picard, B. 1960. *The Iliad of Homer*. New York: Walck.

———. 1952. *The Odyssey of Homer Retold*. New York: Walck.

Pyle, H. 1946. *The Merry Adventures of Robin Hood of Great Renown in Nottinghamshire*. New York: Scribner.

Reeves, J. 1962. *Fables from Aesop*. New York: Walck.

Riordan, J. 1982. *Tales of King Arthur*. Illustrated by V. Ambrus. New York: Rand McNally.

Rosen, N. 1992. *South and North and East and West*. Cambridge, MA: Candlewick.

Ruoff, A. L., and F. W. Porter. 1991. *Literatures of the American Indians*. New York: Chelsea House.

San Souci, R. D. 1993. *Cut from the Same Cloth: American Women of Myth, Legend, and Tall Tale*. Illustrated by B. Pinkney. New York: Philomel.

———. 1992. *Larger Than Life: The Adventures of American Legendary Heroes*. Illustrated by A. Glass. New York: Doubleday.

Schwartz, A. 1992. *And the Green Grass Grew All Around: Folk Poetry from Everyone*. Illustrated by H. Truesdell. New York: HarperCollins.

Schwartz, H., and B. Rush. 1991. *The Diamond Tree: Jewish Tales from around the World.* Illustrated by U. Shulevitz. New York: HarperCollins.

Singer, I. B. 1966. *Zlateh the Goat and Other Stories.* New York: Harper & Row.

Sutherland, Z. 1990. *The Orchard Book of Nursery Rhymes.* New York: Orchard.

Thurber, J. 1943. *Fables of Our Time and Famous Poems.* Garden City, NY: Blue Ribbon.

———. 1956. *Further Fables for Our Time.* New York: Simon & Schuster.

Tudor, T. 1944. *Mother Goose.* New York: Walck.

Wildsmith, B. 1963. *Brian Wildsmith's Mother Goose.* London: Watts.

Wright, B. F. 1965 (reissue). *The Real Mother Goose.* New York: Rand McNally.

Yep, L. 1989. *The Rainbow People.* Illustrated by D. Wiesner. New York: Harper & Row.

SINGLE SELECTIONS AND RELATED BOOKS CITED IN INSTRUCTIONAL UNITS

Aesop. 1989. *Aesop's Fables.* Illustrated by L. Zwerger. Saxonville, MA: Picture Book Studio.

Barnett, C. 1990. *Lion and the Mouse.* New York: NTC Publishing Group.

Bell, A. 1988. *The Golden Goose by Jacob and Wilhelm Grimm.* Illustrated by D. Duntz. New York: North-South.

Bell, A. 1990. *The Merry Pranks of Till Eulenspiegel.* Illustrated by L. Zwerger. Saxonville, MA: Picture Book Studio.

Bierhorst, J. 1987. *Doctor Coyote: A Native American Aesop's Fable.* New York: Macmillan.

Bishop, C. H. 1938. *Five Chinese Brothers.* Illustrated by K. Wiese. New York: Coward-McCann.

Black, F. 1991. *The Frog Prince.* Illustrated by W. Parmenter. New York: Andrews & McMeel.

Bornstein, H., and K. Saulnier. 1990. *Little Red Riding Hood: Told in Signed English.* Illustrated by B. Pomeroy. Washington, DC: Kendall Green.

Bowman, J. C. 1942. *John Henry.* Illustrated by R. LaGrove. Chicago: Albert Whitman.

Brown, M. 1950. *Dick Whittington and His Cat.* New York: Scribner.

———. 1961. *Once a Mouse.* New York: Scribner.

———. 1988. *Cinderella.* New York: Macmillan.

Carrick, C. 1989. *Aladdin and the Wonderful Lamp.* Illustrated by D. Carrick. New York: Scholastic.

Chase, R., J. Compton, and K. Compton. 1993. *Jack the Giant Chaser: An Appalachian Tale.* New York: Holiday House.

Climo, S. 1989. *The Egyptian Cinderella.* Illustrated by R. Heller. New York: Harper Trophy.

Coady, C. 1992. *Little Red Riding Hood.* New York: Dutton.

Compton, K., and J. Compton. 1993. *Jack and the Giant Catcher. An Appalacian Tale.* Illustrated by K. Compton. New York: Holiday.

Craig, J. 1986. *The Three Wishes.* Illustrated by Y. Salzman. New York: Scholastic.

Croll, C. 1989. *The Little Snowgirl.* New York: Putnam.

D'Aulaire, I., and E. D'Aulaire. 1962. *D'Aulaires' Book of Greek Myths.* New York: Doubleday.

———. 1967. *Norse Gods and Giants.* New York: Doubleday.

Dahl, R. 1961. *James and the Giant Peach.* New York: Alfred A. Knopf.

Dewey, A. 1983. *Pecos Bill.* New York: Greenwillow.

Dodson, B. 1979. *Lazy Jack.* New York: Troll.

Easton, S. 1991. *The Bremen Town Musicians.* Illustrated by M. Corcoran. Kansas City, MO: Andrews & McMeel.

Eisen, A. 1988. *Little Red Riding Hood.* Illustrated by L. Ferris. New York: Alfred A. Knopf.

Evans, E. 1990. *Bremen Town Musicians.* Illustrated by J. Boddy. New York: Unicorn.

Evslin, B. 1987. *The Cyclopes.* New York: Chelsea House.

Fisher, L. 1991. *Cyclops.* New York: Holiday.

Galdone, P. 1969. *The Monkey and the Crocodile.* New York: Seabury.

Garner, A. 1992. *Jack and the Bean Stalk.* Illustrated by J. Heller. New York Doubleday.

Gianni, G. 1988. *John Henry.* New York: Kipling.

Ginsburg, M. 1974. *The Proud Maiden, Tungak, and the Sun: A Russian Eskimo Tale.* Illustrated by F. Galanin. New York: Macmillan.

Gleeson, B. 1988. *Pecos Bill.* Illustrated by T. Raglin. Saxonville, MA: Rabbit Ears Books.

Goble, P. 1978. *The Girl Who Loved Wild Horses.* New York: Bradbury.

———. 1982. *The Gift of the Sacred Dog.* New York: Bradbury.

Goodall, J. 1988. *Little Red Riding Hood.* New York: McElderry.

———. 1990. *Puss in Boots.* New York: McElderry.

Greaves, M. 1990. *Tattercoats.* Illustrated by M. Chamberlain. New York: Crown.

Greenway, J. 1991. *The Three Billy Goats Gruff.* Illustrated by L. Lustig. New York: Andrews & McMeel.

Grimm, J., and W. Grimm. 1983. *Little Red Cap.* Translated by E. Crawford and illustrated by L. Zwergwer. New York: Morrow Jr. Books.

———. 1967. *The Elves and the Shoemaker.* Illustrated by K. Brandt. Chicago: Follett.

———. 1961. *The Elves and the Shoemaker.* Illustrated by J. Hewitt. New York: Holt, Rinehart, & Winston.

———. 1989. *The Frog King and Other Tales of the Grimm Brothers.* New York: Dutton.

Haley, G. 1988. *Jack and the Fire Dragon.* New York: Crown.

Hamilton, V. 1985. *The People Could Fly.* New York: Alfred A. Knopf.

Hastings, R. 1991. *Reynard the Fox.* New York: Tambourine.

Hewitt, K. 1987. *Nathaniel Hawthorne, King Midas and the Golden Touch.* San Diego: Harcourt, Brace and Jovanovich.

———. 1986. *The Three Sillies.* San Diego: Harcourt, Brace and Jovanivich.

Hilbert, M. 1978. *The Golden Goose.* Illustrated by M. Santa. Chicago: Follett.

Hooks, W. 1992. *Peach Boy.* Bank Street Ready to Read Series. New York: Little Rooster.

Huck, C. 1989. *Princess Furball.* New York: Greenwillow.

Isadora, R. 1989. *The Princess and the Frog.* New York: Greenwillow.

Jacobs, J. 1989. *Tattercoats.* Illustrated by M. Tomes. New York: Putnam.

Jarrell, R. 1980. *The Fisherman and His Wife.* New York: Farrar, Straus, Giroux.

Jennings, L. 1986. *The Wolf and the Seven Little Kids.* Illustrated by M. Ursell. Kent, TN: Hodder and Stoughton.

Joyce, W. 1985. *George Shrinks.* New York: HarperCollins.

Keats, E. J. 1965. *John Henry: An American Legend.* New York: Pantheon.

Kellog, S. 1992. *Pecos Bill.* New York: Morrow.

Kimmel, E. A. 1992. *The Tale of Aladdin and the Wonderful Lamp: A Story of the Arabian Nights.* New York: Holiday.

Kimmel, E. A. 1992. *The Old Woman and Her Pig.* New York: Holiday.

La Fontaine, J. 1982. *The Hare and the Tortoise.* Illustrated by B. Wildsmith. London: Oxford.

———. 1986. *The Lion and the Rat.* Illustrated by B. Wildsmith. London: Oxford.

Lanier, S. 1989 (reissue). *The Boy's King Arthur.* New York: Scribner.

Leeds, B. 1990. *Fairy Tale Rap: "Jack and the Beanstalk" & Other Stories.* Illustrated by C. Hamilton. New York: Miramonte Press.

Lewis, N. 1989. *The Frog Prince.* Illustrated by B. Schroeder. New York: North-South.

Lister, R. 1990. *The Legend of King Arthur.* Illustrated by A. Baker. New York: Doubleday.

Littledale, F. 1991. *The Elves and the Shoemaker.* New York: Scholastic.

———. 1985. *The Magic Fish.* Illustrated by W. Pels. New York: Scholastic.

———. 1989. *Snow Child.* New York: Scholastic.

Lobel, A. 1980. *Fables.* New York: Harper.

Louie, Ai-Ling. 1982. *Yeh-Shen: A Cinderella Story from China.* Illustrated by E. Young. New York: Philomel.

Lyman, N. 1980. *Pecos Bill.* Mahwah, NJ: Troll.

Lynch, P. J. 1992. *East O' the Sun and West O' the Moon.* New York: Candlewick.

Mahy, M. 1991. *The Seven Chinese Brothers.* New York: Scholastic Hardback.

Marshall, J. 1987. *Red Riding Hood.* (Big Book.) New York: Puffin.

Martin, R. 1992. *The Rough-Face Girl.* New York: Putnam.

Matsutani, M. 1969. *Fisherman under the Sea.* New York: Parent's Magazine Press

Mayer, M. 1980. *East of the Sun & West of the Moon.* New York: Alladin.

McDermott, B. B. 1975. *Sedna, An Eskimo Myth.* New York: Viking.

McDermott, G. 1992. *Zomo the Rabbit: A Trickster Tale from West Africa.* New York: Harcourt.

Mills, L. 1993. (Translated from P. Asbjornsen and J. Moe). *Tatterhood and the Hobgoblins.* Boston: Little Brown.

Mosel, A. 1972. *The Funny Little Woman.* New York: Dutton.

Newby, R. 1990. *King Midas: With Selected Sentences in American Sign Language.* Washington, DC: Kendall Green.

Ormerod, J. 1990. *The Frog Prince.* New York: Lothrop, Lee, & Shepard.

Opie, I., and P. Opie. 1991. *Tail Feathers from Mother Goose: The Opie Rhyme Book.* Illustrated by M. Sendak. Avenal, NJ: Outlet Book Company.

Page, P. 1992. *The Traveling Musicians of Bremen.* Illustrated by K. Denton. New York: Little.

Palacek, J. 1988. *The Brementown Musicians.* Saxonville, MA: Picture Book Studio.

Paxton, T. 1991. *Androcles and the Lion: And Other Aesop's Fables.* Illustrated by R. Rayevsky. New York: Morrow Jr. Books.

Perrault, C. 1990. *Cinderella.* New York: Puffin.

———. 1989. *Puss in Boots.* Translated by M. Arthur and illustrated by F. Marcellino. New York: Farrar, Strauss.

Plume. I. 1991. *Shoemaker and Elves.* San Diego, CA: Harbrace.

Porter, A. P. 1991. *Kwanzaa.* Illustrated by J. Porter. Minneapolis: Carolrhoda Books.

Porter, W. 1979. *The Hare, the Elephant, and the Hippo.* Illustrated by J. Behr. New York: Westport Group Book.

Pyle, H. 1990 (reissue). *King Arthur and the Magic Sword.* New York: Dial.

Richardson, I. M. 1988. *The Fisherman and His Wife.* Illustrated by G. Troll. New York: Lippincott.

Roberts, T. 1989. *The Three Billy Goats Gruff*. Illustrated by D. Jorgensen. Westport, CT: Rabbit Ears Press.

Rogers, C. 1992. *John Henry*. Illustrated by B. Jackson. (Video.) Westport, CT: Rabbit Ears Press.

Ross, T. 1990. *Mrs. Goat and Her Seven Little Kids*. New York: Atheneum.

Rounds, G. 1993. *The Three Billy Goats Gruff*. New York: Holiday.

Rowland, J. 1989. *The Elves and the Shoemaker*. Chicago, IL: Calico.

Sage, A. 1991. *Rumpelstiltskin*. Illustrated by G. Spirin. New York: Dial for Young Readers.

Sanfield, S. 1986. *A Natural Man: The True Story of John Henry*. Illustrated by P. Thornton. Boston: D. R. Godine.

Schories, P. 1991. *Mouse House*. New York: Farrar, Straus, Giroux.

Scieszka, J. 1991. *The Frog Prince Continued*. Illustrated by S. Johnson. New York: Viking.

Shorto, R. 1990. *Cinderella, The Untold Story*. Illustrated by T. Lewis. Secaucus, NJ: Birch Lane Press/Carol.

Shute, L. 1986. *Momotaro, The Peach Boy*. New York: Lothrop.

Small, T. 1992. *The Legend of Pecos Bill*. New York: Little Rooster.

Stevens, J. 1989. *Androcles and the Lion: An Aesop Fable*. New York: Holiday House.

———. 1992. *The Brementown Musicians*. New York: Holiday House.

———. 1993. *Coyote Steals the Blanket*. New York: Holiday House.

Stevenson, S. 1992. *The Princess and the Pea*. New York: Doubleday.

Stiles, M. B. 1992. *James, the Vine Puller: A Brazilian Folktale*. Minneapolis, MN: Carolrhoda.

Talbott, H. 1991. *King Arthur: The Sword in the Stone*. New York: Morrow.

Thomson, P. 1992. *The Brave Little Tailor*. New York: Simon.

Townsend, G. F. 1968. *Aesop's Fables*. Garden City, NY: Doubleday.

Vozar, D. 1993. *Yo, Hungry Wolf: A Nursery Rap*. New York: Doubleday for Young Readers.

Wegman, W. 1993. *Cinderella*. New York: Hyperion.

Weil, L. 1986. *Pandora's Box*. New York: Atheneum.

White, E. B. 1945. *Stuart Little*. Illustrated by G. Williams. New York: Harper.

Wilhelm, H. 1992. *The Bremen Town Musicians*. New York: Scholastic.

Williams, M. 1992. *Greek Myths for Young Children*. New York: Candlewick.

Yashima, T. 1967. *Seashore Story*. New York: Viking.

Young, E. 1989. *Lon Po Po*. New York: Philomel.

Zelinsky, P. 1986. *Rumpelstiltskin*. New York: Dutton.

Zemach, H. 1963. *The Three Sillies*. Illustrated by M. Zemach. New York: Holt, Rinehart & Winston.

ADDITIONAL SINGLE STORY BOOKS

Aardema, V. 1991. *Traveling to Tondo: A Tale of Nkundo of Zaire*. Illustrated by W. Hillenbrand. New York: Alfred A. Knopf.

———. 1991. *Borreguita and the Coyote: A Tale from Ayutla, Mexico*. Illustrated by P. Mathers. New York: Alfred A. Knopf.

Arnold, K. 1993. *Baba Yaga*. New York: North-South.

Asbojornsen, P. C., and J. E. Moe. 1992. *The Man Who Kept House*. New York: McElderry.

Bierhorst, J. 1993. *The Woman Who Fell from the Sky: The Iroquois Story of Creation*. New York: Morrow.

Birdseye, T. 1993. *Soap! Soap! Don't Forget the Soap!: An Appalachian Folktale.* New York: Holiday.

Brusca, M. C., and T. Wilson. 1993. *The Cook and the King.* New York: Holt.

Cech, J. 1992. *First Snow, Magic Snow.* New York: Four Winds.

Chocolate, D. M. N. 1993. *Talk, Talk: An Ashanti Legend.* Illustrated by D. Albers. New York: Troll.

Crespo, G. 1993. *How the Sea Began: A Taino Myth.* New York: Clarion.

Croll, C. 1991. *The Three Brothers.* New York: Putnam.

Dugin, A. 1993. *Dragon Feathers.* Illustrated by A. Dugin and O. Dugin. Charlottesville, WV: Thomasson-Grant.

Ehlert, L. 1992. *Moon Rope: A Peruvian Folktale/Un Lazo a La Luna: Una Leyenda Peruana.* New York: Harcourt.

Esterl, A. 1991. *The Fine Round Cake.* Illustrated by A. Dugin and O. Dugin. New York: Four Winds.

Falconer, E. 1990. *The House That Jack Built.* New York: Ideals.

Galdone, P. 1984. *The Teeny Tiny Woman.* New York: Clarion.

Gobel, P. 1985. *The Great Race of the Birds and Animals.* New York: Bradbury.

———. 1988. *Her Seven Brothers.* New York: Bradbury.

———. 1988. *Iktomi and the Boulder.* New York: Orchard Books.

———. 1993. *The Lost Children: The Boys Who Were Neglected.* New York: Bradbury.

Gordon, R. 1993. *Feather.* Illustrated by L. Dabocovich. New York: Macmillan.

Greenaway, K. 1888. *The Pied Piper of Hamblin.* London: Fredrich-Warne.

Greene, E. 1993. *The Legend of the Cranberry: A Paleo-Indian Tale.* Illustrated by B. Sneed. New York: Simon.

Grimm, J., and W. Grimm. 1993. *Iron Hans.* Illustrated by M. Heyer. New York: Viking.

———. 1992. *Snow White and Red Rose.* Illustrated by G. Spirin. New York: Philomel.

Han, I. S., and S. H. Plunkett. 1993. *Sir Whong and the Golden Pig.* Illustrated by O. S. Han. New York: Dial.

Hastings, S. 1993. *The Firebird.* Illustrated by R. Cartwright. New York: Candewick.

Hodges, M. 1990. *The Kitchen Knight: A Tale of King Arthur.* Illustrated by T. S. Hyman. New York: Holiday.

Hodges, M. 1984. *Saint George and the Dragon.* Illustrated by T. S. Hyman. Boston, MA: Little, Brown.

Hong, L. T. 1993. *Two of Everything.* New York: Whitman.

Hutton, W. 1992. *The Trojan Horse.* New York: McElderry.

I Know an Old Lady Who Swallowed a Fly. 1990. Illustrated by G. Rounds. New York: Holiday.

Jeffers, S. 1979. *The Jovial Huntsmen.* New York: Macmillian.

Kellog, S. 1985. *Iva Dunnitt and the Big Wind.* New York: Dial.

———. 1988. *Johnny Appleseed.* New York: Morrow.

———. 1984. *Paul Bunyan.* New York: Morrow.

———. 1988. *Pecos Bill.* New York: Morrow.

Kimmel, E. A. 1993. *Asher and the Capmakers: A Hanukkah Story.* Illustrated by W. Hillenbrand. New York: Holiday House.

Knutson, B. 1993. *Sungur and Leopard: A Swahili Trickster Tale.* New York: Little.

Kwon, H. H. 1993. *The Moles and the Mireuk: A Korean Folktale.* Illustrated by W. Hubbard. New York: Houghton.

Lacome, J. 1993. *Walking through the Jungle*. New York: Candlewick.

Lagerlof, S. 1990. *The Legend of the Christmas Rose*. New York: Holiday.

Longfellow, H. W. 1983. *Hiawatha*. Illustrated by S. Jeffers. New York: Dail.

McDermott, G. 1993. *Raven: A Trickster Tale from the Pacific Northwest*. New York: Harcourt.

Maddern, E. 1993. *The Fire Children: A West African Creation Tale*. Illustrated by F. Lessac. New York: Dial.

Mantinband, G. 1993. *Three Clever Mice*. Illustrated by M. Gourbault. New York: Greenwillow.

Martin, C. 1992. *Boots and the Glass Mountain*. Illustrated by G. Spirin. New York: Dial.

Martin, R. 1993. *The Boy Who Lived with Seals*. Illustrated by D. Shannon. New York: Putnam.

Merrill, J. 1992. *The Girl Who Loved Caterpillars*. New York: Philomel.

Mike, J. M. 1993. *Gift of the Nile: An Ancient Egyptian Legend*. Illustrated by C. Reasoner. New York: Troll.

Mollel, T. M. 1993. *The King and the Tortoise*. Illustrated by K. Blankley. New York: Clarion.

Paterson, K. 1990. *The Tale of the Mandarin Ducks*. Illustrated by L. Dillon and D. Dillon. New York: Lodestar.

Peppe, R. 1985. *The House That Jack Built*. New York: Delacorte.

Poole, J. 1991. *Snow White*. Illustrated by A. Barrett. New York: Alfred A. Knopf.

Raffi. 1990. *Baby Beluga*. Illustrated by A. Wolff. Westminster, MD: Crown.

———. 1989. *Tingalayo*. Illustrated by K. Duke. Westminster, MD: Crown.

San Souci, R. D. 1991. *Sukey and the Mermaid*. Illustrated by B. Pinkney. New York: Four Winds.

———. 1993. *Young Guinevere*. Illustrated by J. Henterly. New York: Doubleday.

Scieszka, J. 1992. *The Stinky Cheese Man and Other Fairly Stupid Tales*. Illustrated by L. Smith. New York: Viking/Penguin.

Stevens, J. 1992. *The Bremen Town Musicians*. New York: Viking House.

———. 1985. *The House That Jack Built*. New York: Holiday.

Stow, J. 1992. *The House That Jack Built*. New York: Dial.

Wahl, J. 1992. *Little Eight John*. New York: Lodestar.

Willard, N. 1992. *Beauty and the Beast*. Illustrated by B. Moser. New York: Harcourt.

Yolen, J. 1990. *Tam Lin*. Illustrated by C. Mikolaycak. New York: Harcourt.

Young, E. 1992. *Seven Blind Mice*. New York: Philomel.

Zeman, L. 1992. *Gilgamesh*. Platsburgh, NY: Tundra Books.

INDEX

❋ ❋ ❋ ❋ ❋ ❋ ❋ ❋ ❋

by Linda Webster

217